ecpr PRESS
monographs

Series Editors:
Alan Ware (University of Oxford) and
Vincent Hoffmann-Martinot (Sciences Po Bordeaux)

deliberation behind closed doors:
transparency and lobbying in the european union

Daniel Naurin

ecpr PRESS

First published by the ECPR Press in 2007

The ECPR Press is the publishing imprint of the European Consortium for
Political Research (ECPR), an independent, scholarly association, which supports
and encourages the training, research and cross-national cooperation of political
scientists in institutions throughout Europe and beyond. The ECPR's Central
Services are located at the University of Essex, Wivenhoe Park,
Colchester, CO4 3SQ, UK

Typeset in Times 10pt by the ECPR Press
Printed and bound by Lightning Source

British Library Cataloguing in Publication Data
A catalogue record for this book is available from the British Library

ISBN: 978-0-9552488-4-9

ecpr PRESS
monographs

The ECPR Monographs series is published by the ECPR Press, the publishing imprint of the European Consortium for Political Research (ECPR).

As an independent, scholarly, institution, one of the ECPR's objectives is to facilitate research in political science among European universities. To that end, the ECPR has developed a strong publishing portfolio since the 1970s.

The policy to extend that portfolio by launching its own publishing imprint was discussed by the Executive Committee of the ECPR in 2002, and the decision to proceed was taken in early 2003.

It was decided that the first two series to be published under the imprint should be complementary. The ECPR Classics series facilitates scholarly access to significant works from earlier eras of political science by re-publishing books that have been out of print. The ECPR believes this will enable contemporary students and researchers to develop their own work more effectively.

The ECPR Monographs series publishes major new research in all sub-disciplines of political science including revised versions of manuscripts that were originally submitted as PhD theses, as well as manuscripts from established members of the profession.

To the memory of my father
Torbjörn Naurin 1943–2006

contents

tables

figures

chapter one | taking transparency seriously

There is general agreement among theorists addressing the democratic legitimacy problems of the European Union that increased transparency is a must.[1] 'Although it is difficult to formulate easy recipes', says one scholar:

> ... it seems obvious that any significant progress presupposes a huge leap towards increased transparency. ... A reversal of the still dominant tradition of closed-door negotiations and the opening up of European institutions to both public and media scrutiny is not only a normatively sound request, but also a major precondition for effective, efficient and high-quality European governance. (Neyer 2003: 703)

What is less clear in this discussion, however, is precisely why more transparency is needed. What is it, more specifically, that transparency is expected to do for the European Union?

One possible answer is that it is not a question of consequences; it is a question of rights. Access to information from public institutions, according to some, is a fundamental democratic, liberal and/or human right (e.g. Harden 2001: 185, Curtin 2000: 8, Davis 1999: 2, Öberg 1998: 1, Birkinshaw 1997: 3). Such a view could fall back on Immanuel Kant, who writes in his *Perpetual Peace* (1795) that 'all actions relating to the right of other human beings are wrong if their maxim is incompatible with publicity.'[2] If publicity is perceived as a necessary condition for justice, and if the EU is correctly described as an opaque political system, it certainly seems 'obvious' that reforms are needed.

But even if one would agree to a fundamental-rights approach to transparency, reformers of the EU or any other democratic political institution must still face the tricky question of how far this right should be stretched. Would it be undemocratic, anti-liberal or inhuman not to televise Council of Ministers meetings or publish the minutes of the European Central Bank? What if this fundamental 'right to know' (Öberg 1998: 1) was found to collide with other values and rights, such as problem-solving capacity or private integrity? Should transparency always be prioritised? Few would deny that secrecy under some circumstances may be legitimate (Cf. Mill 1861 [1928]: 189, Gutmann & Thompson, 1996: 105f.). Even Kant leaves room for secrecy in practice, as his publicity test applies to the maxim of an action rather than the action itself.[3] At some point institutional designers and reformers will have to weigh the pros and cons of transparency.

So the question remains; what might the positive consequences of transparency be with respect to democracy and legitimacy for the EU? In the scholarly and popular debate, three main types of positive effects are considered: transparency is believed to affect elite behaviour, citizen attitudes and the exercise of democratic control by the citizens of their elites.

This book deals with the first type of effect, the idea that transparency may 'civilise' political behaviour at the elite level. As will be seen this proposition has strong support in political theory, but is on somewhat more ambiguous terms with evidence from the real world.

Before I dig into the civilising effect, however, I will argue, in the spirit of the title of this chapter, that the other two suggested effects deserve more scrutiny than they have so far received. Transparency is argued to affect citizen attitudes, in the sense of strengthening the public legitimacy of a political system, and to affect democratic control through increased possibilities for citizens to hold decision-makers accountable for their actions (e.g., Neyer, 2003: 703, Gronbech-Jensen 1998: 186, and the references in note 1 of this chapter). Without implying for a moment that I have a case for refuting these claims, I do believe that I can at least question their 'obviousness'.

If we look at the democratic control, or accountability, argument first, it seems that transparency is a necessary condition for accountability. Citizens must be able to get hold of independent information about the doings of their representatives in order to evaluate their actions and impose sanctions on them (Manin, Przeworski & Stokes 1999: 24). But transparency is not a sufficient condition for democratic accountability.[4] An essential part of the concept of accountability is that bad performance attracts sanctions (Mulgan 2000: 555) and it is the question of sanctions which, in Fritz Scharpf's terminology, is the essential 'input oriented' democratic problem for the EU (Scharpf 1999: 6). The constitutional design of the EU makes it difficult for European citizens to 'throw the scoundrels out, in Weiler's words (Weiler 1997: 152), irrespective of the degree of transparency.

The transparency debate has centred mainly around the European Commission, which is the main agenda-setter in the system, and the Council of Ministers, which is the primary legislative body. But the Commission is deliberately designed as an independent authority, which is not supposed to be accountable to majority opinions among European citizens (Cf. Majone 1996). The Commission cannot be dismissed from office unless serious malpractice is discovered, which is closer to a judicial rather than democratic conception of accountability (Cf. Harlow 2002: 144 f, Lord 1998: 80). No matter how transparent the Commission is, there will be no democratic political accountability, in the sense that European citizens cannot choose another if they do not like the policy of the Barroso or any other Commission. Neither can the Council of Ministers be held collectively accountable, regardless of the degree of transparency. All the governments are accountable to their respective electorates but uncoordinated national elections, where EU policies usually play a minor role,[5] are hardly sufficient mechanisms for punishing poor decisions taken by the Council as a whole. To what extent, one wonders, would increased transparency make EU institutions more democratically accountable, when key decision-makers do not face democratic sanctions for their EU-policy decisions?

The public legitimacy argument also seems intuitively strong but it, too, is vulnerable to criticism. It certainly seems reasonable to assume that transparency may demystify elite policy processes, making them easier to understand and control and therefore to accept as legitimate.[6] But one could ask—as does Juliet Lodge, for instance (Lodge 1994: 360f)—how important this factor really is for explaining public support for political institutions? For example, when it comes to document access and availability of information, EU institutions have become much more transparent than they were in the early 1990s.[7] Nevertheless public support for EU membership has not changed much (or rather has fallen slightly) since 1993, when the first internal regulations concerning access to documents were introduced.[8]

Furthermore, one can also make a completely opposite argument, postulating that transparency may be destabilising and leads to less public acceptance of the political system. In the literature on corporatism and consociational democracy it is argued that insulated negotiations between elite representatives can be an effective means of securing subjective (although not necessarily objective or normative[9]) legitimacy and social stability, in the face of tensions between different groups in a society (Cf. Lijphart 2002, Williamson 1989). In a corporatist or consociational system, confidentiality during elite negotiations makes compromise easier. The decisions taken can be defended afterwards and legitimised to citizens at the grass-root level via the internal communication channels of the organisations, parties or nation states involved, rather than in a common public sphere. Would not the risks involved with open conflict be especially relevant for the EU, considering its heterogeneity as a political entity?[10]

The purpose of making these critical remarks, however, is not to argue that transparency is a weak factor for improving accountability or public legitimacy or that transparency should not be considered a fundamental right[11] My point is merely that there is more uncertainty here than is usually recognised. The claims about the positive consequences of transparency—the civilising effect, the legitimacy effect and the accountability effect—have become more or less axiomatic in the debate on the democracy and legitimacy deficits of the EU. They tend to be made routinely rather than argumentatively. While transparency may promote accountability and legitimacy under some circumstances—as well as a civilised behaviour among the elite actors, a claim to which I will return below—we need to know more about how, when and why it may do so.[12] If the importance of increased transparency becomes a cliché in the discussion on how to democratise and legitimise the European Union our understanding of these issues will suffer. As John Stuart Mill—who was himself a strong proponent of publicity—argued, positions and arguments that remain unquestioned for too long tend to lose their vigour. Challenging such statements, then, is not making the case for murky elitism, it is taking transparency seriously.

OVERVIEW OF POSITION, ARGUMENT AND METHODOLOGY

A common argument in the debate about the democratic status and the legitimacy of the EU is that increased transparency may help to civilise elite behaviour. It is argued that transparency will promote high quality decision-making in line with the public interest. Transparency will prevent 'wrong-doing' (Scharpf 2003: 4), make decision-makers more 'responsive' (Héretier 1999, p. 272) to the public and 'secure the adoption of more impartial decisions'. (Gargarella 2000: 202. See also, for example, Lord 1998: 88, Curtin 1997: 23, Peterson 1995: 473) This is an 'output-oriented' effect, in Scharpf's terminology (Scharpf 1999: 6). It focuses on government *for* the people, rather than government *by* the people. Since EU institutional structures for 'input-oriented' legitimacy (i.e. democratic political institutions) are weak, such output-oriented legitimacy may be a welcome compensation; a 'substitute legitimation' in Adrienne Héritier's words (Héritier 1999: 271). The legitimacy of the political system is strengthened, in spite of its lack of democratic quality, if decision-makers are forced to 'clean up their acts' and make decisions that can withstand public scrutiny.

The idea that public exposure has a civilising effect on political action has a long history in political philosophy. Jeremy Bentham defended publicity on utilitarian grounds, arguing that it motivates public officials to do their duty.

> The greater the number of temptations to which the exercise of political power is exposed, the more necessary is it to give to those who possess it, the most powerful reasons for resisting them. But there is no reason more constant and more universal than the superintendence of the public. (Bentham 1816 [1999]: 29)

Mill defended the open ballot on the basis that it would put a check on 'the selfishness, or the selfish partialities, of the voter' (Mill 1861[1928]: 194). Mill assumed that private motives would be morally inferior to public justifications and that publicity would encourage people to take a more moral standpoint.[13]

> The best side of their character is that which people are anxious to show, even to those who are no better than themselves. People will give dishonest or mean votes from lucre, from malice, from pique, from personal rivalry, even from the interests or prejudices of class or sect, more readily in secret than in public. (Mill 1861 [1928]: 201f)

Another famous advocate of transparency and publicity was the American president Woodrow Wilson, with his plea for 'open covenants, openly arrived at'.

Wilson claimed that 'publicity is one of the purifying elements of politics' (Mill 1861 [1928]: 201f).

In the 1980s and 1990s the suggestion that publicity has the power to censure selfish and immoral behaviour and promote considerations of the common good had something of a comeback with the 'deliberative turn' (Dryzek 2000: 1) in democratic theory.[14] A common assumption among deliberative democratic theorists is that arguing, rather than bargaining or voting, is at the heart of democracy. Drawing on Jürgen Habermas's notion of communicative rationality it is assumed that politics should be—and can be—more about giving good reasons than forcing or striking deals (Habermas 1984, 1996). Assuming accountability for one's political actions by justifying them to one's fellow citizens is a question of treating these fellow citizens with respect. 'When properly conducted', thus, in Joshua Cohen's words, 'democratic politics involves public deliberation focused on the common good' (Cohen 1989: 19).

To what extent modern democratic politics actually can be described in deliberative terms, or whether it is better understood as a game of naked power and interest, is one of the grand debates of political philosophy and political science. Deliberative theorists often position themselves in contrast to economic conceptions of democracy, where politics is 'understood mainly in terms of conflict of competing interests—and thus more in terms of bargaining than of public reason' (Bohman & Regh 1997: xii). A central distinction made in the deliberative literature is that between 'the market and the forum'. Theorists such as Jon Elster, Bernard Manin and Joshua Cohen have developed the view that decision-making over public policy must be governed by a different behavioural logic from the market sphere of society (Elster 1986, Manin 1987, Cohen 1989). In the marketplace, actors are only asked to consider the personal consequences of their actions. Markets, therefore, are legitimately governed by bargaining and self-interest. Political actions, on the other hand, affect the community at large and should therefore be justified to the community at large.

One way of describing the role of publicity in the deliberative school of thought is to picture it as an institutional device which works to liberate politics from illegitimate market behaviour. When political actors are exposed to publicity they have to face the norms of the forum. In order to avoid the social and political costs of norm-violation they will substitute self-interested bargaining for public-interest argument. Publicity, therefore, can be seen as a part of an institutionalist program of designing 'deliberative processes that favour broader over narrower interests [and] puts a premium on moral deliberation rather than power politics and bargaining' (Macedo 1999: 10).[15]

A note on the relationship between the concepts of transparency and publicity is needed at this point. Even though publicity is 'a fundamental requirement of deliberative democracy' (Gutmann & Thompson 1996: 95), and thus a core part of deliberative democratic theory, the precise meaning of the term is seldom defined in the literature. Consequently, there are different usages by different deliberative theorists. The most relevant interpretation of publicity for this study, focusing on potential civilising effects on elite behaviour, is publicity as the opposite of secrecy. This is also perhaps the most common usage of the term. According to this interpretation then, publicity could be defined as having one's actions exposed to a broad audience.[16]

The connection between transparency and publicity may be described as transparency promoting publicity. While publicity is what political actions are exposed to, transparency is a characteristic of the political process, and on an aggregate level of political systems. A transparent political process is one which is easy to follow for anyone who is interested. There is freedom of information and easy access to decision-makers for the media. The decision-making procedures are comprehensible, the language used is understandable, and those interested can easily get the information they need to form opinions about issues on the agenda.[17] But the correlation between transparency and publicity is not perfect. There will be no publicity, i.e. no actual exposure of political actions to a broad audience, no matter how transparent the policy-making process, if the available information about political actions is left unattended. The mass media is therefore a crucial link between transparency and publicity. Transparency promotes publicity by increasing the chances of a political action reaching a broader audience by making information about this action available.[18]

The fact that the concept of publicity is hardly ever defined in the deliberative literature is, to some extent, symptomatic. Just as transparency is, unfortunately, uncontested in the discussion on democracy and legitimacy in the European Union, so is the civilising effect of publicity in deliberative democratic theory. While 'all theories of deliberative democracy' according to Simone Chambers, 'contain something which could be called a publicity principle' (Chambers 2004), publicity's effect on political behaviour is surprisingly underdeveloped theoretically within the deliberative literature (Chambers herself being an exception).

One notable objection to the civilising effect can be found in classical negotiation theory (e.g., see, Schelling 1960, Walton & McKersie 1965, Lax & Sebenius 1986, Fisher, Ury and Patton 1999) as well as in more recent game theoretical works (see Stasavage 2004, Groseclose & McCarty 2001). The claim here is that transparency and publicity impede the problem-solving capacity of political systems. With a generous interpretation, as will be discussed in the next chapter, this may be considered a side-line objection from a deliberative point of view. Even though effective problem-solving may suffer to some extent, deliberative theorists would still argue that on the whole 'public discussion tends to promote the common good' (Elster 1986, p: 113), since public interest argument is substituted for self-interested bargaining. However, this book will present another challenge which goes to the core of the theory of publicity's civilising effect.

This challenge can be illustrated by two puzzles. Two very different pieces of research (which will be described more in the following chapter), neither of which has aimed at studying effects of transparency or publicity on decision-making, have produced results which are difficult for the theory of publicity's civilising effect to explain. First, Christian Joerges and Jurgen Neyer claim to have found evidence of deliberative behaviour in one of the most opaque political arenas one can possibly imagine, namely the EU Comitology committees (Joerges & Neyer 1997a, 1997b). The fact that these shielded decision-making forums, which are not just opaque but whose mere existence is largely unknown to most people, are characterised by public-spirited arguing, seems difficult to reconcile with the assumption that secrecy tends to invite 'market behaviour'. At the least it suggests that publicity is not a necessary condition for political actors to behave according to the norms of the forum.

Second, Nina Eliasoph has demonstrated that publicity is not always conducive to a public-spirited behaviour. Her study of civic group activists in America, based on participatory observations, found that these activists 'sounded better backstage than frontstage' with respect to the use of self-interested arguments (Eliasoph 1998: 7). In backroom conversations the activists and volunteers Eliasoph met during her fieldwork articulated broad concerns about social justice and environmental deterioration. In public forums, however, and when media came around, they switched to arguments like 'it's close to home' and 'it affects my family' (Eliasoph 1998: 6). These activists actually seemed to find it inappropriate to express public-interest in public settings. Thus, publicity does not seem to be a sufficient condition for public-spiritedness either.[19]

Is it possible that opaque 'backstage' areas of politics may in fact, under some circumstances, be more civil in the deliberative sense—more characterised by arguing with reference to public interests and ideals and less affected by self-interested bargaining and pressure politics—than the public 'frontstage'? At the least, Joerges and Neyer's and Eliasoph's findings demonstrate the prevailing ambiguity about the effects of transparency and publicity on political behaviour.

This ambiguity constitutes the starting point for the empirical study of this book, which is outlined in chapters three, four and five. This study focuses on business lobbyists—presumably the most 'market-based' and self-interested actors in politics—acting in public and non-public settings. The question to be explored is: what does a change in the degree of transparency and publicity of the setting do to lobbyists' willingness to argue rather than bargain, and to use other- and ideal-regarding rather than self-regarding justifications? The study of business lobbyists provides an easy test for the validity of the theory of publicity's civilising effect when it comes to the non-public ('backstage') areas of politics. The backstage is assumed by the theory to be dominated by market behaviour. If politics is just like a market when the public light is turned off, business men and women should be among the first to adopt market behaviour. It constitutes a tougher test, on the other hand, on the public frontstage, where, according to the theory, political actors are forced to switch to other- and ideal-regarding argument in accordance with the norms of the forum. If such a switch is made even by the most market-based actors in politics the theory would be significantly strengthened.

The methodological challenge for a study of effects of transparency and publicity is to get hold of data from the non-public backstage, which can be compared with similar data from the public 'frontstage'. That problem is approached in two different ways in this study.

First, rather than speaking to the main actors (and potential norm-breakers) themselves—company leaders and business association managers—I have chosen to speak with their guides to the political sphere. Interviews with the best-reputed public affairs consultants in Brussels and in Stockholm have been carried out. It is the job of these consultants to help business leaders succeed in the forum. The interviewees were given a fictitious case study to comment on. A road transport organisation having a problem with a new proposal for eco-taxes on trucks, this story goes, asks for their advice. The Secretary-General of this hypothetical association has private meetings with officials and public appearances before a broad audience. The consultants explain how they would advise the Secretary-General to act in each of the different settings.

The degree of transparency and publicity in the case study was varied both by switching of scenarios within the interviews and in the comparison between the Brussels and the Stockholm interviews. The notoriously opaque European Commission, on the one hand, and the Swedish governmental ministries, with its centuries-old institutionalised publicity principle, on the other, are two extreme points on the transparency scale. If the degree of transparency does affect the norms inherent in the decision-making processes within these institutions, in the way described by the theory of publicity's civilising effect, professional lobbyists should be aware of it.

The second data collection involved the gathering of a unique sample of confidential letters, sent by industry lobbyists in Brussels to the European Commission under the assumption that they would remain secret. These letters are compared, in chapter five, with public position papers and press releases from the same Brussels organisations, on the one hand, and letters addressed to the Swedish ministries, where the sender knows that all incoming mail will become publicly available, on the other hand. Thus, while the study of the consultants' guided tour to politics seeks to analyse the incentive structures for behaviour coming from the different institutional settings by means of a fictitious case study, the letters and press releases document real action.

The results of the study, discussed in the final chapter, reinforce the doubts raised above about the theory of publicity's civilising effect. Just like Eliasoph's civic group activists, the industry lobbyists studied here sounded better, with respect to self-interest, behind closed doors than in public. That could be seen as bad news for deliberative theorists championing the idea of a civilising effect of publicity, as well as for promoters of increased transparency in the EU building on this deliberative idea. The notion of using transparency to civilise politics is less effective, according to these results, than is assumed by many supporters of increased transparency in the EU. In fact, the effect may be quite the contrary. One lesson for the transparency debate, then, should be that increasing transparency with the purpose of strengthening the 'output side' of the democratic legitimacy equation (government for the people, by means of a civilised elite behaviour), should not be used as an excuse for refraining from reforms on the input side (government by the people).

The good news for deliberative theorists, on the other hand, is that the basic idea of deliberative democratic theory—that the forum is governed by a different logic from the market—is in fact supported. The reason is that the theory of publicity's civilising effect not only failed the tougher 'frontstage' test but also the easier backstage test. The private lobby meeting—which from outside seems to be an almost archetypical case of a political backstage area—was in fact found to be dominated by what the theory would describe as the logic of the forum. This book demonstrates that business lobbyists—often conceived of as the most genuinely self-interested actors operating in politics—in private communications with a political institution lacking almost all forms of formal political accountability (the European Commission) and in one of the least transparent political systems in the democratic world (the EU), have found that in order to promote their interests they have to argue carefully with reference to public interests and ideals rather than bargaining from self-interest. To be successful as lobbyists these actors of the market have to get dressed for politics. While the theory of publicity's civilising effect is based on an overrating of the positive force of transparency and publicity, at the same time it underestimates the inherent civilising force of democratic politics itself.

NOTES

1   Following are some examples from the 'DemDefLit' (democratic deficit literature), as Weiler calls it (Weiler 1999: 268): Föllesdal & Hix 2006: 555, Lord 2004: 220, Héritier 2003: 824, Karlsson 2001: 281, Bunyan 2000: 9, Gargarella 2000: 200f, Schmitter 2000: 29, Zurn 2000: 204, Weiler 1999: 351f, Abromeit 1998: 138, Joerges & Neyer 1997a: 285, Curtin 1997: 22f, Curtin 1996: 95f, Majone 1996: 292. For discussions on the importance of transparency for international organisations in general, see Stasavage 2004, Keohane & Nye 2003, Grigorescu 2003.

2   Quoted from Luban 1996: 155.

3   See Luban 1996: 156.

4   This point is developed further in Naurin 2003b. Cf. Dyrberg 2002: 96.

5   In fact, even European Parliament elections are dominated by national rather than European issues. See Franklin, van der Eijk & Marsh 1996: 370f.

6   Cf. Ferejohn 1999, who argues that elected representatives may have incentives to increase transparency in order to strengthen their trust among the voters.

7   See, for example, the contributions to Deckmyn 2002.

8   'Membership is a good thing', said 57 per cent of the EU citizens in 1993 and 54 per cent in 2006. Eurobarometers 40 and 66.

9   In Beetham's words; 'A given power relationship is not legitimate because people believe in its legitimacy, but because it can be justified in terms of their beliefs.' Beetham 1991: 11.

10   Social stability, on the other hand, which should not be confused with social legitimacy, is of course dubious as a normative goal. 'Glasnost', which means openness, contributed to the fall of the Soviet Union when people fully realised how utterly corrupt the system was.

11 Furthermore, accountability is a democratic value primarily linked to representative models of democracy. Proponents of more participatory models could argue that transparency increases the possibilities of citizens of making their voices heard in other ways than in general elections. See, for example, Curtin 2003: 66f.

12 For two attempts at analysing the differential effects of transparency for democracy and legitimacy in the EU, depending on timing and institutional context, see Naurin 2004 and Héritier 2003.

13 For a more recent attempt of making the case for unveiling the vote, see Brennan & Pettit 1990.

14 See, for example, Dryzek 2000, Macedo 1999, Elster 1998, Bohman & Rehg 1997, Gutmann & Thompson 1996, Habermas 1996. For overviews of the literature, see Delli Carpini, Cook & Jacobs 2004, Chambers 2003, Bohman 1998.

15 The deliberative version of the civilising effect thus has a clear moral content. There may be other less political (but not necessarily less important) effects of transparency as well, having to do with 'good governance' in general, such as trying to be as cost-effective as possible and securing high technical quality and efficacy in policy. Cf. Curtin 2000: 11. Transparency is also considered to be one of the most important elements of anti-corruption reforms. See, for example, Rose-Ackerman 1999.

16 Another existing usage of the term, which is important especially to participatory interpretations of deliberative democracy, is to make publicity approximately equivalent to 'dialogue'. To Habermas, for instance, the 'public' is not an audience watching other people's deliberations, but a critical-rational public engaged in debate (see Habermas 1996). Having to defend one's views in dialogue with others then tends to be perceived as a form of publicity, even though there are only two people in the room. Consequently, any political discussion becomes public per definition. The confusion, in my view, starts when the 'in dialogue with others' conception of publicity is combined with the concept of deliberation into 'public deliberation', which in turn is said to promote 'reason-giving' or 'arguing'. If publicity means deliberation, which in turn means reason-giving, there is no room for any causal relationship between these concepts. And if deliberation is public by definition then the concept of 'public deliberation' seems tautological.

17 An additional component which is often mentioned in the discussions on transparency in the European Union is easy access to decision-makers for interest groups. See, for example, Héritier 2003: 822, Gronbech-Jensen 1998: 187. In my view that is a less obvious component of the concept. Rather it is a factor which may promote the spread of information to a broader public, i.e. publicity.

18 The distinctions and relationships between the concepts of transparency, publicity and accountability, and the subsequent implications for empirical research using these concepts, are developed further in Naurin 2006.

19 In Eliasoph's study, this applies both to the 'being exposed to a broad audience' conception of the term (as when speaking to the media) and the 'in dialogue with others' interpretation.

chapter two | the theory of publicity's civilising effect

'Political correctness' is no isolated phenomenon limited to left-leaning intel-
lectuals. It is a pervasive fact of social life. It appears whenever prevailing
norms discourage people from taking issue with a widely held social belief.
Those interested in democratic politics should notice the omnipresent role of
public constraints on public statements. (Sunstein 1996: 1180)

The concept of political correctness is inflected with a negative tone of social
conformity. According to Cass Sunstein, social norms 'may prevent people from
offering arguments that are productive, reasonable, or even right' (Sunstein 1996:
1181). Furthermore, Timur Kuran has argued that 'preference falsification', that
is, 'the act of misrepresenting one's genuine wants under perceived social pressures', may have important negative consequences for a society (Kuran 1995: 3).
According to Kuran, preference falsification contributed to the stability of the
unjust political institutions of Eastern Europe before the fall of the Berlin Wall.
Perhaps the most powerful critique of unreflective acceptance of public norms,
however, is that of Michel Foucault. Norms, rules and laws, in Foucault's view,
however reasonable they may seem, mirror power struggles of the past and tend
to contribute to the domination of some over others.[1]

Whether the fact that people adhere to a social norm should be taken as itself
normatively good or bad and obviously depends on one's judgement of the norm
in question. The theory of publicity's civilising effect, as described in this chapter,
is based on a normative proposition central to deliberative democratic theory. It
assumes that political actors should focus on public rather than private concerns
and that decision-making should be based on arguing rather than bargaining. In
this view, therefore, publicity is civilising rather than intimidating if it forces
actors to adhere to that ideal. This normative bias inherent in the term 'civilising'
should be kept in mind throughout this book.[2]

This chapter first describes the normative background that forms the basis of
the theory of publicity's civilising effect, as I interpret it from the literature on
deliberative democracy. The theory of publicity's civilising effect is a part of the
'deliberative turn' in democratic theory, although it has a long history in political philosophy. It is based on empirical propositions that, as such, can and will be

tested in this study. The normative defence of deliberative democracy, however, does not rest on these empirical propositions. Deliberation may still be defended as the most legitimate way to reach decisions, regardless of the validity of the theory of publicity's civilising effect. Empirical research cannot test normative theory in that sense. However, deliberative democratic theory, like any normative theory, includes empirical assumptions. The extent to which these assumptions are correct largely determines the relevance of the normative theory to the real world.

Since the deliberative literature mainly speaks of publicity rather than transparency, the concept of transparency will be used less frequently in this chapter. As described in the introduction, the two concepts are linked; transparency usually increases the chances of publicity. In theory, anticipating the risk of publicity should be enough to bring about the civilising effect. Whether or not transparency (accessibility of information) is sufficient, or if actual publicity (exposure to a broad audience) is required, is an empirical question that will be tested in chapters four and five.

In the theory of publicity's civilising effect the crucial mechanisms are the social norms inherent in the forum—i.e. the political sphere of society—which, according to the theory, differ from those of the market sphere. These norms follow from the deliberative democratic ideal of politics as being 'public in nature'. The norms of the forum are not created but activated by publicity and forced upon 'weakly socialised' actors: those who would break the norms if they could get away with it without being discovered. According to the theory, the result is that, in the light of public scrutiny, public-interested arguing is substituted for self-interested bargaining. Initially, the change in rhetoric may amount to no more than hypocrisy. However, deliberative theorists continue, rhetoric is not 'just rhetoric'. The civilising effect has an impact not only upon the arguments but also the on actual decisions taken. Hypocrites are forced not only to 'talk the talk' but also to 'walk the walk'. Eventually, behaving according to the norms of the forum may become a habit.

The second section of this chapter considers some objections to the theory of publicity's civilising effect. First, the most common objections against publicity, such as that it leads to ineffective, emotional and/or insubstantial rhetoric rather than constructive discussions aimed at problem-solving, are discussed. Thereafter, the puzzling results, from the theory's point of view, of Joerges and Neyer's and Eliasoph's studies, which were mentioned in the introduction, are raised. That discussion leads to the conclusion that there is a fundamental ambiguity about the effects of publicity which calls for more empirical research. The final section of this chapter, before the research design is described in chapter three, discusses the use of business lobbyists as a case for studying such effects and examines the interest group literature's ability to verify the hypotheses posed by the theory of publicity's civilising effect.

THEORY AND MECHANISMS

The market and the forum

The basic idea behind the theory of publicity's civilising effect, as derived from the literature on deliberative democracy, is that different spheres of society are legitimately governed by different standards for behaviour, but that social actors tend to have a less than perfect respect for these standards. This idea is most clearly expressed by Jon Elster, who illustrates it by making a distinction between three basic motivations for behaviour: passion, interest and impartial reason (Elster 1995: 239). While passion may be a great motivational base for people's love lives, it is probably, in many people's view, less suitable for directing business deals or guiding consumption. And while private interest is a legitimate principle for behaviour in the marketplace, in modern Western societies at least it is a less appropriate justification for marriage. In the same way, according to Elster, passions and interests are unsuitable for politics. Political actions should be guided by impartial reason.

Not all deliberative theorists would subscribe to this view. The deliberative turn in democratic theory is broad and diverse, and the notion of impartiality is especially contested. According to Simone Chambers there is a movement within deliberative democratic theory towards a more 'flexible and pluralistic idea of reason-giving' than that represented by Elster's rationalistic model of impartiality 'rising above all difference' (Chambers 2003: 321).[3] Nevertheless, in most of the deliberative literature it is assumed that the drive behind political action should be some kind of impartial reason, such as the common good or the general interest. In the spirit of Rousseau, politics is assumed to be public in nature. 'Public policy belongs to us all and is exercised over us all, and we should exercise it together based on reasons and arguments we can share in spite of our differences.' (Macedo 1999: 8) According to John Dryzek political communication 'that cannot connect the particular to the general should be excluded' (Dryzek 2000: 68).

The major theoretical opponents of deliberative theorists, therefore, have traditionally been the 'market' or 'competition' theories of democracy[4] in which politics is perceived as 'a public means of pursuing the satisfaction of personal preferences' (Brennan & Pettit 1990: 315). 'The economic theory of democracy', according to Elster, 'rests on the idea that the forum should be like the market, in its purpose as well as in its mode of functioning. The purpose is defined in economic terms, and the mode of functioning is that of aggregating individual decisions', (Elster 1986: 127). The political process, according to the market theories of democracy, is fundamentally a 'struggle for power among competing interests rather than a search for the common good', (Bohman & Regh 1997: xi). Politics becomes 'a contest in which actors compete for advantage'(Dryzek 2000: 31). Such a model of democracy is inadequate from a normative point of view, according to deliberative theorists. Politics as a contest creates winners and losers rather than consent and legitimacy.

An important source of inspiration for the deliberative literature in this respect has been Jürgen Habermas's theory of communicative action. The concept of communicative action involves actors engaged in arguing with the sincere purpose of understanding each other and seeking agreement. In this model only the better argument counts. Actors communicate by challenging each other's validity claims with respect to facts and moral principles. In contrast to 'strategic action', actors engaged in communicative action recognise each other as equals and put forward only such arguments which they genuinely believe to be right. 'The actions of the agents involved are coordinated not through egocentric calculations of success but through acts of reaching understanding' (Habermas 1984: 285f).

In his article 'The market and the forum: three varieties of political theory' Elster discusses 'the relation between economics and politics', (Elster 1986: 127). Elster contrasts social choice theory with a view of politics in line with the concept of communicative action. While Habermas understands the goal of politics to be 'the transformation of preferences through rational discussion', according to Elster, social choice theorists assume politics to involve the aggregation of fixed private preferences into optimal compromises (Elster 1986: 104). The mistake of social choice theory, according to Elster, is that it fails to recognise the differences of the behavioural logics governing the market sphere and the political sphere:

> It [social choice theory] embodies a confusion between the kind of behaviour that is appropriate in the market place and that which is appropriate in the forum. The notion of consumer sovereignty is acceptable because, and to the extent that, the consumer chooses between courses of action that differ only in the way they affect him. In political choice situations, however, the citizen is asked to express his preference over states that also differ in the way in which they affect other people (Elster 1986: 111).

A market theory of politics could perhaps suffice, according to Elster, if the task of politics was 'only to eliminate inefficiency'. But since politics is also about 'creating justice', the 'principles of the forum must differ from those of the market' (Elster 1986: 111).

Similar arguments have subsequently been put forward by other deliberative theorists. Habermas has argued that 'politics finds its paradigm not in the market but in dialogue' (Habermas 1996: 273). Bernard Manin, criticising Robert Dahl's theory of a pluralism of interest competition and Anthony Downs' economic theory of democracy, argues that, while competition between self-interested actors in the market in the long run is beneficial for all, this is not the case in politics. If a consumer makes a bad choice in the market place, she will be the only one to suffer. In politics, on the other hand, many more people will be affected by the decision.

> If the voters behave just like consumers in the marketplace, they are apt to choose from among proposed policies those whose consequences they perceive as affecting their particular situation most deeply and clearly. But the

consequences that affect them only marginally will tend to be neglected, regardless of their importance for society as a whole. (Manin 1987: 356)

The uncertainty of the single individual of the effects for society at large of her political choice necessitates deliberation, Manin argues. The only way to find out which is the socially best option is to talk to others about it. 'Citizens must be persuaded to adopt a policy because they cannot simply choose according to the immediate effects that they perceive themselves' (Manin 1987: 356). Bargaining in the market, on the other hand, Manin implicitly assumes, does not require buyers and sellers to justify their wants. It is enough to make clear what one wants and negotiate an outcome on the basis of competing wants.

Similarly, Joshua Cohen states that 'the ideal of deliberative democracy' contains the notion that 'collective decision-making ought to be different from bargaining, contracting and other market-type interactions [in its] explicit attention to considerations of the common advantage' (Cohen 1989: 17). Citing John Rawls, Cohen argues that:

In a well-ordered democracy, political debate is organized around alternative conceptions of the public good. So an ideal pluralist scheme, in which democratic politics consists of fair bargaining among groups each of which pursues its particular sectional interests, is unsuited to a just society. Citizens and parties operating in the political arena ought not to 'take a narrow or group-interested standpoint'. (Cohen 1989: 18)

A classic defence of the notion of 'horizontal accountability' (See Gosseries 2005)—citizens' duty to act in accordance with their perceptions of the common good—is John Stuart Mill's. For Mill, voting was a trust, rather than a right, since it implies exercising power over others. Voting is not something which citizens can dispose of as they like (for instance by engaging in vote trading): 'His vote is not a thing in which he has an option; it has no more to do with his personal wishes than the verdict of a juryman. It is strictly a matter of duty; he is bound to give it according to his best and most conscientious opinion of the public good', (Mill 1861[1928]: 191).

Mill's uncompromising view of the voters' duty to suppress any personal wishes may not be widely shared today. Nevertheless, the main conclusion from the deliberative literature remains that while the market sphere of society is legitimately expected to be dominated by competition and self-interested bargaining, the appropriate principle to govern political behaviour is arguing with reference to the public interest. In Elster's words, the 'ideas of impartiality and universality [are] generally recognised as the basis for political life', (Elster 1995: 245).

From philosophy to politics
The argument of deliberative theorists about how politics best should be 'understood' or 'conceptualised' is both a normative and an empirical one. Although the

distinction is often blurred in the literature, deliberative theorists argue against the perception of politics as being 'just like a market' on both normative and empirical grounds. Politics should be something more than a struggle between competing interests, and it can be.

The theory of publicity's civilising effect—which is, as noted before, one part of deliberative democratic theory—rests on the assumption that the ideal of politics as being public in nature, rather than based on market forces, is more than an interesting theoretical standpoint in political philosophy. It is a real ideal, in the sense that it is actually recognised as morally right by a substantial part of the people in modern democratic societies. To paraphrase John F. Kennedy, the theory assumes that many of us believe that we should not ask what Society can do for us, but what we can do for Society. Or at least we believe that this is what we ought to believe. Even though our most private motives often are somewhat obscure even to ourselves, our public selves will generally acknowledge the public nature of politics. As Brian Barry notes: 'I think there would be a general tendency among people to say when asked that when evaluating a policy the proper reference group is comprised of all those who are affected by it', (Barry 1965[1990]: 13). Similarly, James Coleman claims to have identified a norm in collective decision-making that operates 'to constrain members from expressing interests that are not shared by others in the collectivity'. This norm says 'that no one should take a position that cannot be justified in terms of benefits to the collectivity or to all its members', (Coleman 1990: 383).

It is crucial for the theory of publicity's civilising effect that the normative deliberative ideal has this counterpart social norm which affects behaviour. In fact, the theory assumes that there are two norms corresponding to the ideal of the political process as a public-spirited exchange of rational arguments: a 'force of the better argument' norm and a 'non-selfishness' norm.

The force of the better argument'norm states that collective decisions should be based on a discussion on the merits of the available options. 'In trying to reach agreement people can interact in two main ways', according to Elster. 'On the one hand, they can try to persuade each other by rational argument. On the other hand, they can try to induce agreement by threats and promises', (Elster 1995: 237). The dominant public view in modern democracies, the theory of publicity's civilising effect assumes, is that at the forum arguing is the appropriate method for reaching agreement. 'We no longer think that bashing each other over the head is an acceptable method of dispute resolution within liberal democracies', according to Chambers (1996: 1). Nor do we accept buying and selling support for public policy. Thus, the mode of communication promoted by the 'force of the better argument' norm is arguing rather than bargaining.

The usual definition of bargaining in deliberative democratic theory is that it is 'a form of interest-aggregation that builds on the exchange of threats and promises'; while arguing 'is based on claims of validity', (Zurn 2000: 192). Arguing focuses on preference transformation—changing people's minds about what they want or what they believe is right—while bargaining involves coordinating fixed preferences into a decision.[5]

The non-selfishness norm, on the other hand, is based on the assumption that private interests belong to the market sphere.[6] In politics, the theory of publicity's civilising effect assumes, self-regarding arguments are not only unconvincing, they are illegitimate bases for justification. There is 'something embarrassing or even shameful', according to Fearon, about publicly revealing one's self-interested motives (Fearon 1998: 54). Using politics to further one's own ends is unethical.[7] The non-selfishness norm, therefore, affects the types of justification used by political actors, forcing them to use other- and ideal-regarding justifications rather than self-regarding ones.[8]

However, even though it may be widely agreed that public-spirited argument should guide the behaviour of political actors it is a well known fact that this is not always the case. While 'deliberative theorists are in general agreement', according to Bohman and Regh, on the belief that 'the political process involves more than self-interested competition governed by bargaining and aggregative mechanisms' (Bohman & Regh 1997: xiii), that does not mean that they deny that such behaviour exists in politics. It would be naïve to assume that all traces of market behaviour automatically disappear when consumers and business-people step over from the market sphere to act as citizens and representatives at the forum. The existence of a 'force of the better argument' norm and a non-selfishness norm in the political sphere does not rule out that some market behaviour survives the crossing of spheres and continue to play a role on the other side.

In fact, there would be no need, from a deliberative perspective, for these norms if all actors had already perfectly internalised the deliberative ideal. On the other hand, as Elster argues, if no one acknowledged the deliberative ideal as normatively right there would be no such norms (Elster 1999: 373). 'Where there is no public-spirit, there is no arguing', as Zurn put it (Zurn 2000: 197). For the non-selfishness norm to arise, not all political actors can be motivated only by self-interest all the time. Why bother to follow the norm if everyone knows that the only purpose of political action is to get as much as possible out of it for oneself? Why the theatre if no one believes in it? The non-selfishness norm thus applies to self-interested actors but is dependent upon the presence of at least 'some genuinely non-self-interested actors in the system' (Elster 1995: 248). In fact, the theory of publicity's civilising effect assumes that these latter actors have managed to set the standard for the rest.

The theory of publicity's civilising effect also rests on the assumption that there is uncertainty about who the self-interested actors are. If it was already clear to everyone that actor A is genuinely and utterly self-interested, A would not have to bother pretending otherwise. Likewise, if A already knows that B is only interested in closing a bargain, there is no need for A to try convincing B by using public-spirited arguments, unless there is a public audience watching who will punish norm-violations. The uncertainty of the motives of the actors is necessary for the norms to be produced. If the motives of all were clear to all there would be no norms. Public-spirited arguments would still be used, since some actors would be known to demand such arguments in order to be persuaded but that would not be a case of norm-induced behaviour.[9]

In sum, while people of modern democracies are civilised enough to produce and publicly acknowledge the norms of the forum, according to the theory, that is not to say that they will actually follow these norms if they do not have to. This is where publicity comes in.

The backstage and 'frontstage' of politics

Publicity raises the costs of norm violation. While marrying for money may be the real motive behind a marriage proposal, it is not one that is ordinarily declared publicly. For deliberative democrats, the problem at hand is the risk of politics being unduly invaded by passions and interests. Of these two 'outlaws', the main worry in the literature has been about interests. The institutional mission has focused on promoting impartiality, forcing self-interest back to the market sphere where it belongs.

Even if breaking the 'force of the better argument' norm or the non-selfishness norm is not a problem *per se* for an actor who has failed to internalise the principles of the forum, if the violation is discovered it may become a problem. If an actor's norm-violating behaviour is exposed to a broad public audience he might incur social and political costs in the form of lower credibility, status, or sympathy. Publicity, therefore, does not create the norms—they are inherent to the forum according to the theory of publicity's civilising effect—but it activates them. Publicity civilises political debate by imposing the norms of the forum upon political actors who have in their hearts not yet fully left the market behind.

Elster has furthest developed the idea of publicity's civilising effect within the deliberative democratic literature. According to Elster, 'there are certain arguments that simply cannot be stated publicly. In a political debate it is pragmatically impossible to argue that a given solution should be chosen just because it is good for oneself' (Elster 1986: 112f). In order to 'avoid the opprobrium associated with the overt appeal to private interest in public debates' (Elster 1998: 102), political positions must be publicly justified with reference to impartial reason. David Miller argues similarly: 'Even if initially my aim is to support the claims of a particular group to which I belong or which I represent I cannot in a general discussion simply say "I claim that group A—farmers, say, or policemen—should get more money"' (Miller 1992: 75). Rather 'we must argue in terms that any other participant could potentially accept, and "It's good for me" is not such an argument' (Miller 1992: 82). Similar claims about the civilising effect of publicity abound in the deliberative literature.[10]

The theory of publicity's civilising effect thus applies to 'weakly socialised actors', in Frank Schimmelfennig's terms: actors who are aware of the norms of the forum but treat them as 'regulative' rather than 'normative' (Schimmelfennig 2001: 63). They do not genuinely care about following norms but know they ought to. Public scrutiny of such actors will force them, for strategic purposes, according to Elster, to 'pay lip service to the idea of the common good' (Elster 1995: 244). Thus, 'publicity does not eliminate base motives, but forces or induces speakers to hide them' (Elster 1998: 111).

According to the theory of publicity's civilising effect, publicity affects not only the type of justification—shifting from private-interested to public-spirited justifications in order not to violate the non-selfishness norm—but also the mode of communication. 'The absence or presence of an audience is [an] important determinant of the location of communication on the arguing-bargaining continuum', according to Elster. '[One] effect of secrecy [is] that of shifting the mode of the proceedings toward the bargaining end of the continuum' (Elster 1998: 109, 110). Naked appeals to bargaining power—threats and promises—are assumed to be censored by publicity as they violate the 'force of the better argument' norm.

However, the distinction between types of justification and modes of communication is seldom made clear in the deliberative literature. It is often implicitly assumed that arguing is connected to public-spiritedness and bargaining to self-interest. But while there is probably a strong empirical correlation in many cases, this relationship is not logically entailed thereby. While deliberative theorists may be right that it is 'pragmatically impossible' (Elster 1986: 112) to make self-regarding claims in public debate—although that proposition is empirically challenged in this book—it is not conceptually impossible. In fact, as will be demonstrated later, letters and press releases from business actors often contain arguments like; '[this proposal] creates an uncertainty which is absolutely unacceptable from a business perspective' (from the battery producer SAFT).[11] At the same time, bargaining does not have to be based solely on self-interested claims. As Barry notes: 'Bargaining is quite consistent with publicly-oriented attitudes. ... To say that a man is a tough bargainer is not necessarily to say that he uses his bargaining skills for selfish purposes (either his or anyone else's). Indeed, he may be easy-going where privately-oriented matters are at stake but inflexible and unscrupulous in advancing ends which he conceives to be good', (Barry 1965 [1990]: 88). Types of justification and modes of communication, which are the two dependent variables of the theory of publicity's civilising effect, should therefore be kept conceptually distinguished from each other.

In sum, democratic politics, according to the theory of publicity's civilising effect, is characterised neither solely by market behaviour (self-interested bargaining) nor by behaviour appropriate for the forum (public-spirited argument). Both types of behaviour exist, but they are separated, at least partly, within the sphere of politics, by the curtain of secrecy. Politics has a 'backstage' and a 'frontstage', demarcated by publicity. In the private—backstage—areas of the forum, the logic of the market dominates. In the smoke-filled rooms, behind the scenes, deals are still struck and self-interested pressure and 'bashing over heads' is still practised. On the public stage—the frontstage—on the other hand, the non-selfishness and 'force of the better argument' norms rule. The role of publicity is to draw the curtain and force political actors backstage to clean up their acts.

The idea that social actors follow different norms depending on which 'stage' they are acting on is familiar from Erving Goffman's classic 'The Presentation of Self in Everyday Life' (Goffman 1959). On the frontstage—in social settings—people wear masks and perform roles. The performance is determined by the actors' interpretation of the expectations of the audience. The backstage, on the other hand, is a place for people to 'be themselves', to throw away their masks and being free not to care about social conventions.

However, deliberative theorists would not argue that the distinction between public and private arenas perfectly coincides with public-spirited argument and self-interested bargaining. The private areas of politics will include argumentative behaviour from those actors who are more strongly socialised into the norms of the forum. But the separation between public and private arenas is assumed to be important enough, at least, to conclude that the more of politics that is exposed to public scrutiny the less room there will be for market behaviour in the political sphere.

The argument so far is illustrated in Figure 2.1, which models publicity's effect on the mode of communication and the types of justification used by political actors. Publicity is an interaction variable in this model. When publicity is in operation the actors must face the norms of the forum and subsequently switch from bargaining to arguing and from self-regarding to other- and ideal-regarding justifications.

Figure 2.1. Publicity's civilising effect: The first step

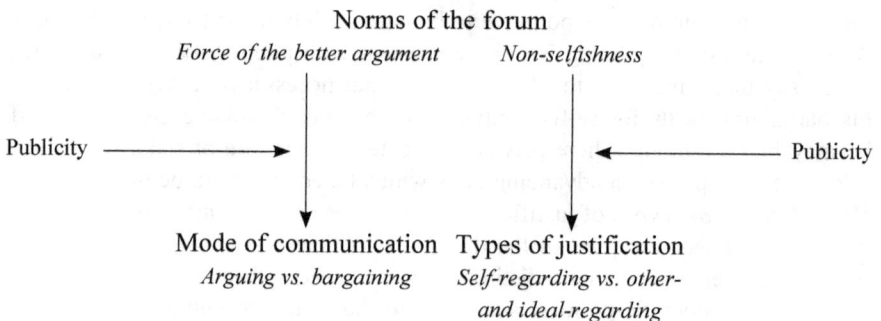

Norms of the forum

Force of the better argument   *Non-selfishness*

Publicity ⟶   ⟵ Publicity

Mode of communication   Types of justification
Arguing vs. bargaining   *Self-regarding vs. other-*
and ideal-regarding

Note: Figure 2.1 illustrates the effects of publicity on the mode of communication and the types of justification used by the actors. When publicity is in operation, the "force of the better argument' norm forces actors to change the mode of communication from bargaining to arguing. At the same time, the non-selfishness norm produces a change in the types of justification used as actors substitute self-regarding for other- and ideal-regarding justifications when publicity is introduced.

Rhetoric is not 'just rhetoric'

The first effect of publicity in the model above, however, is plain hypocrisy. Rather than saying 'if you give me X, I'll see to that Y will happen', when publicity is in operation actors will say that 'X is the preferred public policy because of public-interest argument Z'. Not because speakers actually believe that Z is the right answer, however, but because they find it strategically useful.

Schimmelfennig calls this practice 'rhetorical action'; it is the 'strategic use of norm-based arguments in pursuit of one's self-interest' (Schimmelfennig 2001: 63). Such 'pseudoarguments' are, in Elster's words, 'parasitic' on the norms of the forum (Elster 1995: 244).

So why would deliberative theorists prefer hypocrisy to honest norm violations? They may agree with La Rochefoucauld that 'hypocrisy is the homage that vice pays to virtue', but that is not much of a comfort if vice still carries the day in the end. There should be more to the civilising force than that. The answer given by the theory of publicity's civilising effect is that rhetoric is not 'just rhetoric'. And the reason why rhetoric is not just rhetoric is that there are limits to how much hypocrisy political actors can handle.

First, following deliberative theory's fundamental assumption about human nature in politics—not everyone is purely selfish—using 'the voice of reason' for strategic purposes may later backfire on a hypocritical user. There is one softer and one harder version of this mechanism, both of which involve preference transformation as an effect of publicity. The softer version is the 'alarm-clock effect'. Exposing actors to publicity, this argument goes, can work as a reminder for those who really want to behave well, and who know deep inside how one should behave but who tend to forget when there is no pressure on them to keep up the good behaviour (Goodin 1992: 137f). The harder version invokes a psychological dissonance reduction mechanism. Even if one starts hypocritically, according to this line of reasoning, in the long run the gap between what is said and what is genuinely believed will become difficult to bear. Most people want to be able to look themselves in the mirror and feel reasonably comfortable with what they see. The result may be that over time, in order to close the gap, one starts to believe what one first only pretended to believe. Not only the rhetoric but also the actual preferences are laundered in that process (Elster 1986: 113). According to Risse and Sikkink, who have studied the international politics of human rights norms, even the hypocritical and instrumental adoption of such norms may set into motion 'a process of identity transformation, so that norms initially adopted for instrumental reasons, are later maintained for reasons of belief and identity' (Risse & Sikkink 1999: 10. See also Risse 2000).

Acting for too long on the frontstage, the argument goes, will eventually transform one's original preference for self-interested bargaining into one for public-spirited argument. The more strongly socialised into the norms of the forum the actors are to begin with, the more likely it is that reason will be able to touch their genuine preferences. But preference transformation is not the only way in which the civilising effect of publicity may give virtue at least part of the victory in the end. The really tough nuts—the genuinely self-interested actors who will not be bothered about the picture in the mirror—may not be cracked by the alarm clock or the dissonance reduction mechanism, in the sense that they will start to genuinely embrace the norms of the forum as a result of being exposed to (their own and others') reasoned arguments. Nevertheless, they may still have to compromise their self-interest as a result of their rhetorical action. When the rhetoric is civilised in order to fit with the norms of the forum, there may be strategic reasons to adjust positions as well. Because if positions remain unchanged the actor may run the risk of being revealed as a hypocrite. Therefore, Elster argues, actual policy proposals 'will be modified as well as disguised' (Elster 1998: 105). There are three components of this non-hypocrisy constraint:

First, if the self-interested actor wants to deceive the audience about her real (self-interested) motives in order not to break the non-selfishness norm, the position taken must not be too close to the actor's objective interest. This 'imperfection constraint', as Elster calls it, assumes that the audience has some knowledge about the interests of the actor, but is uncertain of the actor's motives.

> An impartial argument that coincides too well with the interests of those who deploy it tends to arouse suspicion. If the well-off advocate tax breaks for all the well-off and only for the well-off, the impartial argument that such policies will benefit all by a trickle-down effect is probably not optimal. If, however, an impartial argument is made that supports a diluted conclusion, with tax breaks for most but not all who are well-off and for some of the badly off as well, it is more likely to be accepted. (Elster 1995: 246).

Second, if the purpose of using a public-spirited argument is to persuade some audience of the merits of one's position, rather than being just a face-saving cover for one's self-interested motives, there must be a credible connection between argument and position. This is a plausibility constraint. If you are not able to credibly demonstrate that your self-interested position X actually will bring about the public-interested outcome Z, which you may consider claiming, you cannot use Z as an argument for X. Thus, if the brewing industry wants to argue for lower taxes on beer with the argument that it will 'save jobs', it must be able to demonstrate that with facts and figures for the argument to be persuasive. If it is too obvious that the public-spirited justification given is just an arbitrary cover-up for a self-interested position no one will be persuaded, regardless of whether they care about the non-selfishness norm or not.

The imperfection and plausibility constraints assume that the public audience can only be fooled up to a certain extent. But 'while the proposal has to be sufficiently diluted to deflect suspicions... it must not be so much diluted that the interest in question is harmed rather than promoted', (Elster 1998: 102). Advocating tax-breaks only for the poor would certainly look good with respect to the non-selfishness norm, and it would persuade those sympathetic to the poor, but it would hardly be the optimal solution for the rich (given that they are driven mainly by self-interest).

The third component of the hypocrisy constraint, which contributes to forwarding the civilising effect on the rhetoric on to the actual policy decisions, is the requirement to be consistent. 'Once a speaker has adopted an impartial argument because it corresponds to his interest or prejudice, he will be seen as opportunistic if he deviates from it when it ceases to serve his needs', (Elster 1998: 104).

Hence, there will be pressure on the actors to hold on to publicly-expressed positions and justifications through the whole decision-making process. Actors will be punished if they first support policy option A publicly, 'because it is good for the environment', and then in the end vote for option B. An important condition for this constraint to work is that the political process is transparent all the way through to the actual decision-making, so that the hypocrisy can be discovered.[12]

In conclusion, according to the theory of publicity's civilising effect, publicity has the power to make political actors argue and act in favour of policy A instead of policy B. It is not good enough to 'talk the talk', if one is not also, at least partly, prepared to 'walk the walk' (Cf. Risse 2000: 32).

Conclusion
Elster concludes that there exists a 'civilising force of hypocrisy', which tends to 'on the average…yield more equitable outcomes', (Elster 1995: 251). This phrase, which has been frequently used in subsequent deliberative works (e.g., Eriksen & Fossum 2000: 13, Sunstein 1996: 1181), is a bit misleading since it gives the impression that the positive effect on behaviour stems from hypocrisy itself. In fact, the effect is a product of the norms of the forum—the non-selfishness norm and the 'force of the better argument' norm—which are activated by publicity and forwarded into policy positions and decisions via the requirements to be consistent and to have a credible fit between justifications and positions.

Figure 2.2. Publicity's civilising effect: The whole chain

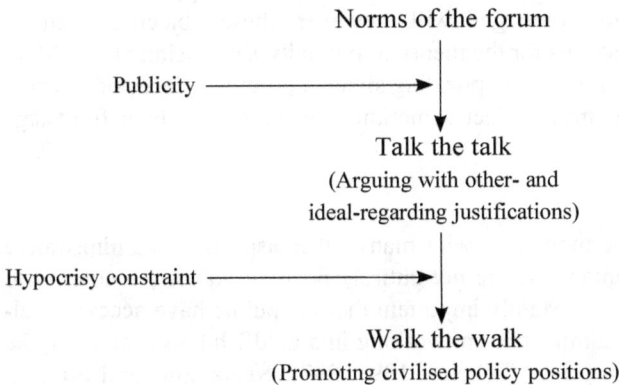

Norms of the forum

Publicity ⎯⎯⎯⎯⎯⎯⟶

Talk the talk
(Arguing with other- and
ideal-regarding justifications)

Hypocrisy constraint ⎯⎯⎯⎯⎯⎯⟶

Walk the walk
(Promoting civilised policy positions)

Note: Figure 2.2 describes the causal chain which produces the civilising effect of publicity. When publicity is in operation the norms of the forum are pressed upon political actors, forcing them to talk the talk: to shift from self-interested bargaining to arguing with other- and ideal-regarding justifications. In the second step the actors become entrapped by their own rhetoric due to the hypocrisy constraint. In the end, therefore, not only the rhetoric but also the actual policy positions will be civilised.

Figure 2.2 illustrates the causal chain from the norms of the forum, via the mode of decision-making and types of justification on to the policy positions promoted by political actors. In the Figure, publicity is in operation, forcing actors to talk the talk—to argue (or at least use the form of arguing, as will be discussed later) with other- and ideal-regarding justifications—as a first step. The hypocrisy constraint, in the second step, makes sure that the shift on the rhetorical level also affects the actors' policy positions and eventually, it is assumed, the actual decisions taken.

If one agrees with the normative assumption of deliberative theory that the logic of the forum should be distinguished from the logic of the market—that public-spirited arguing is a more legitimate way of conducting politics than self-interested bargaining—this model provides a strong argument in favour of transparency, as discussed in the introduction. If decision-making processes are opened up to be more comprehensible and visible, thereby increasing the risk for publicity for political actors, there will be positive effects on elite behaviour.

QUESTIONING THE CIVILISING EFFECT

There are, however, counter-arguments to the theory of publicity's civilising effect that must be faced. The most common objection to institutionalising higher degrees of transparency in political institutions is that it spoils the effectiveness, in terms of problem-solving capacity, of the decision-making processes. Publicity may also contribute to a less rational and a more emotional type of behaviour, according to some. With some goodwill, however, these objections can be considered side-line objections for the theory of publicity's civilising effect. More directly problematic is that there are puzzling signs in previous pieces of research that backstage behaviour may in fact sometimes be more civil than frontstage behaviour.

Side-line objections
'Publicity and open government, as with many other aspects of administrative responsibility and accountability, are not entirely positive values', according to Guy Peters. 'Although it is certainly important that the public have access to relevant information about administration, working in a goldfish bowl can rarely be as efficient as working in private', (Peters 1995: 297). Negotiators and officials in the European Union Council of Ministers and the Commission argue similarly. They need 'a space to think', they claim, shielded from the public, in order to make decisions and reach agreements in an efficient way (Bunyan 2000: 5. Cf. Héritier 2003: 825, Hayes-Renshaw and Wallace 1997: 7). This claim is supported by negotiation theory and is acknowledged also by several deliberative theorists. Amy Gutmann and Dennis Thompson, for instance, admit that, in spite of their strong plea in favour of publicity, 'deliberation itself is not always enhanced by complete openness' (Gutmann & Thompson 1996: 101). In the same way Jurgen

Neyer notes that, while 'publicity is an important condition for promoting the argumentative orientation of speakers', it is 'no guarantee of constructive discourse' (Neyer 2003: 695).

According to negotiation theory, publicity impedes effective problem-solving capacity primarily because actors become less willing to reveal private information and to change their positions once they have stated them publicly.[13] Beside the non-selfishness and 'force of the better argument' norms emphasised by deliberative theorists, publicity also seems to activate a decisiveness norm. There is a certain expectation on political actors to appear principled and sure of themselves.[14] This decisiveness norm, in combination with the consistency requirement discussed before, contributes to giving positions a 'high degree of finality' (Walton & McKersie 1965: 93. Cf. Schelling 1960: 28). In negotiation theory, going public with a position is equivalent to saying 'this is our last offer, take it or leave it'. Positions become less flexible and the risk of negotiation breakdown increases. Negotiators sometimes use publicity to tie themselves to a position, in order to pressure their opponent to yield. The credibility of one's commitment to a certain position is increased if one would seem to risk losing face by changing it. However, if one violates the other party's resistance point (for example, by bidding too low), negotiations may break down, which could lead to a costly conflict. Making commitments with exactly the right degree of flexibility, therefore, is part of the art of negotiation.

The decisiveness norm activated by publicity thus hampers constructive discussions by making the participants cling more rigidly to their positions. Furthermore, negotiation theorists argue, positive-sum 'integrative bargaining'— reaching compromises which all around the negotiating table may be satisfied with—requires that the actors are prepared to reveal private information, including 'base motives' (Walton & McKersie 1965, chapter 4). If the 'force of the better argument' norm and the non-selfishness norm censor such information, that becomes a problem, rather than a virtue, from the point of view of making an agreement.

> [The parties] will not engage in problem-solving behavior unless the activity is relatively safe. Both Party and Opponent need to be assured that if they freely and openly acknowledge their problems, if they willingly explore any solution proposed, and if they candidly discuss their own preferences, this information will not somehow be used against them. [...] The use of transcripts or a stenographer may inhibit exploratory and tentative discussions. Large galleries and disclosure to outside persons have the same effect. (Walton & McKersie 1965: 159)

Negotiation theorists therefore usually recommend secrecy during the process of decision-making, which does not preclude the outcomes being made public. Fisher, Ury and Patton, in fact, argue that 'a good case can be made for changing Woodrow Wilson's slogan "open covenants openly arrived at" to "open covenants privately arrived at"'. In order for negotiating parties to reach a 'wise outcome', they claim, 'it is useful to establish private and confidential means of communicating with the other side', (Fisher, Ury & Patton 1999: 36f). Similarly, Groseclose and McCarty, who have modelled the impact of an audience in bargaining games, conclude that publicity increases the risk of negotiation breakdown and Pareto inefficient outcomes. 'Although there may be benefits to "sunshine laws" and other measures to make negotiations open, our results show that they may actually harm efficiency' (Groseclose & McCarty 2001: 114. See also Stasavage 2004 and Prat 2005).

It is usually (implicitly) assumed among negotiation theorists that publicity is something which the negotiators have or not as they please. Bargaining without any secrecy is hardly even considered, in theory or in practice. If the parties are exposed to unwanted publicity, their logical response, from a negotiation theory perspective, would be to lower the 'degree of specificity' of their positions (Walton & McKersie 1965: 94). The actors would try to counter the higher degree of finality of their statements, and the subsequent increasing risk of inflexibility, by making them more vague. The less specific the public position, the lower the risk of negotiations getting stuck and the participants losing face.

But the strategy of lowering the degree of specificity in order to safeguard flexibility assumes that publicity is just temporary. To negotiation theorists the frontstage is not a decision-making arena. It is an arena on which you act so as to strengthen your position before the private bargaining—where the real decisions are made—starts (or restarts).

Taking negotiation theory into account, it is not so clear that publicity will cause arguing to be substituted for bargaining as the mode of communication, at least not if arguing is defined as involving genuine attempts to persuade with the purpose of reaching agreement, which is the common interpretation of the term.[15] What publicity may introduce, by unleashing the 'force of the better argument' norm, is a requirement to use the form of arguing. Pretending that one is arguing, however, is clearly different from the real thing. While the 'force of the better argument' norm may deprive the actors of the possibility of bargaining, that does not mean that they will automatically choose to solve their conflicts by arguing. The effect of having an audience may rather be to diminish the parties' interest in each other altogether, as they focus more on their appearances in the views of the audience. Opening the doors to the Council of Ministers of the European Union, for example, may promote the use of other- and ideal-regarding justifications but at the same time it could lead to less arguing and bargaining between the member state representatives.

But if political actors neither bargain nor argue sincerely with each other when debating in public then what are they doing? Making commitments is one part of it, as explained by negotiation theory. Public relations is another part. The actors are making statements in order to show off, both to the public and to the other parties. That means that they have temporarily stopped the process of attempting to reach agreement. Efficiency, in terms of problem-solving capacity, may suffer as a result of publicity: not only because the actors become more unwilling to back down from their positions but also because they stop talking to each other. The audience becomes a distraction, bringing the decision-making process to a halt until the veil of secrecy is drawn again (Cf. Checkel 2001: 570).[16]

Nevertheless, while inefficient and time-consuming decision-making processes may be a disadvantage of publicity, and while the decisiveness norm certainly is problematic from a deliberative point of view,[17] it is more of a side-line objection than a core objection for the theory of publicity's civilising effect. It is an unwanted by-product of publicity but it does not disrupt the causal chain of the theory (see Figure 2.2). The fact that the actors have to use the form of arguing and other- and ideal-regarding justifications is still enough to activate the hypocrisy mechanisms of imperfection, plausibility and consistency. The actors will still become trapped by their own rhetoric. Assuming that a decision will eventually be taken in one way or another—be it over lunch or in a vote—the publicity of the process before that, it can be assumed in line with the theory, will have set the agenda in such a way that policy options reflecting purely partisan interests will already have been forced off the agenda. If the parties bargain an agreement based on two public-spirited options, then virtue has already won the day.

Another problematic aspect of publicity, one that pre-occupies Elster in particular, comes from the risk for an increase of 'rhetoric' in its pejoratively negative sense. The promise of publicity, from the perspective of deliberative democratic theory, lies in its ability to make political actors behave according to the norms of the forum, where impartial reason should be the governing principle. Usually it is self-interest which is conceived of as the major threat to reason but, as discussed earlier, people are also driven by passion. To be passionate, according to Elster and other deliberative democratic theorists (but not all), is fine as long as one is engaging in love, sports, arts etc. But it is not an appropriate motivation for politics.[18]

Unfortunately, from this point of view, while publicity may guard against the pursuit of self-interest in politics—if the theory of publicity's civilising effect is correct—it also tends to invite passion. Using emotional rhetoric in order to induce others into a certain position is an alternative way of changing people's minds. Both impartial argument and self-interested bargaining rest on rational communication, in the sense that it is the cognitive reasonableness of the content of the message that counts (the rhetorical term is *logos*): the validity of the argument or the consequences and credibility of the threat or the promise. Passionate rhetoric (*pathos*), to the contrary, does not provide a causal logic for why policy X should be chosen. Its purpose is to awaken those feelings of anger, fear, jealousy, hatred, shame, nostalgia, pride, admiration, gratitude, compassion, hope, love, etc., that make people feel that policy X is the best solution.

Elster believes that the probability that passionate rhetoric will be successful is higher when employed to persuade a large public audience rather than a handful of people at a private meeting. Open doors and large assemblies give demagogues a chance to play on the emotions of their audiences. In his study of discussions within historical constituent assemblies, he finds that passionate rhetoric played a more important role at the open French Assemblée Constituante in 1789 than in the closed American Federal Convention of 1776. 'In closed proceedings among a small number of delegates, expressions of passion will be derided as cant. In a public forum, with large numbers of delegates, passionate argument serves both as a sword and as shield' (Elster 1995: 244).

Classical rhetoricians were also clear on this point. Since people are emotional, they argued, political orators standing before public audiences have to rely on emotional rhetoric. Cicero recommended the orator to 'prefer emotion to reason' (Remer 1999: 42). The audience, according to Cicero, should 'be swayed by something resembling a mental impulse or emotion, rather than by judgment or deliberation. For men decide far more problems by hate, or love, or fear, or illusion, or some other inward emotion, than by reality'.[19] In Cicero's view rational conversation belonged to intimate social gatherings, dinners with friends and philosophical discussions, not to the senate or other public assemblies (Remer 1999: 44).

Chambers also recognises that publicity may negatively affect the qualitative content of rhetoric but not, however, because it induces speakers to use emotional rhetoric. Emotional rhetoric is not inconsistent with a deliberative perspective, according to Chambers. 'If deliberation and seeking out public reasons requires that we attempt to see things from the other's point of view, then the skills associated with rhetoric appear to be very much part of successful deliberation. Thus a successful orator truly knows her audience, their desires, concerns, fears and interests, and uses that knowledge in order to speak to the heart' (Chambers 2004). For Chambers, *pathos* steps over the line into the unacceptable 'when it appeals to a set of emotions that are destructive of democracy itself [such as] resentment, hatred, envy and blame' (Chambers 2004).

But while emotional rhetoric is nothing to be afraid of from a deliberative point of view, according to Chambers, publicity may lead the argumentation to become shallow and poorly reasoned. This happens when the public setting involves 'little or no critical accountability'. Such 'plebiscitory reason', as Chambers calls it, involves making vague references to some broad public interest while lacking a coherent argument to back this up (Chambers 2004). The objective of such rhetoric is not to reach understanding but to please or manipulate the audience, assuming it to be incapable of critically holding the speaker to account.

For Elster, taking into account publicity's unfortunate tendency to produce emotional rhetoric, as well as ineffective decision-making processes, results in a dilemma. The optimal degree of publicity is found by a delicate balancing act, which has to be determined case by case. 'With total secrecy, partisan interests and logrolling come to the forefront, whereas full publicity encourages grandstanding and rhetorical overbidding. Conversely, secrecy allows for serious discussion, whereas publicity ensures that any deals struck are capable of withstanding the light of day.' (Elster 1998: 117). Nevertheless, Elster concludes, on the whole publicity 'will lead to more equitable conflict resolutions', (Elster 1995: 258). 'If we take account of equity effects as well as efficiency effects, arguing in public is probably a superior form of collective decision-making than bargaining in private'(Elster 1999: 402).

Most deliberative theorists are in fact much less worried about the objections to the publicity effect coming from negotiation theorists and classical rhetoricians than Elster is. According to James Bohman, 'while there are conflicting accounts of the nature of deliberation all proponents of this conception argue that the publicity of the process of deliberation makes the reasons for a decision more rational and its outcomes more just' (Bohman 1997: 322). On the whole, from a deliberative point of view, the fact that self-interested bargaining is driven out of the forum by publicity compensates for the eventual loss of efficiency and the increase in emotional rhetoric. Even though decision-making processes may become a bit slower, and the rhetoric a bit less rational and substantial, the fact that publicity spurs a more argumentative and public-spirited process is more important. The pros and cons of publicity may require a balancing act from institutional designers but, from a deliberative perspective, increased public-spiritedness weighs heavily in the favour of publicity. However, this proposition can also be questioned.

Two puzzles

Two interesting pieces of research will help to outline two puzzles for the theory of publicity's civilising effect. These go right to the core of the theory, rather than just pointing to unwanted by-products of publicity.

First, Christian Joerges and Jurgen Neyer's study of decision-making within the Comitology committees of the European Union is probably the most cited empirical study focusing on the deliberative qualities of the decision-making processes of the EU (Joerges & Neyer 1997a, 1997b). The Comitology committees consist of delegates from national authorities assisting the Commission in the implementation of European law. According to Joerges and Neyer, these committees are to a large degree governed by deliberative norms of behaviour, where impartial arguments rather than interest-based bargaining carry the day. The interaction between the delegates within the committees is characterised by 'persuasion, argument and discursive processes' rather than 'command, control and/or strategic action' (Joerges & Neyer 1997a: 298).

The puzzle from the point of view of the theory of publicity's civilising effect is how these committees came to develop such norms, in spite of their almost complete lack of transparency and publicity. The Comitology committees are the very symbol of the opaque EU. Not only are the proceedings of the committees confidential but most people probably do not even know that the committees exist. A report from the Swedish Agency for Public Management revealed that not even the Swedish ministries themselves knew fully which committees included Swedish delegates and who those delegates were (Statskontoret 2000: 52).

Joerges and Neyer themselves do not connect their findings to the transparency debate. To the contrary, in a later article Neyer argues, with reference to the theory of publicity's civilising effect, that increased transparency is a 'major precondition' for the realisation of high-quality deliberative practices in the EU (Neyer 2003: 703). But if the Comitology committees satisfy deliberative principles then open doors can certainly not be a necessary condition for making actors adhere to the norms of the forum. In this case openness would seem redundant because this backstage area is already free of market behaviour, if Joerges and Neyer are right.[20] Their result supports the general idea of deliberative democratic theory, that politics is not just like a market; but at the same time it raises questions about the necessity of transparency reforms for promoting behaviour in line with the principles of the forum.

Nina Eliasoph's research also questions the 'backstage-frontstage' logic of the theory of publicity's civilising effect. This logic assumes that public motivations are more public-spirited than private motives. In her study, based on participatory observation of civic groups in America, publicity had completely the opposite effect.

> 'People sounded better backstage than frontstage. … What was announced aloud was less open to debate, less aimed at expressing connection to the wider world, less public-spirited, more insistently selfish, than what was whispered', (Eliasoph 1998: 7). 'The larger the audience, the less eager were speakers to ponder issues of justice and the common good', (Eliasoph 1998: 255). 'They assumed that the public forum was a place for plaintive individuals to expose their side of the story, to "speak for themselves" ' (Eliasoph 1998: 6).

In private conversations, the volunteers and civic group activists Eliasoph met were eager to articulate broad political concerns over environmental deterioration and social injustices. In public forums, and when media were present, they swapped positions and instead motivated their participatory engagement with arguments like 'it's close to home' and 'it affects my family' (Eliasoph 1998: 6). The American public sphere, according to Eliasoph's research, seems to be dominated by a language of self-interest that makes it inappropriate to express one's public-spirited concerns. It was public-spiritedness, not self-interest, which was forced to go underground.

The two 'side-line' objections to the theory discussed in the previous section—the increased risk of lofty and emotional rhetoric and ineffectiveness in the decision-making processes—are fairly uncontroversial, even to deliberative theorists. They constitute unwanted side-effects of publicity but do not really call into question the basic mechanisms of the theory: that publicity produces a shift from self-interested bargaining to a behaviour which at least takes the form of public-spirited arguing and which subsequently traps actors in their own rhetoric. Eliasoph's and Joerges and Neyer's research, however, lead to a different type of criticism, which has not been acknowledged in the deliberative literature. Neither Eliasoph nor Joerges and Neyer make the connection themselves to effects of transparency and publicity but the implications of their results cut right to the core of the theory: could the backstage of politics in reality be more civil—more forum-like—than the frontstage?

On the other hand, the generalisability of these two very different pieces of research should not be over-estimated. Eliasoph shows that, from a grass-roots perspective, the American public sphere seems to be dominated by a 'market-language' of self-interest. But America—the home of individualism and capitalism—one could argue, may be a special case in that respect.[21] Furthermore, her study says nothing of elite reactions to publicity, which is the focus of the theory of publicity's civilising effect and the central question from a transparency-reform perspective. And while it seems surprising, from the point of view of the theory of publicity's civilising effect, to find that such an insulated part of the political sphere as the EU Comitology should be guided by the norms of the forum, that could be explained by the character of the actors involved and the issues on their agenda. The Comitology delegates, it could be argued, are 'Europeanised' experts, with weak links to any political interests, who deliberate over scientific evidence rather than the distribution of costs and benefits. The theory of publicity's civilising effect applies only to actors who are weakly socialised into the norms of the forum. The Comitology delegates may be so strongly socialised to the 'force of the better argument' norm—due to the heavy weight of scientific evidence in the committees—and so decoupled from ordinary interest politics, that they constitute an exceptionally tough case for the theory.

Nevertheless, these two puzzles indicate that the effects of transparency and publicity on the behaviour of political actors are less predictable than assumed by the theory of publicity's civilising effect. This uncertainty of what the effects will be constitutes the starting point for the empirical study of this book, which is described in the next chapters.

BUSINESS LOBBYISTS AS A TEST CASE

The point of choosing business lobbyists as a test case for the theory of publicity's civilising effect is that they, in contrast to Comitology delegates, can be assumed to be the opposite of those strongly socialised into the norms of the forum. Business lobbyists are literally actors of the market. With respect to the back-stage they—if any actors—should be expected to follow the theory of publicity's civilising effect by engaging in market behaviour, i.e. self-interested bargaining. If secrecy invites market behaviour business lobbyists should be among the first to recognise that. Behind closed doors, therefore, industry lobbyists should be an easy case for the theory.

On the front stage, on the other hand, business lobbyists are a tougher case for the theory. Not, however, because they do not care about public norms. Business interest groups and companies should be affected by public norms both directly and indirectly. Directly, because companies care about their public image; being negatively marked makes you more vulnerable both in the stock market and in the political sphere. According to Risse 'even actors such as profit-seeking multinational corporations must justify their actions on the basis of some common goods or shared values' (Risse 2000: 22). Indirectly, business groups should care about public norms because, even though they do not have to win general elections, those who they want to persuade do. Companies and groups with a positive 'social construction', as Ann Schneider and Helen Ingram argue, have more political clout with the decision-makers. 'There are strong pressures for public officials to provide beneficial policy to powerful, positively constructed target populations and to devise punitive, punishment-oriented policy for negatively constructed groups', (Schneider & Ingram 1993: 334). If the non-selfishness norm and the 'force of the better argument' norm dominate the frontstage of politics, therefore, business lobbyists would have to care.

On the other hand, the expectations upon business actors to abide by norms may be lower than for other actors. As described earlier, the non-selfishness norm is dependent upon some uncertainty about the real motives of the actors. If the public audience is in no doubt that some actors are indeed motivated only by self-interest, those actors have nothing to gain from pretending that they are not. They have lost the public's confidence already. While such clear cut cases may not be very common in reality, industry lobbyists presumably have less to lose from being publicly revealed as motivated primarily by self-interest than, for instance, do political parties.

Depending on the outcome of the study, therefore, the generalisability of the results will be stronger for either the backstage or the frontstage behaviour. If the frontstage forces even business lobbyists to cover up their private motives by public-spirited justifications the theory stands strong. On the other hand, if even private lobbying meetings are more civil than the frontstage, the theory seems weak.

The interest group literature

What does previous research on interest groups tell us about such actors' behaviour in public and non-public settings? Can the existing literature be used to draw any conclusions about the prevalence of a civilising effect of publicity on interest group behaviour? Is it really necessary to do more empirical research here?

The subfield within the scholarly interest group literature that comes closest to the description of a backstage-frontstage logic for interest groups, similar to that of the theory of publicity's civilising effect is—paradoxical as it may seem—the economic public choice school. The economist's view of interest groups as rent seekers 'buying' favourable legislation from policy-makers in return for political and economic support describes the ideal-type backstage market behaviour. According to the classical Chicago School of economic interest group theory (see e.g., Stigler & Friedland 1962, Posner 1971, Barro 1973. For an overview see Mitchell & Munger 1991), government

is simply the supplier of regulatory services such as price fixing, restrictions of entry, subsidies, suppression of substitutes, and promotion of complementary goods. In exchange for these highly valuable services, the regulated industry can offer legislators campaign contributions, speaking honoraria, and votes of industry employees and can promise highly remunerative future employ-ment to the regulators. (Mitchell & Munger 1991: 520)

Industry interest groups successfully manage to 'capture' decision-makers and enrich themselves on the expense of the public, according to this literature. Furthermore, the backstage deals that are struck are covered up in a 'public-regarding gloss' in order to 'raise the costs to the public and to rival groups of discovering the true effect of the legislation' (Macey 1986: 251). 'Interest groups and politicians have incentives to engage in activities that make it more difficult for the public to discover the special interest group nature of legislation. This often is accomplished by the subterfuge of masking special interest legislation with a public interest façade', (Macey 1986: 232).

There are two major differences between public choice theory's 'subterfuge' and the deliberative theory of publicity's civilising effect. First, there are no strong hypocrisy constraints in the public choice models. Rhetoric is just rhetoric, in the sense that words do not have to be followed up by deeds. This is a result of the assumption that ordinary voters are 'rationally ignorant' of the foul game played backstage. They cannot see through the rhetorical fog of the frontstage.[22] Therefore interest groups and policy-makers get away with talking the talk with-out walking the walk.[23]

Second, as described before, deliberative theorists assume that there are 'at least some genuinely non-self-interested actors in the system' (Elster 1995: 248), who set the standards of the forum. And while publicity has an important job to do in encouraging weakly socialised actors to adhere to these standards, deliberative theorists do not assume that the backstage is completely empty of public-spirited arguing. Public choice theorists, on the other hand, develop their models from the assumption that no actors are socialised by the norms of the forum, which gives the conspiracy-like results just described.

While the political science literature on interest groups is less cynical about the relationship between lobbyists and government officials than the economic literature, the notion of backstage lobbying as an exchange of goods rather than a discussion on the merits of the proposals is also dominant in this literature. A common view of pluralist interest group systems today, among political scientists, is that lobbyists contribute with 'costly information' to policy-makers (Austen-Smith & Wright 1994: 29). This is information about the impact of different policy options which legislators cannot easily obtain on their own. According to Jeffrey Berry: 'If lobbyists are to do anything to influence members of Congress or administrators beyond the opinions they already hold, they must have something new to bring to their attention.' (Berry 1997: 99). Lobbyists are 'merchants of information', in one classical formulation (Milbrath 1960: 35).[24]

Typically, the pluralist interest group literature depicts lobbyists as either pressur-ing opponents or informing already convinced allies. Neither the informant nor the pressure group is assumed to argue on the merits of a proposal. Informants do not need to persuade those already on their side, merely to provide back-up information to strengthen their positions. Those who attempt to apply pressure, on the other hand, threaten legislators 'that if they do not work with them there may be consequences at the next election, either because the group will withhold cooperation and contributions or because the group will mount an active campaign against the legislator or in support of a rival' (Baumgartner & Leech 1998b: 218).

John Heinz and his colleagues derive from the interest group literature five different perspectives on the nature of the relationship between interest groups and government—pressure, bargaining, aggregation, mediation and symbiosis—none of which emphasise arguing about the merits of different proposals. 'It seems fair to say', they claim, 'that the prevailing mode of thinking about interest group politics has employed some version of the pressure model'. According to this model, 'groups know what they want and make their demands on officials accordingly, offering incentives or threatening disincentives in the event of non-cooperation' (Heinz et. al. 1993: 13).

While there is an impressive empirical literature on interest groups' use of different tactics—insider and outsider strategies, coalition-building, agenda-setting, litigation strategies, campaign contributions etc.[25]—these studies typically neglect the substance of the messages put forward. Little consideration has been given to the actual content of the costly information. Hojnacki and Baumgartner note that there has been little empirical research on the use of different types of arguments by interest groups. With respect to public-interest arguments, which they call 'symbolic appeals', they note that; 'efforts to specify and test under what conditions these appeals are used and are more or less effective have not been undertaken'.[26]

The pluralist interest group literature is largely dominated by American scholars, working on the Washington political system. In Europe the pluralist picture of the role of interest groups has, since the 1970s, been complemented by corporatist theory. European scholars have noted that pluralist theory, picturing a highly competitive group system, does a poor job of explaining the patterns of close cooperation between strong state actors and a few large and centralised interest organisations, which have traditionally characterised much of European politics. With respect to the backstage-frontstage logic, corporatist theory draws largely on negotiation theory, suggesting that elite negotiations between the organisation leaders and the government should be kept private in order to be effective (Streeck & Schmitter 1985: 13). Deals are struck behind closed doors between the elites and legitimated to the grassroots via the hierarchical structures of the organisations. In traditional corporatist theory, the interactions between the negotiating parties are assumed to be cooperative bargaining based on the interests of the participating actors, rather than arguing about the common good. The public interest is safeguarded in this process to the extent that the organisations are encompassing enough to actually represent all, or nearly all, interests in society.[27]

In the wake of the 'deliberative turn' in democratic theory, however, some theorists have suggested that corporatist arrangements can induce arguing about public interests.[28] According to this view, corporatist institutions, including long-term face-to-face interactions, can have an effect on actors similar to that predicted by the theory of publicity's civilising effect. It may 'hamper the exercise of raw power' (Mansbridge 1992: 496) that is assumed to characterise pluralist systems and encourage deliberation between the parties. PerOla Öberg claims to have found 'strong indications of deliberation' in one case study of administrative corporatism (Öberg 2002: 468).

Partly due to the methodological difficulties of getting access to the private meetings of corporatist institutions, there are few empirical studies that focus on the mode of communication within such institutions. If corporatist institutions are better interpreted as arenas for deliberation, rather than bargaining, a similar puzzle to the one arising from Joerges and Neyers' research on Comitology challenges the theory of publicity's civilising effect. Again, the backstage seems to be compatible with arguing, in that case. There will thus be little market behaviour in the corporatist settings for publicity to civilize.

In sum, the scholarly interest group literature is not unsupportive of the backstage-frontstage logic of the theory of publicity's civilising effect but nor does it clearly verify the theory either. It seems that we simply know too little of what exactly is being said when lobbyists meet decision-makers. The concept of pressure—the actual substance of the messages put forward by lobbyists to decision-makers—has not been adequately problematised and investigated in the pluralist tradition. The dominant picture, however, is one of an exchange of goods, rather than arguing aimed at convincing decision-makers of the merits of a proposal. Corporatist theory, on the other hand, does not apply to competitive lobbying as much as to especially state-organised decision-making institutions. These are usually assumed to be dominated by a problem-solving style of bargaining. Deliberative corporatist theorists, on the other hand, question that assumption. Paradoxically, the greatest support for the existence of a civilising effect on the rhetoric (although based on formal modelling rather than empirical research) comes from public choice theorists, while the least support comes from theorists who emphasise the deliberative qualities of non-public corporatist arrangements. Publicity is more of a disturbing than a civilising factor in the later case.[29]

So far, however, there has been no systematic comparison of the content of interest group argumentation backstage and frontstage. In the next chapter I will describe how I have designed my study to do just that, with the purpose of putting the theory of publicity's civilising effect to the test.

NOTES

1   For an introduction, see Hoy 1986.

2   For a critique of the deliberative ideal in the spirit of Foucault, see Sanders, who argues that deliberation is a request for 'a certain kind of talk: rational, contained, and oriented to a shared problem. ... Arguing that democratic discussion should be rational, moderate, and not selfish implicitly excludes public talk that is impassioned, extreme, and the product of particular interests'. The consequence, according to Sanders, is a model of democracy

which will favour some and exclude others: 'It favours a form of expression and discourse that makes it likely that the talk of an identifiable and privileged sector of the American public will dominate public dialogue.' Sanders 1997: 370. Also, from a pluralist perspective of democracy, the idea of perceiving a frank defence of self- and group-interests as uncivilized behaviour will be contested.

3   Diversity theorists—emphasising the importance of social differences based on gender, ethnicity, sexuality, class, etc.—challenge such a rationalistic model. Melissa Williams argues that 'whether or not citizens will recognize others' reasons *as* reasons may be a socio-cultural contingent matter'. Moreover, 'it seems likely that the contingency of this recognition may tend to be resolved in a manner that systematically disadvantages the reasons of marginalized groups in a discursive exchange'. Williams 2000: 125. See also, for example, Benhabib 2002, Young 1996, and compare Sanders 1997. In a similar vein, James Bohman argues that the dominant view in deliberative democratic theory of the public sphere as an arena where 'citizenship requires adopting a particular role and point of view, which abstracts from all contingent features of oneself, such as social and institutional roles, selfish interests, and particular religious and ethnic identities' is inadequate for a pluralistic and differentiated society. The participating parties must be prepared to broaden their particular perspectives, in order for the public sphere to contribute to cooperation and problem-solving. But they need not be ashamed of taking that particular perspective as their starting point for the deliberations. Instead 'the public use of reason is [dependent on] the capacities of each to engage the other from within its own cultural perspectives, epistemic resources, and social positions'. Bohman 1999: 182.

4   Common references here are Schumpeter 1943, Downs 1957, Buchanan & Tullock 1962, Riker 1982, as well as classical pluralist works such as Truman 1951 and Dahl 1956. Two branches of the rational choice perspective are often depicted as the main competitors of deliberative democratic theory; social choice theory and public choice theory, which share the assumptions of utility maximizing rational actors with (at least in the short term) fixed preferences. Social choice theory must not necessarily be depicted against deliberative democratic theory, however. Dryzek and List argue that social choice theory and deliberative democratic theory, which they claim are 'the two most influential traditions of contemporary theorizing about democracy', are complementary rather than competing theories. The pessimistic conclusions of social choice theory of the possibilities of rationally aggregating individual preferences into a collective decision associated with Arrow's theorem may be overcome, according to Dryzek and List, if deliberative components are included in the decision-making procedure. See Dryzek & List 2003. A similar argument has been put forward by David Miller. See Miller 1992. Knight and Johnson argue that social choice theory may in fact demonstrate the need for deliberative procedures. If deliberation can help voters agreeing about 'what is at stake', thereby reducing the dimensions over which they disagree, instability (cyclical social orderings) may be avoided. Knight and Johnson's conclusion, however, is much less optimistic than Dryzek and List's, as they remain sceptical about whether such common understanding will be possible to achieve in pluralistic societies, given that fair deliberative procedures require equal opportunities for all to participate in the deliberations. See Knight & Johnson 1994.

5   The effect of publicity on the mode of communication thus is derived from the activation in public of the force of the better argument norm. One can also assume that bargaining

becomes more difficult in public due to the fact that publicity opens up for a broader partici-pation of interested actors. According to Fisher, Ury and Patton the more parties involved the more important it becomes, for the sake of the efficiency of the decision-making process that the parties use 'objective criteria'—rather than bargain over positions—when settling their disputes. 'In such cases [many parties involved] positional bargaining is difficult at best.' Fisher, Ury & Patton 1999: 87.

6   The non-selfishness norm can also be seen as a logical consequence of the combination of a 'force of the better argument' norm and an effort on behalf of the actors to reach consensus. If the actors are genuinely trying to reach consensus, and if they are forbidden by the 'force of the better argument' norm from bargaining on the decision, then purely self-regarding arguments are useless as they will not persuade anyone and will therefore not bring the actors closer to a decision.

7   The proposition that self-interested arguments are illegitimate will be too strong, from a normative point of view, for some deliberative theorists. See note 3 in this chapter. Nevertheless, the existence of a non-selfishness norm is one of the basic assumptions behind the theory of publicity's civilizing effect, as defended by many deliberative theorists.

8   A more precise definition of the dependent variables—the mode of communication and the types of justification—is made in the next chapter, in relation to the specification of hypotheses for the empirical study. The concepts of other- and ideal-regarding justifica-tions, it will be seen, are somewhat more nuanced and do a better job for the theory than public-regarding.

9   Cf. Lerner & Tetlock, reviewing experimental work on effects of accountability to an audience, comparing cases when the audience's views are known versus unknown. When the audience's views are known conformity becomes a likely strategy, people adopting positions likely to gain the audience's support—even if this implies inefficient decision outcomes. When the audience's views are unknown, on the other hand, people tend to engage in 'preemptive self-criticism' meaning that they 'think in more self-critical, inte-gratively complex ways in which they consider multiple perspectives on the issue and try to anticipate the objections that reasonable others might raise to positions that they might take'. Lerner & Tetlock 1999: 256f.

10   Some examples are the following: 'The open arena encourages one to direct one's speech and one's voting in a public interest direction.' Brennan & Pettit 1990, p.320. 'Publicity is thought to have a positive effect on deliberation by promoting a democratic mechanism that pushes participants from private to public reason.' Chambers 2004. 'Public debate induces actors to replace the language of power by the language of reason, i.e. they have to appeal to common norms and values. This does not necessarily eliminate egocentric motives, but forces actors to hide them.' Eriksen & Fossum 2000: 27, note 26. 'One advantage of public discussion before a vote would be that the participants might be disinclined to make or support purely self-interested proposals for fear of appearing selfish.' Fearon 1998: 54. 'The condition of publicity [...] removes morally repugnant preferences.' Föllesdal 2000: 92. 'Within an open deliberative framework the representatives are forced to filter out mere self-interested arguments.' Gargarella 2000: 202. 'Certain kinds of argument, power-ful though they may be in private deliberations, simply cannot be put in a public forum.', Goodin 1986: 87. 'Deliberation in the public realm has a certain purifying effect on the arguments brought forward and (ultimately) the preferences formed. Preferences formed

under public conditions are more likely to be directed to the *public* rather than the *private* good.' Karlsson 2001: 61. Publicity works 'as a filter to openly selfish claims'. Neyer 2003: 694. 'It is virtually impossible in public debates to make self-serving arguments or to justify one's claims on self-interested grounds.' Risse 2000: 17.

11 SAFT. App. B, doc 16.

12 Schimmelfennig has demonstrated how the consistency constraint may work in practice and how it can be used strategically in order to entrap actors in their own rhetoric. In his study of the European Union's decision in 1998 to open up full accession to ten Central and Eastern European states, Schimmelfennig shows how those member states whose egoistic preferences were in favour of a weaker form of association, rather than full accession, were gradually manoeuvred towards a decision of accession. This was the result of a process of rhetorical action, where the pro-accession states skilfully pushed the reluctant states towards a positive decision, by confronting them with the choice of publicly subscribing to or opposing small steps towards enlargement. Since enlargement was firmly tied to a norm of pan-European community, it was difficult to raise such opposition. With each small step and public commitment 'the credibility costs of non-enlargement rose'. Schimmelfennig 2001: 74. Eventually, 'the opponents of a firm commitment to Eastern enlargement found themselves rhetorically entrapped. They could neither openly oppose nor threaten to veto enlargement without damaging their credibility as community members'. Ibid: 48. Unfortunately, the consistency constraint will work also when the rhetoric is 'uncivil'. Finel & Lord have argued that transparency and belligerent rhetoric may be a dangerous combination for that reason, making it more difficult for leaders to escape from being drawn into violent conflicts in a crisis situation. Finel & Lord 1999: 335. For a more positive view of transparency's effect on conflict and war, see Schultz 1998 and Fearon 1995.

13 I am referring here primarily to Schelling 1960, Walton & McKersie 1965, Fisher, Ury & Patton 1999, Putnam 1988 and Elgström & Jönsson 2000.

14 Diego Gambetta has argued that there are important cultural variations with respect to the decisiveness norm. In what he calls 'Claro!-cultures', which are characterised by 'discursive machisimo', people are expected to demonstrate strong opinions from the outset on all issues. See Gambetta 1998.

15 Arguing, however, is not the same as deliberation. Deliberation also includes reciprocity, i.e. genuine efforts at respecting, understanding and taking into account the arguments of the other participants (See for instance Gutman & Thompson 1996: 2f). Arguing involves speaking, deliberation involves speaking and listening.

16 Cf. Checkel 2001: 570. For the parties to be able to treat the frontstage as a temporary arena, as assumed in negotiation theory, there must be a non-public backstage available for them to finish the job of reaching agreement. If all formal decision-making forums are opened up for the public, therefore, there is a risk that the negotiations go 'underground', into informal arenas. A common argument against opening up the doors of the EU Council of Minister's meetings is that negotiations would take place in the corridor, over lunch or in the sauna, rather than at the formal meeting. See, for example, Mather 1997. Cf. Curtin 1996: 104, Lord 1998: 88. Increased formal publicity leads to less actual publicity, according to this view. A misguided transparency reform may in fact have the contrary effect of reducing the number of participants having access to the core decision-making. Some

actors, perhaps the less powerful, may get lost between the formal public and the informal non-public, but real, decision-making arena. According to Fisher, Ury and Patton 'no matter how many people are involved in a negotiation, important decisions are typically made when no more than two people are in the room'. Fisher, Ury & Patton 1999: 37.

17 As I have argued elsewhere: 'If deliberation is about transforming preferences, and publicity forces you to know what you want and stand by your position, then 'public deliberation' is something of a contradiction in terms' (Naurin 2003a p: 32). Cf. Gambetta 1998.

18 According to Chambers the passion-reason distinction 'is notoriously problematic for philosophical as well as normative reasons. It opens up a Pandora's box of trouble for any concept of public reason, implying as it does a narrow, philosophically, culturally, and perhaps gender specific view of what is appropriate in the public sphere. Outside of the philosophical debate, common sense should tell us that emotion can and does have a respectable role to play in the public sphere.' Chambers 2004. Cf. note 3 in this chapter. This normative debate does not, however, affect the empirical hypothesis that publicity encourages passionate rhetoric. See also Walzer 1999, who argues that democratic politics would be practically impossible to pursue without the mobilising force of passionate rhetoric. 'It is literally true that parties and movements seek to indoctrinate their members, that is, to bring them to accept a doctrine [...] Whether this sort of thing is good or bad, it is enormously important in political life, because the political identity of most people, or, better, of most of the people who are engaged by politics, is shaped in this way.' Walzer 1999: 59.

19 Cicero, *Brutus* 80.279, quoted from Remer 1999: 42f.

20 For a critique, see Pollack, who argues that the member states use the Comitology to control the Commission. The preferences of the committee delegates, therefore, can not be assumed to be as flexible as Joerges and Neyer's deliberative model suggests. Pollack 2003.

21 Cf. Miller, who argues that in Western cultures there exists a norm which specifies that 'self-interest both is and ought to be a powerful determinant of behavior'. Miller 1999: 1053.

22 Nevertheless, there is at least an implicit argument in the economic theory of interest groups in favour of increased transparency and publicity: The more informed the voters are on an issue the less influential rent-seeking interest groups will be, as the implications of the deals struck will be more easily discovered. Cf. Denzau & Munger 1986.

23 In fact, 'walking the walk' for public choice theorists would in most cases imply deregulation of markets and the withdrawal of politics from large parts of society.

24 Milbrath 1960: 35. Cf. Bouwen 2002, for an application to the European Union.

25 See, for example, Schlozman & Tierney 1986, Walker 1991, Heinz *et. al.* 1993, Kollman 1998. For an overview of the literature see Baumgartner & Leech 1998a (and, in Swedish, Naurin 2001).

26 Hojnacki & Baumgartner 2003: 3. See also Hojnacki *et. al.* 2006, for an explorative study of the arguments used by Washington lobbyists in a sample of 98 policy issues, showing, for example, that the types of arguments used to some extent depends on whether the lobbyist defends or challenges the status quo.

27 For an overview of the literature, see Williamson 1989.

28 See, for example, Mansbridge 1992, Öberg 2002.

29 Cf. Öberg 1994: 281.

chapter three | research design

The key to investigating effects of transparency and publicity on political behaviour is to be able to study political actors moving in and out of the non-public backstage and the public frontstage of politics. Most difficult is getting access to the backstage. This is the place, according to the theory of publicity's civilising effect, where we can expect to see the norms of the forum being violated. Naturally, few political actors will allow a researcher to see that. This methodological difficulty is approached in two different ways in this study of business lobbyists in Brussels and in Stockholm. First, rather than speaking to the main actors involved in the 'play', I have chosen to interview the 'directors'. Second, I have acquired documentation from the people with whom they interact: the institutions that they seek to lobby.

THE PUBLIC AFFAIRS CONSULTANTS

Public affairs (PA) consultants, sometimes referred to as 'hired guns' or 'lobbyists for hire',[1] have as their job to guide business leaders to success in the political sphere. PA consultants make their profit from their knowledge of the terms of the forum. They, if anyone, should know which norms apply to which actors under what circumstances—backstage and frontstage—in the political sphere. To use Goffman's terminology (again), the PA consultants are experts on 'footing' (Goffman 1981: chapter 3), on 'assessing the grounds for interaction' (Eliasoph 1998: 21) with actors in the political sphere. Stepping over from one social context to another, from the market to the backstage to the frontstage of politics, involves making judgments about what to communicate and how. 'Are there stairs here? Loose gravel? Ice? To walk we have to assess the footing. Talking is the same: are we talking to make conversation? To accomplish a task? To show off?' (Eliasoph 1998: 21). Those who misstep and violate the norms of the different contexts may fail to accomplish their task.

PA consultants direct their clients both backstage and frontstage. At the same time they also have a certain degree of outsider's perspective, which make them valuable as interview subjects. Their own businesses are not at stake in the particular cases they are managing. Part of their job is to give a fresh, independent view of the issues. They also have access to the non-political market sphere from which their clients originate. This access is not complete, as will be shown in the next chapter (some clients are unwilling to reveal all relevant private company information to consultants) but at least they have good insights. This is important because the business leader's journey from the world of affairs, markets and consumers to the world of politics and public opinion involves two transitions, according to the theory of publicity's civilising effect. Both transitions are relevant for testing the theory. The business leader's first transition is from the market sphere to the forum. The second involves the business leader moving back and forth between the backstage and frontstage of politics—private communication with decision-makers, on the one hand, and public speeches and statements on the other—which is where the theory assumes that the civilising effect takes place. Interviewing PA consultants makes it possible to study both transitions predicted by the theory through the eyes of those who are responsible for their success.

The methodological function of the PA consultants in this study is to be the antennae for what is right and wrong in different lobbying contexts. Their reactions to the stimulus material in the interviews will be treated as indicative of what they consider to be successful lobbying behaviour. An assumption underlying the design, therefore, is that PA consultants actually do have the expertise that they claim to have.

The sample of consultancy firms chosen for the study is, for that reason, not intended to be representative of the PA consultancy market.[2] Instead I have chosen to interview the best, according to reputation. Of course, reputation—talking to people in the lobbying communities of Brussels and Stockholm (consultants, trade association representatives, companies, civil servants, and researchers)—is not a foolproof method of finding 'the best' but I could not think of any better method either. It turned out that the best, according to reputation, largely corresponded to the largest. In Brussels four large firms were repeatedly mentioned;[3] in Stockholm, three.[4] These firms were selected for the interviews, along with an additional four firms in Brussels[5] and four in Stockholm[6] that were also mentioned. Within these firms, I asked to meet the head of environmental affairs, since the case study designed for the interviews (to which I will return soon) involves environmental policy. If there was no such person I asked to meet the head of public affairs.

Before the design of the study was fixed I conducted several background interviews with consultants, interest groups, and civil servants, both in Brussels and in Stockholm. From those interviews it was clear that the consultants would not be very generous with information on actual cases they had. Even though they are, to some extent, both insiders and outsiders, they would not break confidentiality agreements with their clients for the sake of academic research. Instead, in this study, the consultants were asked to comment on a hypothetical case. The case involves a road transport organisation which has a problem with a new proposal for eco-taxes on trucks. Talking hypothetically clearly made the interviewees more comfortable and decreased the risk of their giving 'politically correct' answers. While not all problems of political correctness are thereby solved, at least they are partly neutralised. The best evidence for that is probably that the interviewees were in fact quite frank in their discussions of when and how they would let their hypothetical client use 'market behaviour'. They were also frank about the fact that their job implies getting paid to influence public policy in favour of private interests. 'We're not NGOs. At the end of the day companies will try to lobby something for profit' (Brussels IP 2). Neither would they pretend to be morally bound by any particular argumentative method if it failed to promote their clients' interests. 'What's important when it comes to arguments is not to be in the right, but to win the argument' (Stockholm IP 3).

An additional advantage of constructing the case to be used in the interviews from scratch was the possibility of controlling for other factors. The case is designed to control for as many potentially disturbing variables as possible (such as size of actor, policy network, type of issue, degree of media attention, etc.). The interviews then could concentrate attention on the three relevant settings: 1) the pre-political (market) stage of the first meetings between the consultant and the client; 2) the backstage meetings with lower-level civil servants responsible for the drafting of the eco-tax proposal; 3) a public frontstage appearance at an open conference on the future of transport policy where 'everybody', including the media, is present. The case study is described in detail in the next chapter.

The degree of transparency and publicity was varied in two ways in the interviews. First, scenarios were switched within each interview, between closed meetings with officials and a public conference speech. Second, interviews with eight PA consultants in Brussels, lobbying the allegedly opaque European Commission, were compared with interviews with seven consultants in Stockholm whose job it is to influence the uniquely transparent Swedish governmental ministries.

The comparison between Stockholm and Brussels is motivated by the varying levels of transparency in the two settings. The Swedish 'publicity principle' is protected by the constitution and has been an integral part of Swedish politics since the eighteenth century. Freedom of information laws in Sweden are exceptionally far-reaching. Almost everything that is put on paper by any member of the government's administration is made publicly available. 'Whenever a decision is made by an administrative authority, not only the decision itself but also all the documents forming the basis for the decision become public' (Larsson 1998: 34). All incoming mail is publicly available, a situation frequently utilised by the media. 'Journalists are keen to use this opportunity, and the mass media employ staff whose task it is regularly to check the incoming mail of ministries and larger authorities' (Larsson 1998: 36). Even secret information can be legally leaked to the press by government officials. 'Civil servants have a unique position in the sense that the Constitution guarantees them the right to inform the media of the activities of the administrative authorities—the so called "freedom to impart information" ' (Larsson 1998: 34). The information may only be leaked to the media, and only under the provision that it is published, the whole idea being that information about mismanagement should become public.[7]

The EU, on the other hand, is usually accused of lacking transparency, as noted in the introductory chapter. 'The political process within the Union suffers from a lack of openness and transparency that makes it difficult for the citizens of the Union to acquire reliable and accurate information on community affairs', according to Christer Karlsson (Karlsson 2001: 64). 'None of the main European institutions fully satisfies what are usually considered as the important democratic principles of popular responsiveness and accountability; nor is much of the business of government subject to the normative publicity associated with transparent decision-making and freedom of information', argue Richard Bellamy and Dario Castiglione (Bellamy & Castiglione 2000: 69).[8]

The EU has only recently developed a freedom of information act, which was still in the process of being implemented during the fieldwork of this study (2001–2).[9] If a Commission or a Council official is found to have leaked without a superior's permission, that official's job will be at risk. 'Officials of the Union are not at liberty to reveal secret information to the media. Indeed, the EU's officials are explicitly required not to disclose information. ... Any information leaked may thus involve repercussions.' (Karlsson 2001: 69). While Swedish officials who leak secret information are protected by the constitution (their superiors being forbidden to investigate who the source is), EU Commission officials can be sacked because of leaked information about fraud and mismanagement.[10] That is not to say that confidential documents are not being leaked from the EU institutions—they certainly are—but on a much more *ad hoc* basis. The Commission is also less exposed to media and public scrutiny than the ministries in Stockholm, not least because politics in Brussels is distanced from the general public. In Scharpf's terminology, EU politics is 'below the threshold of political visibility' (Scharpf 1999: 23).

The interviews with the public affairs consultants focused on lobbying lower-level officials. Both in Stockholm and in Brussels, these officials are subject to an indirect publicity pressure coming from the ministers and commissioners, who need to have arguments at hand that can be used in the public sphere should the media become interested in a particular policy proposal. Interest groups can be expected to take this factor into account when lobbying these administrations. Swedish civil servants, in addition, also have a *direct* link with the public due to the 'sunshine acts'. Torbjörn Larsson argues that this affects their behaviour:

Civil servants in the [Swedish] administration know that everything they write or include in the formal act of the decision may become public material, and this fact in itself influences their writing and behaviour. Therefore it is fair to assume that the image of the activities of administrative authorities created by public records is to a certain extent arranged with this in mind. In a government where almost all official documents are public it becomes even more important to find arguments that can be defended to the public and, even more importantly, to give the impression that this decision is not only the best but also the only possible solution to a certain problem. (Larsson 1998: 35)

If the theory of publicity's civilising effect is correct, it seems reasonable to assume that Swedish civil servants have stronger incentives to draft their proposals using justifications that they can put on paper and defend publicly. Therefore, if institutionalising transparency—and thereby increasing the risks/chances for publicity—is an important determinant of political behaviour, different signals to those who wish to influence them should come from the Swedish ministries compared to the European Commission. The PA consultants are the ones who should be able to notice and interpret those signals.

Obviously, the degree of transparency is not the only factor distinguishing Swedish politics from the politics of the EU. All comparative studies are vulnerable to 'omitted variables' disturbing the comparison (King, Keohane & Verba 1994: 186). One such factor could be the long tradition of corporatism and consensus politics in Sweden. Swedish political actors are used to negotiation and seeking compromises, while the EU lobbying system is often described as more competitive and pluralist.[11] If the theorists who emphasise the deliberative character of corporatism are right, as discussed in the previous chapter, Swedish actors may have been socialised into a deliberative behaviour that is not a result of transparency but rather of long-term face-to-face interactions. Another difference between the two settings that may affect the results is the fact that the European Commission is not accountable to voters in democratic elections. The Swedish government, therefore, should be more worried about its public image than the Commission is.

However, given the fact that the results of the study, as will be demonstrated, do not indicate any civilising transparency effect, this potential weakness of the design rather strengthens the validity of the results. In spite of the high degree of corporatism in Sweden, and the low degree of accountability of the Commission, there was no indication of a higher level of adherence to the norms of the forum in Stockholm than in Brussels.

There may be more factors that disturb the comparison between Stockholm and Brussels—few comparative studies are watertight in this respect—but if variation in the degree of transparency makes a significant difference it should be possible to detect that from a comparison of two extreme points on the scale.

THE LETTERS

The second way in which the empirical study is designed to gain insight into the backstage performance of lobbyists and compare it to frontstage activities is through analysis of documentation obtained from the lobbied institutions themselves. The fact that this was possible is largely a result of the increasing drive towards transparency in the EU, which was the starting point of the study. Thanks to the new regulations on access to the documents of EU institutions—EC No

1049/2001—it was also possible to study the potential effects of transparency and publicity on paper. Formerly confidential letters in Brussels are compared, in chapter five, to publicly available Swedish letters, on the one hand, and published position papers and press releases on the other.

In Sweden, letters sent from companies and organisations to officials in the government ministries are publicly available. The letters are carefully archived by the administration in a searchable public database, and copies of letters can be ordered. Letters to the European Commission, on the other hand, have until recently been confidential and only arbitrarily archived. When my search for such letters started, the initial idea was to take advantage of the fact that the Swedish Environment Commissioner, Margot Wallström, had publicly taken a high profile on the question of transparency. Her cabinet had been sending out the message that DG Environment was a forerunner within the Commission on this issue, archiving records and publishing information widely.[12] My hope, in the early fall of 2001, was that it would be possible to receive confidential letters from DG Environment, under the provision that the identity of senders would not be revealed. Informal contacts with Wallström's cabinet were vaguely positive and investigations started within the directorate into how this could be accomplished (which letters could be searched for, where they could be found, who should make the judgments on whether they could be given out, etc.). The cabinet worried somewhat about the reactions of the civil servants involved ('we can't force them to give out the letters if they don't want to'[13]), but they were nevertheless prepared to provide some support, for instance by sitting in on meetings with civil servants and myself concerning the search for letters. Involved in that process, when consulted by DG Environment, was also the General Secretariat of the Commission, which is the unit responsible for internal administrative rules and procedures. At that time they were working on the details of the implementation of the new regulation on access to documents in the EU institutions. The new regulation, which was agreed upon in May 2001 and would come into force in December, would make third-party letters publicly available in principle, subject to certain exemptions. To the surprise of this author, as well as the staff-members of DG Environment who were engaged in the issue, the General Secretariat eventually made it clear that they intended to interpret the new regulation as applying also *retroactively* to documents already received by the Commission. It would therefore be possible to apply formally for access to letters which were sent to the Commission before the new regulation was taken, and under the assumption of the sender that they would be treated confidentially. This would apply not only to DG Environment but to all directorates.

The main problem, after the legal issues had worked out unexpectedly well, turned out to be finding the letters. I was told that searching in central archives of the Commission or the DGs would yield very little. Letters were kept—if they were saved—in the individual archives of the civil servants responsible for the dossiers. The advice was to direct any requests directly to the Heads of Units and hope that they would be able to engage their staff in searching their personal

archives. The support of the cabinet would increase the odds of receiving cooperation from DG Environment.

This request for letters from the Commission was definitely one of the first,
probably the first, of its kind. Taking into account, first, that the interpretation
from the General Secretariat of the new regulation as applying retroactively was
not evident from the legal text and appeared to be rather controversial and, second,
the fact that the success of the request was highly dependent on the cooperation of
the units involved, there was a limit to how many letters that could be requested.
It was clear from communications with DG Environment civil servants that,
although they would 'of course do anything to assist this important project', this
would also be an additional burden on their already much-too-heavy workloads.
The implicit conclusion was that my request should take their workload into consideration. This constraint affected the sample of letters which could be collected.
The number of letters could not be in the thousands.

Ideally, the sample would include both confidential letters and public position papers from the same organisations in Brussels, concerning the same policy
issues, and publicly available letters from, if not the same, at least similar organisations in Stockholm, also concerning similar policy issues. Before the request to
the Commission was made, therefore, it was necessary to ensure that those senders and policy issues for which letters were requested had comparable cases in
Stockholm. Consultations were made with civil servants and interest organisations
in Brussels and Stockholm in order to identify potential candidates: which policy
issues had been on the agenda both in Sweden and in Brussels the last couple
of years? Which organisations and companies were active on those issues? Two
environmental policy areas seemed to be suitable; dangerous substances, including chemicals, and transport policy. An additional methodological advantage with
choosing environmental policy, apart from the possibility of making comparisons
between the national and the EU level, is that it is a policy area where it is possible to make a clear distinction between self-interest (industry profitability) and
common interests and ideals (macro-economy, environment).

A search was conducted in the Swedish public archives for letters from organisations and companies within these policy fields. Comparing the result of that
search with the information from people who knew these sectors in Brussels, a
list of fifteen senders (nine companies, six business associations) and five policy
issues was compiled for the request to the Commission. The request was then
directed to the relevant units within DG Environment, as well as to the director-
generals of DG Enterprise, DG Transport and Energy, DG Competition, and DG
Internal Market. It applied for access to all letters (including faxes and e-mails)
received from these senders relating to the specified policy issues during a time
period of three years (1999–2001).[14]

The response was a total of 143 letters from thirteen senders. After having sorted out, first, letters which did not directly address the policy issues (instead containing only invitations to conferences, confirmations of or requests for meetings,
requests for information, discussions of who should be on which committees and

other procedural issues, and so on) and, second, letters that were official position papers rather than confidential letters, 69 letters remained. Of these 69 confidential letters sent to Commission officials, 58 contained a clear position on the issue at hand on behalf of the sender (others contained information relevant to the issue but without explicitly promoting any particular position) and could therefore be used in the analysis of whether and how these companies and associations argued for their preferred position. The ten senders of those letters (of whom three contributed only one letter each) dealt with chemicals policy and hazardous substances in electronic equipment (48 letters, of which sixteen came from the European chemicals industry association Cefic), and transport policy (ten letters from the car and oil industries).

A similar sorting of letters received from the search in Stockholm gave 63 letters from seven senders within the same policy sectors, of which 55 contained a position which was promoted by the sender. After the sample of confidential letters was finalised, a search on the websites of the remaining senders for position papers and press releases gave 45 documents, 41 with a clear position. The time period was stretched to ten years (1991–2000) for the Swedish letters and eight years (1996–2003) for the public documents, in order to be able to collect an approximately equal number of documents from each category. (Appendix A gives an overview of the sample of documents, focusing on the comparability of the confidential Brussels letters, the Stockholm letters and the press releases and public position papers. A list of all the documents used in the analysis is given in Appendix B.)

The document analysis not only provides a complementary method to the interviews. It also provides a check on whether the stories coming from the PA consultants are relevant to the real world. The purpose of interviewing the consultants was that they should be able to indicate how a successful lobbyist should behave, taking into account the norms of the different stages on which they act. In that way, the different incentive structures of the backstage and the frontstage in Brussels and in Sweden could be studied. They are not a credible source, however, for drawing conclusions on how interest groups in general actually do behave, given the fact that not all lobbyists use consultants, and especially not the best. If the incentive structures are difficult to 'read', they will have less effect on actors with 'bounded rationality'. Or to put it differently, if one is unaware of the norms one will not adjust one's behaviour in response. While the interviews focus on hypothetical behaviour under ideal conditions, thus, the letters document real action.

HYPOTHESES

As described, there are two types of variation in the degree of transparency and publicity used in the study. The shifting of scenarios between closed meetings and a public conference speech in the interviews, and the comparison between confidential letters and public positions and press releases, investigates what I will call the publicity effect. The comparisons between Brussels and Sweden, on the other hand, both in the interviews and in the letters, analyses the transparency effect. The publicity effect hits the lobbyists directly as they address a public audience. The transparency effect is indirect, reaching them via the increased need for the civil servants to adhere to public norms and the risk of publicity (which follows from the fact that the publicly available letters may reach a broader audience). The point of studying both types of effects is to be able to give a more nuanced account of the effects of transparency and publicity. Does the civilising effect require actual publicity, i.e. exposure to a broad audience, or is it sufficient that the actors *anticipate* an increased risk of publicity? Furthermore, it seems reasonable to assume that the publicity effect will be stronger than the transparency effect, given the direct relation to the audience.

The mechanism behind the publicity effect is straightforward. A speaker standing before a public audience will be punished by that audience if she violates a norm about which the audience cares. The transparency effect has a somewhat longer distance to travel before it reaches its target. The second part of the following line of reasoning from Elster, concerning different strategic reasons for an actor to misrepresent self-interested motives as impartial reason, describes the transparency effect.

> When A interacts with B before a public consisting of C, D, ..., A has two reasons for misrepresenting his interest as an impartial appeal to reason. First, B might, for all A knows, be one of the genuinely impartial members of society. If A expresses his interest directly, he will both lose the chance of persuading B and run the risk of being punished by B. Second, even if B does not belong to that subset, A knows that B will know that one of C, D, ... belongs to it. A knows that B knows that if B fails to punish A, one of C, D ... will punish B, which gives B an incentive to punish A for expressing purely self-interested concerns. (Elster 1999: 374)

A lobbyist (A) in Stockholm sending a letter including an explicit bargain such as 'if you do X, we'll give you Y' would not only run the risk of being revealed as breaking the force of the better argument norm herself, should the letter reach a broader audience. She would also force the Stockholm civil servant (B) to make calculations based on the risk of publicity. A risk-averse civil servant will reject the offer and possibly punish the lobbyist in some way, for instance, by exclusion from an advisory committee, in order not to be regarded as a norm-breaker by the public (C, D, ...). In the Brussels case, on the other hand, there would be a much smaller risk of the public coming to know about the bargaining offer, since the letter would be confidential.[15]

The third type of effect studied is the forum effect, which is the change in behaviour forced upon a market actor, a company CEO, for instance, stepping over from the market sphere to the backstage of the political sphere. Following the theory of publicity's civilising effect, we should assume that this step is not a very dramatic one. Self-interested bargaining is assumed to dominate not only the market but also the non-public areas of politics. The forum effect is studied in the first part of the interviews, in which the consultants were asked to describe the first meetings with a new client about to enter the political sphere to influence a policy proposal.

Due to the differing degrees of transparency in Brussels and Stockholm, the forum effect and the publicity effect will, if the theory is correct, have different strengths in the two settings. The Brussels backstage will be more of a 'real' backstage in the Goffman sense, where actors relax from the norms of the frontstage, than the Swedish 'goldfish bowl'. Even though private meetings between lobbyists and civil servants are formally just as private in Stockholm as in Brussels, the former are held under a stronger 'shadow of publicity' than the latter. This leads up to two propositions about the forum effect and the publicity effect. First, the step from the market to the backstage of politics will be larger in Stockholm than in Brussels, i.e. there should be a stronger forum effect in Stockholm. Second, in Brussels, consequently, the largest step for the business lobbyist will be that between the private lobbying meeting and the public appearance. In Stockholm this move should be less dramatic, since the norms of the forum can be assumed to be in at least partial operation even in private meetings. The publicity effect, if the theory is correct, will thus be stronger in Brussels than in Stockholm. The difference in strength of the forum and publicity effects in Brussels and Stockholm in effect measures the transparency effect.[16]

This discussion can be summarised into three main hypotheses following from the theory of publicity's civilising effect:

- H1 (the forum effect): The move from the market to the private backstage of the forum will involve little or no civilising effect in Brussels, but some effect in Stockholm.
- H2 (the transparency effect): The private backstage will be more civilised in Stockholm than in Brussels.
- H3 (the publicity effect): The move from the private backstage to the public frontstage will involve a significant civilising effect in Brussels and a lesser effect in Stockholm.

In the interviews, the footing for the norms of the forum is analysed qualitatively and described primarily by a generous use of quotations from the interviewees. The document analysis, on the other hand, is based on a quantitative content analysis. Figure 3.1 summarises the different comparisons made in the interviews and the document analysis.

Figure 3.1. Summary of the different comparisons and the main hypotheses

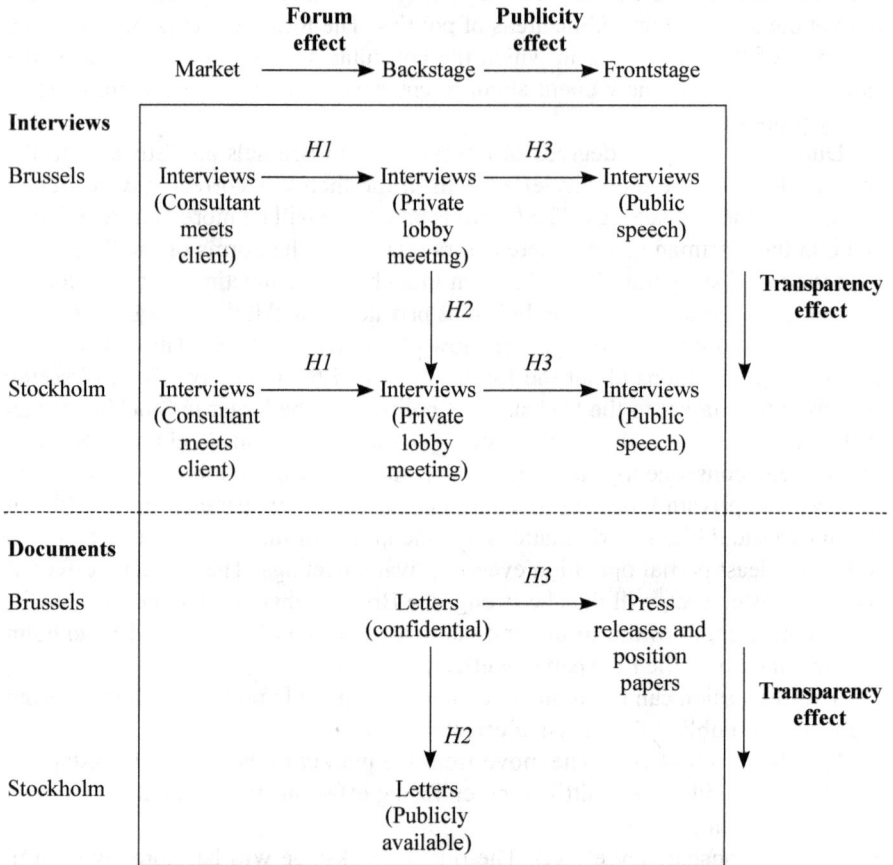

Note: The arrows in Figure 3.1 do not illustrate causal relationships but the different comparisons made in the analysis and the hypothesised civilising effect. The forum effect is studied in the interviews when the consultants describe the preparations necessary before the client is ready to step over to the political sphere (H1). The transparency effect is captured in the comparison between Brussels and Stockholm, both in the comparison of confidential letters to the European Commission and publicly available letters to the Swedish ministries, and by comparing the interviews with Brussels consultants with those in Stockholm (H2). A strong transparency effect would imply a larger forum effect in Sweden than in Brussels and a larger publicity effect in Brussels than in Stockholm. The publicity effect is also investigated both in the interviews—the switching of scenarios between the closed lobby meeting with civil servants and the public speech—and in the written material in the comparison between confidential letters in Brussels and public position papers and press releases from the same organisations (H3).

SPECIFYING THE DEPENDENT VARIABLES

Before the results of the interviews and the content analysis of the letters are presented in the following chapters, a further specification is needed on the actual content of the civilising effect. What exactly should we be looking for in the empirical data?

First, as illustrated in Figure 2.1 in the previous chapter, due to the force of the better argument norm, increasing degrees of transparency and publicity are expected to affect the mode of communication, forcing actors to argue instead of bargain. Deliberative theorists usually define bargaining as 'a form of interest-aggregation that builds on the exchange of threats and promises', while arguing 'is based on claims of validity' (Zürn 2000: 192). An actor who aims at convincing the other participants of the merits of a certain policy option is arguing. Barry uses the term 'discussion on merits', which 'involves the complete absence of threats and inducements. ... If agreement is reached by means of discussion on merits, the parties to the dispute have changed their minds about what they want' (Barry 1965 [1990]: 87). The purpose of arguing, therefore, is the transformation of preferences; the method is giving convincing reasons concerning the merits of the proposal.

If, on the other hand, the communications are focused on reaching a common decision but include no efforts to change the minds of the other parties involved about what they want or what they perceive to be right, then bargaining is occurring. Bargaining implies attempting to change the positions of the other actors rather than their preferences. The cooperative version, which presumably is what deliberative theorists have in mind when referring to 'promises', is known in negotiation theory as 'integrative bargaining' (Walton & McKersie 1965: chapter 4). This involves efforts at reaching agreements by comparing and matching fixed preferences, searching for solutions which will satisfy all participants given their existing preferences. The goal in an integrative bargaining game is not to transform preferences but to clarify them, put them on the table and, in a common effort among the participants, seek to maximise preference-satisfaction for all present at the table. For integrative bargaining to occur, the participants should perceive the situation as variable-sum, including opportunities for package-deals and log-rolling. Communication is characterised by a cooperative attitude, brainstorming, rich information-sharing and participants candidly speaking their minds about what they want.

'Distributive bargaining', on the other hand, denotes a conflict-based bargaining game, where actors try to 'solve' the conflict by pressuring the other participants to make concessions. The goal is neither to transform preferences, nor to search for compromise solutions but to make the others comply with one's demands. The term 'distributive' comes from the notion of having a fixed sum of utilities to allocate, making one participant's gain a loss to the others. A distributive bargaining process involves manipulating information about the utilities and costs of policy alternatives, making strong commitments and using threats.[17]

As Jurg Steiner *et al.* notice, not many empirical studies have tried to distinguish between arguing and bargaining behaviour in real world politics (Steiner *et al.* 2004). A problem with some of those that have is that they fail to make the distinction between integrative bargaining and arguing. Steiner *et al.* themselves, for instance, in their 'Discourse Quality Index', include 'constructive politics'—putting mediating proposals on the agenda—as a criterion for deliberation (Steiner *et al.* 2004). But cooperative and constructive behaviour is equally compatible with integrative bargaining ('if you give us X, we'll give you Y') as with arguing ('X is the best alternative, because of argument Z'). A highly cooperative attitude by the parties does not itself indicate whether they are arguing or bargaining.xviii

What we should be looking for, with respect to the mode of communication, is lobbyists either trying to persuade officials by using arguments that they believe will change the official's perception of the merits of different policy options (arguing); or lobbyists trying to persuade officials to shift policy in return for something—a positive compensation of some sort (promising, in the case of integrative bargaining) or the relief of a negative consequence over which the lobbyist has power (threatening, in the case of distributive bargaining).[18]

The second dependent variable we should look for is the types of justification used by lobbyists. Justifying one's position is the most fundamental part of arguing. It is the cognitive reasonableness of the reasons given that must have the power to persuade. But what about bargainers, do they also need reasons? It might seem that actors involved in bargaining would not care at all why the other participants have certain preferences and how these could be justified. The hard currency in a bargaining process is not the power of the better argument but the credibility of threats, the generosity of offers and the creativity of preference-linkages. But bargainers do need justifications, although not for the same reason as actors who are arguing to convince. Actors involved in distributive bargaining, for instance, use justifications to show their opponents how committed they are to a certain position. Sometimes actors may want to give the impression that under no circumstances will they back down from their positions. In other cases it may be a better strategy to communicate a certain degree of flexibility. Justifying one's position may be a useful instrument in that communication (Walton & McKersie 1965: 84ff). Reason-giving is also important in integrative bargaining, as the participants need as much information as they can get about each others' preferences, in order to find the optimal solutions. Knowing why the other participants want X may help to solve the problem (Fisher, Ury & Patton 1999: chapter 3).

The claim made by the theory of publicity's civilising effect is that the non-selfishness norm affects the justifications given. I find it useful to distinguish between three types of justification: self-regarding, other-regarding and ideal-regarding. A self-regarding justification implies making reference to the preferences and interests of oneself, one's family or one's 'group'. 'Policy Y should be chosen, because it is good for us (students, farmers, Londoners, women, Somalis, etc.)', or 'because that is what we want', or 'what we need'. A justification is self-regarding only if one's reference group is just one group among several, or at least two, constituting the community. Thus, justifying a policy with reference to the interests of consumers should not be considered self-regarding even if the speaker represents a consumers' organisation, since it is hard to think of anyone not being (at least potentially) a consumer.

Consequently, an other-regarding justification implies making reference to the preferences or interests of others: people not belonging to one's family or one's group. 'Policy Y should be chosen, because it is good for the children' (or for the unemployed, the Somalis, etc. (provided the speaker is not specifically representing children, unemployed or Somalis) or 'for society at large'. The reference may be explicit, as in 'it is good for the children', or implicit, as when invoking a distributive norm. 'Policy Y should be chosen, because it is fair' is an other-regarding justification, even in the case where Policy Y in practice would mean more money for the speaker's own group, since the norm potentially applies to all individuals. Other-regarding justifications thus are distinguished from self-regarding justifications in that they make reference to the interests or preferences of individuals belonging to other groups than the speaker. This does not necessarily preclude speakers from also including themselves in the reference-group, as when referring to 'the public interest' or to a distributive norm such as justice, fairness or equality.[19]

Using an ideal-regarding justification, on the other hand, implies justifying a proposal by making reference to the ideals of the speaker. While self- and other-regarding justifications only deal with interests and satisfaction of wants (one's own or others'), ideal-regarding motives also involve making judgements about wants, valuing some higher than others. A certain policy is advocated, not because that it is what 'we' or 'they' want, but because that is what we all should want, according to some higher principle. As soon as other considerations than satisfying existing preferences are introduced, an ideal-regarding justification is being used. 'Policy Y should be chosen, because it promotes democracy (or multiculturalism, or the environment, or civic virtues, or the pride of the nation and so on).'

The important distinction for the empirical study is that between other- and ideal-regarding justifications, on the one hand, and self-regarding on the other. The non-selfishness norm is assumed to force actors to substitute self-regarding justifications for other- and ideal-regarding ones. However, any ideal-regarding justification may not conform to a civilising effect, from the perspective of deliberative democratic theory. Deliberative theorists emphasise that arguments should be potentially 'acceptable' to all parties.[20] Purely self-regarding arguments are not acceptable, according to deliberative theorists, but neither are arguments that refer to sectarian or religious beliefs shared only by a particular social group. From a deliberative point of view, therefore, in order to count as 'civilised' ideal-regarding justifications must not be too particularistic. A speaker should not refer to ideals that she knows cannot be shared by others. Since the data of this study concerns industry lobbyists, rather than religious or ethnic groups, however, there is little risk that such private ideals will play any role here.

The mode of communication and the types of justification are the dependent variables of the study (transparency and publicity being the independent variables). The empirical study thus stops at the first step of the causal chain of the theory of publicity's civilising effect, as described in Figures 2.1 and 2.2 in the previous chapter. The argument for why it is relevant to study effects at the rhetorical level, without examining whether the rhetoric is followed up by action, has already been stated. Given the existence of a hypocrisy constraint, rhetoric is not just rhetoric. The assumption that any civilising effect in the first step is translated into policy positions in the next step is left unchallenged. What is clear, however, is that if there is *no* civilising effect in the first step, there will be no second step. Political actors who do not even bother to talk the talk will definitely not walk the walk.

NOTES

1   Cf. Moloney 1996.
2   According to one survey there were about 80–90 'political consultancies' (i.e. excluding law firms and PR consultancies) active in Brussels in 2000, with a total staff of 850 (including secretarial staff, etc.) and an annual turnover of more than 100 million euros. The market is highly fragmented, however, with many small firms employing just a handful of people and a few large firms with more than fifty people. See Lahusen 2002: 702f. A study of the Swedish PA consultancy market in 1999 claimed that there were only about 10–15 firms active employing some 30–40 consultants (most of who were part-time PAs or part-time PR consultants). Hermansson *et al.* 1999: 137f. Cf. Johnson 1999.
3   APCO, GPC, Hill & Knowlton and Weber Shandwick/Adamson.
4   Gullers Grupp, JKL, KREAB (Stockholm office). Some large firms have offices both in Brussels and in the national capitals, including Stockholm. Two such firms –KREAB and EPPA – are represented in the study both by their Brussels office and their Stockholm office.
5   Burson-Marsteller, EPPA (Brussels office), INTEREL, KREAB (Brussels office).
6   EPPA (Stockholm office), Geelmuyden Kiese, Jerry Bergström AB, Westander Publicitet & Påverkan.
7   See Ziller 2001: 108f, Gronbech-Jensen 1998, Österdahl 1998.
8   Bellamy & Castiglione 2000: 69. See also, for example, Eriksen & Fossum 2000: xi, Zurn 2000: 204.
9   EC No 1049/2001.
10 A fact illustrated by the famous case of Paul van Buitenen, who was sacked after having leaked information about fraud in the Commission. See van Buitenen 2000.
11 Cf. Streeck & Schmitter 1991, Mazey & Richardson 2001.
12 The European Commission is organised in a way similar to a government. The 25 commissioners resemble ministers, as they preside over a small cabinet of hand-picked political advisors and one or more sectoral directorates-generals (DGs) (such as DG Environment, DG Transport and Energy, DG Agriculture, etc). The DGs, which are comparable to ministries in the national context, make up the civil service staff of the Commission.
13 Quote from a conversation with Marie Söder-Higgins, a member of Wallström's cabinet.

14 Letters from the following senders, and in relationship to the following policy issues, were requested: 1. Communications concerning the White Paper on chemicals strategy from: CEFIC (European Chemical Industry Council), CEPE (European Council of Paint, Printing Ink and Artists' Colors Industry), CONCAWE (Oil industry organisation), BASF (Chemicals company), Degussa (Chemicals company), Rhodia (Chemicals company), Shell (Oil company) 2. Communications concerning Waste Electrical and Electronic Equipment from: Electrolux (Electronic equipments company), Ericsson (Electronic equipments company). 3. Communications concerning the regulation of batteries from: CollectNicad (Battery producers and users organisation), SAFT (Battery company). 4. Communications concerning the Auto-Oil program and the White Paper on Transport Policy from: CONCAWE (Oil industry organisation), Shell (Oil company), ACEA (European Automobile Manufacturers' Association), IRU (International Road Transport Union), Volvo (Automobile company), DaimlerChrysler (Automobile company)

15 It must be assumed that the civil servant (B) is not 'one of the genuinely impartial members of society', in which case the lobbyist (A) would also have to use impartial arguments in private meetings, or that the lobbyist is uncertain about the motives of the civil servant.

16 It should be noted that the transparency effect may have two potential sources, one short term and one longer term. The short-term effect comes from the actor's efforts to avoid the 'opprobrium', as Elster calls it, of breaking the norms of the forum. This effect is captured in the comparison between the different strengths of the forum and publicity effects in Brussels and in Stockholm. A longer-term effect, which also may affect the results, could come from the fact that the publicity principle has been an institutionalised part of Swedish politics for almost 250 years. If Swedish political actors have been exposed to the voice of reason for so long, one could argue in line with deliberative theory, there might be a higher degree of socialisation into the norms of the forum in Sweden from the start. If the analysis of the letters had shown a strong transparency effect, therefore, it could have been produced by a combination of the genuine predisposition of Swedish actors to argue with strategic calculations over short-term regulative norms. However, as already revealed, no such transparency effect was found.

17 'Integrative' and 'distributive bargaining' is the terminology used by Walton and McKersie. Walton & McKersie 1965: 4f. Other terms used in the negotiation literature for basically the same distinction are 'creating value' and 'claiming value' (Lax & Sebenius 1986: 30f.) and 'problem-solving' and 'bargaining' (Elgström & Jönsson 2000: 685). Cf. Schelling, who speaks of the 'efficiency' and the 'distributional' 'aspects of bargaining' (Schelling 1960: 21).

18 Öberg makes the distinction between 'deliberation' and 'contending interests', where the latter form of interaction involves representatives who 'defend positions their organizations have instructed them to take', i.e. a conflictual game. (Öberg 2002: 464). In his operationalisation of deliberation he includes both transformations of opinions in response to arguments (which indicates that arguing is present) and accepting compromises (which is rather a feature of integrative bargaining). Ibid: 469.

19 The two concepts of self-regarding and other-regarding justifications used here are close to Barry's 'privately-oriented' and 'publicly-oriented' principles, but with certain important differences. Both privately-oriented and publicly-oriented principles as defined by Barry

are too narrow to do a proper job for the theory of publicity's civilising effect. Barry only includes 'oneself or one's family' in his concept of privately-oriented principles, but the theory of publicity's civilising effect also makes claims towards representatives of broader societal groups, defined by exogenous factors such as occupation, residential area, age, class, sex, ethnic origin, etc. Therefore a concept is needed which includes references to the interests of one's group. This is not least important since group-oriented preferences are far more politically relevant than the family or oneself. Barry's concept of being publicly-oriented, on the other hand, is a particular subcategory of being other-regarding, in which all individuals of society are included in the reference-group (or at least where no particular individuals are *a priori* excluded). See Barry 1965 [1990]: 12f, 297.

20 See, for example, Gutmann & Thompson 1996: 53.

chapter four | dressed for politics

Business leaders (such as a CEO of a company or a Secretary-General of a business association) who find that their businesses are affected not only by the usual market forces but also by politics, and who decide that something needs to be done about that, will have to manage two different transitions. In accordance with the theory of publicity's civilising effect, as described in chapter two, they must first enter the political sphere—the forum—from their home base in the market sphere, taking meetings with decision-makers in the political institutions. Second, their visits to the forum will most likely include not only private meetings but also public appearances. They will therefore have to move back and forth also between the backstage and the frontstage of the forum.

The degree of transformation of behaviour necessary at each of these transitions indicates to what extent the mechanisms of the theory of publicity's civilising effect are at work. The theory assumes that the first transition is less dramatic than the second. Secrecy in politics allows the standards of the market, with which business leaders should be familiar, to dominate behaviour in the forum as well. However, in the transparent Swedish context, the first transition should involve a somewhat larger change in behaviour—towards more arguing and other- and ideal-regarding justifications—than in Brussels. On the other hand, the transition between the backstage and the frontstage of the forum should involve a more significant transformation towards forum behaviour in Brussels.

This chapter describes these two transitions from the perspective of those actors whose job it is to guide business leaders to success in the political sphere: the best, according to reputation, public affairs consultants in Brussels and in Stockholm. In interviews, the consultants were asked to discuss a hypothetical lobbying case about which they had received information some days previously. The case, which was used as the basic starting point and discussion material for all the interviews, involved road hauliers having problems with a draft proposal for eco-taxes on trucks. The road hauliers were represented by the European Road Haulage Association (the ERA) in the Brussels case and the Swedish Road Haulage Association (SRA) in the Stockholm case. The European Commission, in the Brussels case, and the Ministry of the Environment in the Stockholm case, were considering a differentiated tax-system. According to the draft proposal, less environmentally friendly trucks would be burdened with higher taxes and the most polluting trucks were to be off the road within five years. The Secretary-General of the ERA/SRA was approaching the consultant for help lobbying against the proposal. This hypothetical case will be explained in more detail shortly. In one of the first meetings, according to the case story, the Secretary-General of the ERA/SRA had brought to the consultant a list of nine arguments against the eco-tax proposal, which he thought could be useful in the lobbying campaign. The list included six other- and ideal-regarding arguments: two environmental arguments, two macroeconomic arguments, one argument having to do with implementation efficiency and one argument referring to a 'cherished ideal' (undistorted competition in Brussels and international cooperation in Stockholm). There were also three self-regarding arguments on the list, with the basic message that this proposal will be bad for the haulage industry. The content of these arguments, which operationalise the dependent variable types of justification, will be described in a later section (p.78). First, however, I want to give a snapshot of the consultants' reactions to the arguments. The consultants were asked to select three arguments from the list, which they would advise the ERA/SRA Secretary-General to bring to a private meeting with the civil servants responsible for drafting the proposal. They were also asked to reject the three arguments which they would be least eager to use in such a meeting. Table 4.1 shows the results of this exercise. As illustrated in the table the self-interested arguments are the least preferred both in Brussels and in Stockholm. Both on the opaque Brussels backstage and in the more transparent Stockholm context the lobbyists prefer other- and ideal-regarding arguments before self-regarding ones. (The reason why the categories are not ranked exactly the same (one environmental argument, for instance, is ranked higher than the other) is because they have different content, even though the basic grounds for justification (environmental) are the same.)

After the private meeting with civil servants, the consultants were faced with a different situation. The context was changed from private meetings with civil servants to a public appearance at a conference on the future of European/Swedish transport policy. In this situation, the Secretary-General of the ERA/SRA was invited to give one of the opening speeches and had decided to address the issue of eco-taxes. 'Everybody' was to be in the audience, including civil servants, politicians, NGOs, the media and members from the Secretary-General's own association. The list of arguments was the same as in the private meetings, and again the consultants were asked to select three and reject three arguments.

Table 4.2 shows the results of this second round of choosing arguments. While the self-regarding arguments are still rather unpopular, the picture is less clear in the public speech than it was in the private meeting. Some of the self-regarding arguments in fact have a higher rank in the public speeches than they had in the private meeting.

Table 4.3 summarises the results of table 4.1 and 4.2 with respect to the self-regarding arguments. As can be seen there is no difference in the popularity of the self-regarding arguments between Brussels and Stockholm.[1] Furthermore,

Table 4.1. Preferred arguments in private meetings with civil servants (selected minus rejected)

Arguments	Brussels	Stockholm	Total
Environment (number 3 on the list)	6	7	13
Competition/Cooperation (number 2 on the list)	3	7	10
Implementation (number 6 on the list)	1	1	2
Macroeconomic (number 7 on the list)	4	-2	2
Environment (number 9 on the list)	1	-1	0
Macroeconomic (number 4 on the list)	-2	-1	-3
Self-regarding (number 8 on the list)	-2	-3	-5
Self-regarding (number 1 on the list)	-3	-5	-8
Self-regarding (number 5 on the list)	-7	-4	-11

Notes: Table 4.1 shows the results of the Brussels and Stockholm consultants' selection and rejection of arguments for the private meetings with civil servants. From the list of nine arguments they were asked to select those three arguments they would be most willing to use in the meeting and reject those three they were least eager to bring to the civil servants. Since there are eight interviewees in Brussels and seven in Stockholm the scale ranges from 8 (all consultants select the argument and no one rejects it) to -8 (no consultants select the argument, everyone rejects it) in Brussels and from 7 to -7 in Stockholm. In total the scale goes from 15 to -15. (The precise content of the arguments are described on page 78).

Table 4.2. Preferred arguments in public speeches (selected minus rejected)

Arguments	Brussels	Stockholm	Total
Environment (number 3 on the list)	7	6	13
Competition/cooperation (number 2 on the list)	2	6	8
Macroeconomic (7 on the list)	4	1	5
Self-regarding (number 1 on the list)	2	-2	0
Environment (number 9 on the list)	2	-2	0
Macroecomic (number 4 on the list)	-3	0	-3
Self-regarding (number 8 on the list)	-3	0	-3
Implementation (number 6 on the list)	-4	-4	-8
Self-regarding (number 5 on the list)	-5	-4	-9

Notes: Table 4.2 shows the results of the Brussels and Stockholm consultants' selection and rejection of arguments for the speech at the public conference on the future of transport policy. From the list of nine arguments they were asked to select those three arguments they would be most willing to use in the speech and reject those three they were least eager to use in such a context. The scale ranges from 8 to –8 in Brussels (eight interviewees), from 7 to –7 in Stockholm (seven interviewees) and from 15 to –15 in total. (The precise content of the arguments are described on page 78).

Table 4.3. Popularity of self-regarding arguments in private meetings and public speeches (selected minus rejected)

	Brussels	Stockholm
Private meetings	-12	-12
Public speeches	-6	-6

Notes: Table 4.3 shows the results of the Brussels and Stockholm consultants' selection and rejection of arguments for the private meetings with civil servants and the public conference speech, with respect to the three self-regarding arguments. From the list of nine arguments they were asked to select the three arguments they would be most willing to use and reject those three they were least eager to use. The scale ranges from 24 to –24 in Brussels (three arguments, eight interviewees) and from 21 to –21 (seven interviewees) in Stockholm.

contrary to the hypothesis of publicity's civilising effect there is a tendency for self-regarding arguments to be preferred more in the public speeches than in the private meetings, both in Brussels and in Stockholm.

Following these figures there seems to be no civilising effect of publicity on the types of justification. There is no sign of any transparency effect—implying less self-interest in the argumentation—in the comparison between Stockholm and Brussels. The institutionalised Swedish publicity principle does not seem to make any difference at all here. When it comes to the publicity effect there is instead an effect in the opposite direction: self-regarding justifications seem to be somewhat more popular in the public arena compared to the private meetings both in Brussels and in Stockholm.

However, this simple counting of arguments from a handful of public affairs consultants, although strategically chosen, is hardly enough to convince a deliberative theorist that the theory is not working here. The tables, furthermore, give no clues at all to why publicity would have such a contradictory effect. Neither do they address the second dependent variable—the mode of communication, i.e. whether the lobbyists prefer arguing or bargaining.

The rest of this chapter is devoted to understanding the reasons for the consultants' choices of action, with respect to both the mode of communication (arguing versus bargaining) and the types of justification (self-regarding versus other and ideal-regarding), by analysing the motivations they gave and the judgements they made of the different situations during the interviews. From the fifteen interviews came a story of a business leader from the world of markets and consumers on an involuntary visit to the world of politics and public opinion that was remarkably consistent and told in almost exactly the same way in Sweden as in Brussels. Furthermore, in the next chapter the validity of this story is supported by the results of the content analysis of private and public letters and documents.

It will be seen in this chapter that there are two major reasons why publicity does not have the effect posited by the theory of publicity's civilising effect. The first reason is that private lobbying meetings, even in the opaque Brussels setting, is in fact not a backstage area at all for lobbyists in Goffman's sense of allow-ing actors to feel free to express their 'market selves'. Instead the real trans-formation—from an attitude and behaviour in line with the logic of the market to an appearance appropriate for the forum—occurs at the first transition of spheres. This is the forum effect, i.e. when business-people carefully step into the private office of the civil servant. The consultants' job at this stage is to get their client dressed for politics, to avoid a clash between the differ-ent logics of the market and the forum. If that job is done when the curtain of secrecy is drawn not much bargaining or pressure is left to be revealed.

However, as will be demonstrated, only one of the norms of the forum comes into force at this point, namely the force of the 'better argument' norm, affecting the choice of mode of communication (whether the lobbyists prefer arguing or bargaining). The types of justification are also affected by the step from the mar-ket to the forum but not because self-regarding arguments are illegitimate due to a non-selfishness norm. The reason why the self-regarding arguments are the least preferred in Table 4.1 is because they are not persuasive. 'This is going to be bad for the haulage industry' is simply not a very interesting argument for a public policy-maker, even though it is not illegitimate to use it.

Second, the reason why the lobbyists in this study, with respect to the use of self-regarding justifications, sounded better backstage than frontstage—just like Eliasoph's civic group activists, as described in Chapter two—is because the pub-lic itself is not always public-regarding. The theory of publicity's civilising effect is based on an oversimplification of the public as a coherent unit of public-spirited citizens. The interviews show, however, that there is very little pressure from any non-selfishness norm also in the public setting. In fact, at least for industry lobby-ists, there is an 'imperfection constraint' working in the opposite direction from the imperfection constraint that is assumed by the theory of publicity's civilising effect (see page 22). Trying to hide your self-interest is just not credible and will weaken rather than strengthen your position.

Furthermore, from the Secretary-General's perspective, the public audience is a heterogeneous entity, containing many wills and interests. Among them are the wills and interests of the organisation representative's own members. When the curtain of secrecy is drawn aside, representatives of organisations and groups face not only the general public but also their constituents, explaining why self-interested rhetoric grows rather than diminishes in public settings.

This chapter first describes the consultants' picture of the introductory meet-ings with their clients and their preparations for forthcoming lobbying activities in the forum. Thereafter the chapter deals with the consultants' advice to their cli-ents attending private meetings with civil servants. In the Brussels interviews, the Secretary-General of the ERA was meeting with people in the Air and Noise unit of the environment directorate (DG Environment) of the European Commission. The Stockholm consultants were asked to prepare the Secretary-General of the SRA for meetings with the Ministry of the Environment. The consultants were also asked to describe what difference it would have made if the meeting instead had been held at a more industry-friendly department, where the chances for a 'capture' relationship, as described by the economic theory of interest groups, could be assumed to be higher. In the third part of the chapter the consultants develop their thinking about their client's speech at a public conference on the future of transport policy.

PREPARING FOR THE FORUM

The case of the ERA/SRA and eco-taxes on trucks presented to the consultants gave a basic frame to the interviews. The discussions frequently and fruitfully drifted from that into generalisations and real-world examples from different sectors. The first part of the hypothetical case's introductory text is presented below, as it was written for the Brussels interviews—with adaptations for the Swedish context in the Stockholm interviews shown in square brackets:

> You have been contacted by the Secretary-General of the European Road Haulage Association (ERA) [the Swedish Road Haulage Association (SRA)], an organisation with which you have not worked before. They are concerned about a proposal for a new directive on taxation on trucks according to an environmental classification system, which is being prepared within DG Environment [the Ministry of the Environment].
>
> The ERA [SRA] is representing the European [Swedish] road hauliers, which makes it one of the larger players on the European [Swedish] transport market. The organisation's members are national [regional] road haulier organisations and a handful of large forwarding firms. The members are following developments within transport policy and keep an eye on the doings of their trade association. The ERA [SRA] represents an important business sector, although it is not one of the 'giants' of European [Swedish] industry in terms of economic turnover and jobs.
>
> DG Environment [the Ministry of the Environment] is drafting a proposal for an EU [Swedish] system of differentiated vehicle taxes on heavy trucks, and a timetable for phasing out the least environmentally friendly vehicles. According to the information which has reached the ERA [SRA] a taxation system is considered which would impose a lower tax on the most environmentally friendly trucks (Class 1). Standard vehicles (Class 2) would be substantially taxed, and the most polluting vehicles (Class 3) would not only be burdened by a high vehicle tax but must be off the roads within five years.
>
> The initiative to prepare a proposal using eco-taxes within transport policy originates from a request from the Council of Ministers [originates from a government commission]. The issue will most likely be politically salient—transport and environmental issues usually are. The environmental NGOs will be active. Representatives of competing modes of transport (rail, air, waterways), will also try to have a say in the process.

Environmental issues are being addressed by the ERA [SRA]. It has adopted a Charter for Sustainable Development, etc. Still, the hauliers are probably perceived by the public as a typical special interest organisation in these kinds of issues (which does not mean that the ERA [SRA] is suffering from any particular image problem as a 'bad duck'). The proposal will hit many hauliers hard since Class 1 vehicles are rather uncommon, and building up new fleets of trucks is a long and costly process. The ERA's [SRA's] position on this issue is that the proposal should be trashed.

It is against this backdrop that you meet the ERA [SRA] secretariat for introductory talks. You agree to help them with the case and start to draw up the lines for the navigation of the issue. What do these first meetings with the client contain?

The purpose of giving details on the political context around the issue (salience, actors involved, etc.) as well as the characteristics of the ERA [SRA] (size, image, members, etc.) was to make sure that the case was perceived in the same way by the consultants. The response to the case was positive, in the sense that it was seen to be realistic. 'In fact, the case almost exists' (Brussels IP 2). 'It is a good description of the type of cases we have' (Stockholm IP 1). It was also useful in that it made clear that I was informed about the basics of what a public affairs consultant does, so that the discussions could focus on the core issues of how the interviewees would advise the ERA [SRA] to act.

Amateurs at the forum

While the ERA/SRA and the case of eco-taxes on trucks provided a familiar type of client and situation, PA consultants have considerably varied missions. The answer to the question of what happens during the first meetings with the client depends on who this client is. In general, clients may be categorised along a continuum from amateurs to professionals with respect to their understanding of the world of politics. Some of the companies and trade associations who turn to public affairs consultants for advice are very sophisticated in their approach to politics and public opinion. Many clients, on the other hand, are unaccustomed to acting outside the well-known realms of markets and business. They lack factual knowledge about the political institutions and they are generally unfamiliar with how politics works. In the political sphere, for instance, the business leader is no longer the boss. That may be difficult to handle for a person who is used to running a big company, according to the consultants.

There is a big cultural gap between business people and politicians. Very few business people understand politics. They do not understand the working of democracy. Politicians have grown up in municipal elections, talking to villagers, moving up to the County and the National parliament, talking and listening. But a company is an authoritarian command structure, so business people cannot listen (Brussels IP 5).

> I almost get scared when I meet some clients. First, because they don't know anything—they don't know the difference between the parliament and the cabinet. And that person can hold a high position within the company leadership. Second, they don't understand that when you don't get a response to your arguments, you have to go home and see if there is anything wrong with them. Instead, they end up thinking it is a conspiracy (Stockholm IP 6).

Amateurs—those who have not yet learned the terms of the forum—are recognised by being egocentric, emotional, reactive (rather than proactive) and short-sighted. These are all characteristics which tend to arouse violations of the force of the better argument norm and lead to overly self-interested argumentation.

Egocentric

The first reaction of any company or trade association to a political intervention within their field of business is 'how does this affect us?'. 'That is of course what they worry about most. If they lose their job because of a new tax, which devastates the industry, the first thing they think about is not how it affects small birds in Medelpad [a Swedish County], but they think about how it affects them' (Stockholm IP 3). 'They focus on the detailed impact on their industry' (Brussels IP 8).

When they start to make plans for doing something about the perceived political threat, the professional is distinguished from the amateur by going one step further than looking at the impact on industry. The professional also analyses the effects on other parts of society. The amateurs, on the other hand, tend to get stuck in their own cost-analyses.

> They will focus very much on the technical aspects and the impact on the industry. They will not see things, which we who are working on a regular basis with the institutions see. You need to make them expand from the technical hard facts arguments (Brussels IP 4).
>
> They live in a small world, like the people in [the Swedish County of] Dalarna, like there is a small globe with only us on it. They have a very little grasp of discussions and the societal debate. That is why they cannot understand—when they know exactly what it is like and above all what it should be like—why the politicians don't get it. The world only consists of our company, what is good for our company and everybody should understand what is important to us. They don't understand that there may be contradictions, that democracy to a large degree consists of conflict solving and balancing opposing interests. Many times it is very difficult to see that there are other interests than one's own (Sweden IP 6).

Technical expertise, which is an asset and a major source of profit for many companies in the market, may for this reason actually become a burden in the political sphere. Technical details are simply not as interesting in the political world as

companies are used to from 'home'. This may be difficult to understand for someone who is working day and night with the technical aspects of his or her products
and manufacturing processes.

> Especially engineer and technical companies – like the chemicals industry, oil
> industry, biotech – they all think scientific arguments are an absolute killer,
> which is not true in the political world. I'll give you a very concrete exam-
> ple: The European Parliament can the same day decide to ban phthalates in
> toys and turn down a potential ban on cigarettes. This is not rational [from a
> scientific point of view]! If you're working with scientific evidence and the
> precautionary principle you would ban cigarettes first (Brussels IP 2).

To a large degree, first meetings between the client and the consultant revolve
around this tension between what is interesting and important in the world of the
company or the industry, and the political sphere. 'We have to teach the clients
that what is important to them is not important to the rest of the world. Many people have huge problems understanding that' (Stockholm IP 6).

> Those in industry are experts. We as consultants must spend a certain amount
> of time to understand what they're talking about. They're caught up in a world
> of jargon, and most time they're not connected to the political world. One
> of our primary roles initially is to sift out messages and arguments that have
> political resonance' (Brussels IP 8).

Imagine that an agency has a minimum value and the client is below the limit
and that the product has therefore been questioned. In that case, it is not unusual
that the client wants to discuss the minimum value: 'You don't get cancer at 10
percent, you get cancer at 12 percent and it is wrong to say 10 percent and right
to say 12 percent.' We can possibly agree with the client on that but, at the same
time, we explain that it is difficult to pursue a case about whether it should be 10
percent or 12 percent. 'Is there something else that is the problem?' we may ask.
'Yes, we think the way they made the study is completely wrong,' the client may
say. Maybe they have applied a Swedish model, while the EU applies an entirely
different model and other companies have therefore gotten better results. We
may think that this is an easier argument to pursue. But the client may get very
irritated because there may be a number of civil engineers who have done risk
assessments their whole lives and think that 10 percent is completely insane and
who pull out half a meter of books to show that it really should be 12 percent'
(Stockholm IP 5).

Being egocentric is an obstacle to success in the forum, according to the consultants. In order to develop a winning lobbying strategy you need an open mind
and this is where amateurs typically fail. They overestimate the importance, not
only of technical details in their day-to-day work, but also of themselves, generally, in the eyes of others. 'The client often exaggerates the societal relevance of

their business' (Stockholm IP 3). They tend to think that their problem is everyone's problem, which is not normally the case.

> [The client] wants good conditions for business. Perhaps they want to get into a market that is regulated or they want to lower taxes to get a higher profit for their business. On the most basic level, it is about increased sales, higher profits, higher employment. They don't quite understand that this argument is very small compared to the decision makers' authority, which is to balance an infinite number of different factors and aspects' (Stockholm IP3).
>
> There are a lot of things that are very relevant when the executives meet, when the 'gang' meets, but that nobody else really cares about. Of course, when the trucking industry meets and has conferences a lot of industry problems are discussed. It may be profitability—what do I know—competition from trucks coming from Europe, low wages for Polish drivers or whatever it may be. These arguments reflect their business problem more than any societal problem or any other problem. They are internally logical, applicable and good, but unfortunately they are not anything that anybody else cares particularly about (Stockholm IP 4).

Big multinational companies and trade associations representing major industries, which are regular interlocutors with the political institutions, tend to be more professional than smaller actors—'there is of course a different competence in the largest companies' (Stockholm IP 6)—but the correlation is not perfect. Even top business leaders are vulnerable when their businesses are affected by politics rather than market forces. Most CEOs of multinational companies are no doubt admirable persons in many respects, in the views of the consultants, intelligent and competent in what they do—managing businesses, marketing, product development, etc. But some have a blind spot when it comes to politics, according to the consultants. 'You do not manage a company like Volkswagen if you are not a very clever person. But you also do not get to the top of Volkswagen if not all your life has been focused on the car-market, if you're a sort of vague, broad-minded philosopher' (Brussels IP 5).

Therefore, even the most successful business leaders are sometimes handicapped by 'a closed mind' in the management of political issues. One of the interviewed consultants mentions that he was advising a client who was lobbying against Volvo's proposed acquisition of the truck manufacturer Scania. The affair was eventually turned down by the European Commission, due to the monopolistic market share Volvo-Scania would have achieved on trucks in the Nordic countries. The Volvo Chairman was managing this issue poorly, according to the consultant, by not taking the arguments of his critics seriously enough, because:

> he was so narrow-minded. He wanted so much the Volvo-Scania truck deal to go through and he wasn't looking at anything else, which is why his mind was

also closed to making concessions to the Commission, DG Competition, until they said 'No'. And this can happen anywhere! Volkswagen has had so many fines for the same reason. Piëch [the Volkswagen CEO] is a person with a closed mind. A brilliant car-manufacturer, perhaps one of the best, admired also by politicians, but with a closed mind (Brussels IP 5).

Emotional
Clients are often emotionally involved in the issues. The professionals are distinguished from the amateurs by being able to control these emotions. The amateur lets the emotional engagement spill over to the lobbying campaign. 'Basically there is an outrage—"why do you do this, it's going to cost us money"—and then they translate that into astronomical figures in terms of plant losses and job losses' (Brussels IP 8). 'If it happened to you, you get emotionally affected, right. You get angry, you get disappointed, you think it is about raising your voice' (Stockholm IP 3). It is their business, their products, their markets, their way to make a living, they are putting their lives into this. And then some ham-fisted bureaucrat comes up and tells them they can not use that particular substance anymore! Just because some stupid researcher from a low-status university thinks it could cause cancer! They have always used that substance, they know it is safe, why should anyone come and make their lives a mess?

> Clients are often very emotional. They may feel that authorities or politicians work against them. That is classic, right. This happens very often, and we have to try to explain that the political process is irrational. It is not a technical process; it is not a process where decisions are made based strictly on facts. Decisions are made based on political values and based on an agenda which is more or less set every day. And we cannot moralize about that, there is no point as a representative for the private sector, to moralize about ignorant politicians who made the wrong decisions—they have a different agenda. But this recurs often: 'we must go out and explain how ignorant the politicians are, they do not consider facts' (Stockholm IP 5).

Being angry and emotional, however, is not very helpful for industry lobbyists. Industry representatives are not expected to be emotional, according to the consultants. Showing emotions may underline an argument, it is a rhetorical trick which may be suitable for some types of actors under some circumstances. But industry lobbyists are not among those actors and the lobby-corridor is an especially unsuitable context for waiving arms. 'Policy makers switch off as soon as industry becomes emotional on jobs and starts hitting the table. They expect someone from the trade union to hit the table, not an industry that is making a lot of money. They expect them to be constructive and parts of the process' (Brussels IP 8).

Emotions also tend to cause 'attitude problems' for the client. 'If the client for example says that "politicians are idiots and the only people you can listen to are the Conservative Party", then you have a problem, right' (Stockholm IP 1). In order to find the winning arguments you have to cool off first. An important part of the public affairs consultant's job, therefore, is to dampen frustrations.

> There's often this perception of 'let's kill this directive' which leads to a shotgun approach: 'BANG, this is going to ruin our industry, people's jobs, there are whole families out there doing these things'. And there's a hope, I wouldn't even say expectation, that this is going to put so much pressure on the decision-makers that they will say 'ok, let's forget about it'. But it's not going to work that way. Brussels is the capital of compromise (Brussels IP 8).

Reactive

The amateur clients would not come near politics if they did not have to. 'A given company does not tend to think about how transport policy is developing. They're concerned about doing their business, and then they come across restrictions as they're going along' (Brussels IP 8). They are reactive in two ways. First, they consider politics as something which is there to cause problems, rather than create opportunities. Therefore, they do not initiate political processes themselves and when they analyse the effects of a given proposal they only look for costs. 'The client only sees the negative sides. They will immediately see "oh, we have a problem with that", and they want to have that solved' (Brussels IP 4). They fail to analyse whether there may also be potential business advantages involved in regulating a certain area.

Second, when they lobby they oppose change, but fail to provide decision-makers with alternatives.

> You still see that industry more often than not fights solutions rather than make solutions. They'll be opposing the amendments without proposing alternatives, unless they are quite sophisticated. Especially trade associations—look at their response to the White paper on transport! They go like 'Oh, we welcome the White paper on transport, there was a real need for the Commission to talk to us about the future of the transport sector in the twenty-first century', which is the usual bullshit, and then 'but, we don't like this, we don't like that, we don't like blah blah'. With no alternative solutions! There is no 'This is a good idea, but it can be adapted like this and that' (Brussels IP2).

To be proactive is a common catchword within the public affairs business. It partly refers to an attitude—whether you see politics as an arena in which you can potentially act in order to strengthen your position, or whether you just see it as a source of trouble. But it also denotes a strategy for dealing with issues already on the agenda, by developing alternative solutions rather than just saying 'no'. To be proactive is to 'open doors to policy alternatives, to competing instruments' (Brussels IP 6).

Reactive companies and trade associations tend to underestimate or neglect the importance of a general public affairs 'security policy'. The professionals, on the other hand, foresee what is coming from the political sphere. 'If your security policy is in order, that is your public relations and your relationships to the political institutions, then you can live fairly safely within your borders. No missiles will get into your territory' (Stockholm IP 3). Professionals also seek to manage developments in the political sphere via opinion formation and agenda-setting and by cultivating an image of being a co-operative nice guy, someone you should get in contact with early if you are looking at regulating the field. 'What you should do is anticipate your environment so that you don't end up in this situation [referring to the ERA and the eco-taxes on trucks]' (Brussels IP 6).

The amateur, on the other hand, is taken by surprise. That may happen even to such a big actor as the European chemicals industry association (Cefic):

... so the Commission came out with a new chemicals policy, and they [representatives of the European chemicals industry] turned pale and said: 'This isn't true'. I was speaking to them three days ago. They said: 'How is this possible? What did we do wrong?' I said: 'I can tell you, you were not listening to what's happening in society'. 'Ah... but we do, we do'. 'No', I said. 'I was at your board meeting all afternoon, and you were moaning the whole afternoon, but not once did you mention the Bruntland-report'. And they looked at me and they said: 'What's that?' I said: 'The Bruntland-report, ladies and gentlemen, was written in 1987! And it was the first time that the word sustainable development was used. You should have known this, because if you know these things, then you know what's coming'. And that is exactly the very... you see... business is very good at market detection, but they don't listen to society (Brussels IP 5).

Short-sighted
Amateurs who focus heavily on the immediate costs of a proposal have difficulties in rationally analysing long-term effects. 'The client is often so focused on the issue of costs, which they are acutely facing, that they don't see other solutions, other possibilities' (Stockholm IP 2). If you have an acute pain it is difficult to look ahead. You want to get rid of that pain now, and that is all you can think of. But a company or an industry association which fails to find a long-term solution to their political problem may find it returns, even if they manage to get a temporary delay. 'Things get shelved, but very rarely binned. Look at the environmental liability proposal coming out now. We've been talking about it ever since I've been a consultant and I've been here for ten years. They'll come back, you know' (Brussels IP 8).

The interviewed consultants very firmly underlined that a temporary delay based on the shotgun pressure approach may come with a high long-term political price. 'It antagonises. The shotgun tactic direct from the industry to the officials breaks down the open dialogue you want to be creating. You want to be seen as responsible and engaged. You want them to be aware of other solutions than eco-taxes' (Brussels IP 8). Amateurs tend to make the fatal mistake of not considering their long-term relations with the political institutions.

> You must remember that you never lobby on just one issue and that's it—'bye bye Brussels'. You'll be there for years and years and there will be more issues. You'll have to be on good terms with the institutions in order to make your points to them, you need to have a good attitude and keep a good reputation—that is absolutely key. A Secretary-General is like a diplomat of the association, representing it on many issues (Brussels IP 4).
>
> You have to work on the attitude issue. If the client would say that 'if this proposal goes through the trucking industry will die' and like in this tone of doom 'there won't be another trucker left in Sweden in two years'—and stuff like that—you have to remove that because that is not going to happen! And if you have said that, you are a little discredited the next time you have discussions with the ministry. Sweden is a small country and the people we meet on this issue today are the same people we have to put up with, for better or worse, for at least ten more years, and it is important not to slam doors or make threats. That is not a good idea, I don't know any examples where it has succeeded, on the contrary it is only counterproductive (Stockholm IP 1).

The amateur characteristics of being egocentric, emotional, reactive and short-sighted thus tend to lead to hostile bargaining behaviour, based on the shot-gun approach, which is not acceptable to political institutions and with which clients will incur long-term political costs. Therefore, these characteristics must be removed from or at least subdued in clients before they enter the forum. The consultants' job at this point is to help clients broaden their minds, cool off, be proactive and focus on long-term security rather than single battles.

Fitting into the picture
The consultants' first question to their client is not 'what do you want us to lobby for?', as if they were 'hired guns,' but rather 'why?'. If the client is totally focused on short-term costs, it cannot be taken for granted that she has understood her own interests in the particular issue at hand rightly. This applies both to business interests and political interests, in the short run and in the long run. In the first meetings, therefore, focus lies on what clients need, rather than what they say they want.

> So the first issue really is to discuss, in your case, what an environmental tax on trucks would do to the business. Will it actually shift freight away from trucks or will it not? If the tax is being passed on to the end-consumers it will have no effect on the distribution of freight between rail, maritime, water or road transport. Only if the tax cannot be passed on, and therefore hits the truck industry itself, will it have an effect.
>
> And then you have the question; what effect will it have? Will it drive me out of business because my profit margins are small? Or can I sustain a

smaller profit margin? If I am a large company, which has a variety of services—not just freight transport, but also leasing activities, maintenance activities, etc.—if I have multiple incomes, I can more easily sustain an environmental tax. If I am a small company, with small margins the tax will eat into my margin, reduce my profit, my capacity to expand, to invest, etc. For the big company it may actually be a good thing with an environmental tax, because they will see a lot of small competitors disappear from the market, and ultimately they will increase their market-share. So you first have to make a proper business analysis of the effect of the tax. It often happens that clients change their initial position when you've gone through that discussion (Brussels IP 5).

The amateur client typically wants to lobby for trashing a proposed regulation which will cost money, just as the ERA/SRA does in the hypothetical case of eco-taxes on trucks. For the Swedish road hauliers, according to one consultant, it might in fact be more profitable to support the proposal, but to take it to the European level. 'The best thing would be to have them view the proposal as an opportunity rather than a threat and promote it at the EU level. The Swedish trucking industry would benefit from a higher environmental standard at the EU level' (Stockholm IP 2).

However, even if business analyses show that it would be in clients' business interests to get rid of the proposal, this is seldom a viable solution to the political problem, according to consultants. If you lobby to kill a proposal that is already on the agenda, rather than propose amendments or alternatives, you have to question the already established assumption that there is a need to regulate within the area. One reason why that is difficult, according to one consultant, is simply that 'political institutions rarely regulate on something that does not need to be regulated upon' (Brussels IP 2). And even if they do, they are probably convinced that there is a problem. While you may be able to change that perception in the long term through your security policy (which for some reason has failed you this time), in the short term you will in most cases have to accept the officials' perspective and work from there. In the case of eco-taxes on trucks this would definitely be so, according to the consultants.

In this case the right to formulate the problem has already been passed over, the problem is already formulated. The only legitimate thing to do is to try to solve the problem if you want to be successful. In the case you describe, it would not work to try to move the problem to something that has nothing to do with the environment (Stockholm IP 2).

That is why, in first meetings between clients and consultants, discussions are focused on problems and opportunities more than on positions and arguments. Not until an understanding is reached on what the client's long-term interests in this issue really are can the process of developing positions and arguments start.

A proper business analysis must therefore be conducted in close connection to the political analysis. Doing the political analysis, again, to a large extent involves the question of broadening the perspective of the client. Only an open mind will be able to consider the preferences, positions and arguments of other stakeholders and include that information in the formulation of one's own preferences, positions and arguments. If you decide early what you want to lobby for and how, and fix your mind on that, you run the risk of acting against what is politically feasible and perhaps even against your long-term interest.

The political analysis is about defining the playing field. 'You try to take an incredibly broad view in the beginning; in what context does this question exist?' (Stockholm IP 3). All the players, opponents as well as potential allies, should be mapped out. 'How is the situation in the fifteen member states? Why are the Swedes going to be in favour of an environmental tax? Is this for ideological reasons? Or is this because behind the ideological reason, they are hiding a competitive interest, which in nine cases out of ten is the reality? And why are the French against it, etc.' (Brussels IP 5).

> We'll give the client a situation analysis: 'This is what is happening now within the sector, this is the picture of where you stand in the debate.' Then we'll map out who the key stakeholders are that they are going to have to face, and what their views and positions are. Then we'll work on a definition of key messages: 'This is who you are, this is what you want to achieve, this is why you want to achieve it.' It takes the form of a position paper which will be maximum two pages long (Brussels IP 2).

Special attention should be given to the opponents' best arguments, which amateur clients tend to 'forget' about. 'Always know the arguments of your opponents first!' (Brussels IP 5).

> The client underestimates the depth and strength of the counterarguments that exist. You have to single out the opponents' best arguments very early in the process. What are the good reasons for being against what my client wants to achieve?' (Stockholm IP 3).
>
> Equally important is to make clear (although not public!) the weaknesses of the client's own arguments, 'so that we don't make fools of ourselves' (Stockholm IP 3).

Analysing the political playing field also involves investigating the potential linkages of the single issue at hand with other issues. Political issues are rarely isolated, rather they are nested in each other in complicated ways. If you lobby for a subsidy or a tax reduction 'the politician must ask himself "where do I get that money from?" and "who else might come to see me after I've said yes to you?"' (Stockholm IP1). You must be aware of the chain reaction in order to connect your positions and arguments to the larger context.

There is a myth in the private sector that we call the myth of insight, which means that a company or an organization which has a political problem formulates it something like this: 'If they only realized how things are, they will understand what should be done.' That is why they think it is enough to see the Minister for half an hour so that they can explain the situation. What they don't understand is that most issues are part of extremely large weaves of other questions. If you change something somewhere, it may have enormous consequences somewhere else in the weave. If you, for example, want to achieve a change in a sales tax, it may be connected to a change that has to be made in the entire tax system. And there are principles that cause the system to be constructed in a certain way, which are founded on an entirely different problem than what this little individual question may express (Stockholm IP 3).

If you are unaware of that web of issue-linkages you not only run the risk of misplacing your feet, stumbling over one of those side issues, you also miss an opportunity to find potential allies. If you follow the threads connected to your issue you may find that, at the end of one of them, sits someone who had not previously heard about your issue but who might be an unexpected and valuable voice on your side.

Not until the analyses of the business interest and the character of the political playing field are done should the process of working out positions and arguments start. The professional client is flexible on positions and arguments, which makes that process quite pragmatic. If a particular position or argument does not seem to work politically, i.e. the position is unrealistic and the argument does not persuade those who should be persuaded, it should be sorted out or revised. 'Arguments will evolve over time. If you get stuck you can be left out of the debate very quickly, so we will be defining the arguments on a continuous basis' (Brussels IP 2). Some consultants do regular 'market tests' of arguments, meeting a lot of people within the policy sector. 'I don't think you can decide whether an argument is valid or not before you have tested it' (Brussels IP 2). A 'valid' argument, in this context, is an argument which persuades. 'What's important when it comes to arguments is not to be in the right, but to win the argument' (Stockholm IP 3).

Defining the optimal position, when the short-sighted emotional reactions have been removed from or at least subdued in the amateur, is in essence just a matter of cost-benefit analysis. Normally, when industry lobbies no ideology is involved. It is a question of pure business interests. 'We're not NGOs. At the end of the day companies will try to lobby something for profit' (Brussels IP 2). The position taken will be the one that the client and the consultant perceive as maximising business interests in the long term, taking into account political factors. In order to find that position, as well as the arguments backing it up, a proper analysis of the political playing field has first to be in place. This is where most of the uncertainty in the calculation lies; what can one reasonably hope to get away with, given the information available about the field? 'We're not often in black or white situations so it's about defining which shade of grey are we going for' (Brussels IP 2).

Flexibility with respect to positions and arguments increases the chances of influencing policy. How flexible a given company can be on its position is not only a question of being an amateur or a professional, however. Some companies or industries have no room for manoeuvre at all. 'There are cases where a client has really nothing to give away. If they don't fight for this fundamental piece of thinking, or this particular position, they may lose everything' (Brussels IP 3). In those cases, the ability to engage in dialogue may be very weak and the client is drawn towards conflict. 'Perhaps you represent a product, which will be in trouble regardless of how much security policy you use. There is no stability to be achieved, no strong boundaries, the product version of the old Yugoslavia. Brominated flame retardants may be an example' (Stockholm IP 3).

> In other cases clients just have to give up campaigns in order to avoid incurring even worse damage than the proposed legislation would bring. Especially companies that own well known brands may have a lot to lose from being too stubborn, since they also have broader image costs to think about. Let's say you are a company manufacturing shampoo, and in your bottles of shampoo you've got PVC. Greenpeace starts a campaign saying; 'Oh-oh, PVC is dangerous, could cause cancer,' resulting in the Commission saying; 'Hm, let's check in to this.' You're producing millions of bottles every year, you're personally convinced that there is no risk. Now, up to a certain moment you are going to try to convince the Commission that there is no risk. You've done all the checks, everything is clear, no problems for consumers. But if the debate reaches a certain stage in the public arena, you just pull it out! Because there is no way you want your brand to be attached with the fact that there's a risk on your product (Brussels IP 2).
>
> Generally, companies can be more flexible on their positions and arguments than trade associations, who often have internal negotiation games to think about. The transnational associations in Brussels, the Eurogroups, especially, have a reputation for being slow and for arriving at minimal common denominator positions that are difficult to back away from without the members' consent.[2] 'For a consultant it is much easier to work with companies because you're much more flexible. A trade association secretariat has its own internal clients, and you can't change what they've already decided. They negotiate both on positions and arguments' (Brussels IP 4).

Consultants have clear incentives to make sure that the goals and positions eventually defined are achievable. It is not in their interest to end up with results that look like failures, so they try to avoid impossible missions.

> You have to make it clear to the client that you are rarely a hundred per cent successful. What you describe in your case, that the proposal should be withdrawn, if you think that it is a hundred per cent success, it won't happen anyway. You have to set reasonable goals, sensible criteria on what constitutes

success. Sometimes a thing like a date for taking effect, which may sound very small, may have a large impact. If you can influence that, it may be a success, even if you haven't managed to stop the proposal (Stockholm IP 1).

We have to do a reality check with the client. If a petroleum company comes to see me and says 'I would like to be able to operate with single oiltankers that are 25 years old', I would say 'I don't think your fitting in the picture at the moment, this is not achievable and that wouldn't be good for you anyway' (Brussels IP 2).

If consultants are doing their job well, they criticise and question. The first meetings may therefore include quite frank discussions. 'We often have an argument with our client about what messages and arguments to put forward. Sometimes it's not possible to convince them' (Brussels IP 8). One source of disagreement, as discussed earlier, is the importance of technical details in the argument. Another is the economic impact on the company or industry. 'While this is very often a valid argument, it needs to be used very, very carefully' (Brussels IP 3). The status of the self-regarding 'it's going to be bad for industry' arguments will be analysed more in detail later in this chapter. As already shown in the introduction, this is not one of the more popular arguments among public affairs consultants. That does not mean, however, that it should not be used.

Sometimes clients hide information even from their consultant. One consultant says that he always requests from his clients that they tell him everything:

Sometimes they do, sometimes they don't. One of the classical things is pure economics; companies can do things but they don't want to. They have the technology to change, but they don't want to admit that they can change because it's going to cost them. They are going to have to change their manufacturing processes, they may have to redesign products slightly, it's going to be costly. So they find other arguments to try and block that change (Brussels IP 3).

Another interviewee admits that he sometimes lets clients use arguments which he does not think are effective 'to keep them happy' (Brussels IP 1). At the end of the day, clients have the last say on which positions to take and arguments to use. 'Now ultimately we can really do no more than express our strong reservations, the client has the ultimate say, but we would be quite firm and clear about what we think and we would try as much as possible to explain why we have these concerns and try to find acceptable alternatives' (Brussels IP 3).

You have to agree on the perception of the landscape, otherwise it is difficult to work together. We had a prospective client, who had a traffic solution which involved a kind of a track taxi. He was a very nice person and there were three of us and two from the other group. We discussed it for three hours and we realized we did not have the same idea of reality. 'You have misunderstood the situation,' we said. Because they thought that the issue in principle was politically won, just because there was a proposal in the parliament. We tried to explain that things do not work that way. 'Yes, that is how it works' they said, 'we have assurances from a member of the parliament that he will really push this issue.' We simply could not agree on what reality looked like and in such a case you have to thank for a nice discussion, but it is not going to be more than that (Stockholm IP 1).

Conclusion: travel broadens the mind

Recall the core difference between the rationalities of the market and the forum, as described by Elster: 'The consumer chooses between courses of action that differ only in the way they affect him. In political choice situations the citizen is asked to express his preference over states that also differ in the way in which they affect other people' (Elster 1986:111). The initial phase of public affairs consultants' jobs, when working with clients who are not already sophisticated in their approach to politics, is largely dominated by this required change of perspective. Successful lobbyists, in Brussels and in Stockholm, need to open their minds to the perspectives of others. 'You can't be so damned self absorbed if you are to be a good lobbyist' (Stockholm IP 6). 'Fitting into the picture' means that positions and arguments must be developed with consideration given to the preferences and perceptions of other stakeholders, including the public. The position taken should be able to be presented as a solution not only to the client's own problems, but also to problems perceived by other key players. Companies and trade associations who get stuck in technical details of their own business, who lack the ability to 'view things from the perspective of the rest of the world' (Stockholm IP 7), will have difficulties fitting themselves into the larger picture.

The content of the first meetings between consultants and new clients depend very much on where the clients are situated on the professional-amateur scale. Professionals may appreciate help in order to fine-tune certain aspects of their strategies. 'Sometimes their argument is much more evolved than our input can be, because they've been thinking of an issue for years, and so it can be really just a question of how you present this argument' (Brussels IP 3). Alternatively, professionals may have use for other standard consultancy functions, such as external reviewers with the perspective to 'kill the darling arguments' or providing external support for the in-house communication unit.

The more amateurish clients are, and the more stubborn they are ('it certainly happens that clients are stubborn' (Brussels IP 3)), the greater the challenge for consultants. Much of what is going on during the initial phases of their co-operation has to do with dealing with the downsides of amateur characteristics. The consultants' job is to help clients mitigate their egocentric, emotional, reactive and short-sighted characters, in order to avoid the shotgun approach. Not because public affairs consultants have a particularly strong moral view on how one should behave in the forum but because they get paid to help clients navigate politics, in order to avoid costs and gain advantages. And hard bargaining—according to the consultants themselves—is not the way to do it.

For amateur clients, therefore, the first phase of getting dressed for politics involves rethinking and sometimes substantially redefining preferences, positions and arguments. Some clients find this process of placing oneself in a broader context, looking at oneself from outside and detecting weaknesses in one's own argumentation, stimulating and even 'a revelation' (Stockholm IP 6). Other clients, who are used to being boss, may find this hard to accept. 'They don't think we understand what is important' (Stockholm IP 5).

The picture of the meetings between PA consultants and clients resembles more that of therapists' meetings with patients than the stereotypical image of hired guns. Amateurs may initially behave according to the stereotype, bursting in, swearing over those Neanderthal bureaucrats messing up things, giving orders; 'here is the money, now go and kill that proposal'. However, the consultants' answer does not fit the stereotype. Rather than saying 'thank you, which regulation do you want to get rid of?' the serious consultant puts the client on the couch and asks 'now, what's the problem, really?'.

Of course this is the consultants' picture, not the clients', which makes it biased. Nevertheless, the story is credible. The reason why companies and associations are prepared to pay big sums of money to these consultants is because they believe they need assistance in order to be influential in politics. In order to find the optimal strategy, depending on the political situation, positions and arguments must be flexible. The fact that clients sometimes hide information even from their consultant illustrates how strongly they are resistant to negotiating on their primary position and the perceived threat the consultant poses to that stance. In many respects consultants' advice to their clients is similar to the advice given to negotiators by negotiation specialists Fisher, Ury and Patton: focus on preferences before you decide on positions—and not only your own preferences but also those of the other parties. Those who tie themselves too hard to a particular position are less likely to achieve the optimal agreement (Fisher, Ury & Patton 1999: chapter three).

The theory of publicity's civilising effect assumes that formulating positions and arguments with consideration to the perspectives of others is a behaviour forced upon political actors by the public frontstage. In the next section, however, it will be seen that it applies equally strongly in the closed lobby corridor.

LOBBYING BACKSTAGE

After discussing the first meetings between consultants and clients, and the preparatory phase of developing a lobbying strategy, the interviews proceeded with the concrete management of the case of the ERA/SRA and the eco-taxes on trucks. The second part of the hypothetical case's introductory text is presented below as it was written for the Brussels interviews, with adaptations for the Swedish political context in the Stockholm interviews shown in brackets:

You will advise the European Road Haulage Association (ERA) [Swedish Road Haulage Association (SRA)] on how to act in two different situations.

1. The drafting of the Commission proposal within DG Environment [government proposal within the Ministry of the Environment]. Your client will have contacts with the civil servants responsible for the drafting.
2. A public appearance at the big Transport Conference, where the new developments within European [Swedish] transport policy will be discussed and where the use of economic incentives will be one of the most common topics of conversation. The Secretary-General of the ERA [SRA] is invited to hold one of the opening speeches.

We can assume that you will be using a variety of other communication channels and lobbying strategies as well, but we will not spend time on them during the interview.

Starting with the contacts with the civil servants responsible for drafting the proposal within DG Environment [the Ministry of the Environment], your client will communicate with the Head of Unit and his or her staff at the Air and Noise unit. There will be personal meetings and telephone conversations. The people responsible for drafting the proposal are persons whom your client has had contacts with before. They know each other on a professional basis, but not personally.

Your client suggests the following arguments. The new proposal for an environmental classification system on trucks should be withdrawn because:
1. it will be a serious hit to the European [Swedish] haulage industry;
2. it will distort competition between the different modes of transportation, which will impede the implementation of an effective common market for freight transportation; [Brussels] OR measures against air pollution requires co-operation on a European or global level, not unilateral Swedish rules [Stockholm];
3. a vehicle tax is an ineffective means to reduce emissions from the transport sector;
4. the industry employs a lot of people directly and indirectly – jobs will be lost;
5. the European [Swedish] hauliers industry needs less trouble and cost burdens, not more;
6. the system encourages cheating at vehicle inspections, which will be difficult to control;
7. the European [Swedish] economy is dependent upon letting companies have access to road transports at reasonable prices;
8. it is unreasonable to sacrifice the hauliers like this, when it is obvious that the sources of air pollution are complex and thus a responsibility for the whole society;
9. the heavy focus on road transports prevents the search for a comprehensive approach to air pollution, which has many sources, ultimately hindering effective environmental protection.

Here, the arguments stand in their simplest form. How they should be rhetorically formulated and empirically grounded more precisely is a question we leave aside. For methodological reasons, in order to make the interviews as comparable with each other as possible, we will assume in this particular case that the different lines of argument are equally well underpinned factually. We do not need to specify exactly how well-founded the arguments are, but we assume that they are equally well supported by evidence.

Now, if you would select three of the arguments listed above, to use in your contacts with the responsible officials in DG Environment [the Ministry of the Environment]—which three would you choose? Why? Is any type of argument missing from the list? If you would reject three arguments from the list—the arguments you would be least eager to use in contacts with DG Environment [the Ministry of the Environment] officials—which three would that be?

The simple quantitative results from this question—the selection and rejection of three arguments from the list—was shown in the introduction of this chapter (Table 4.1). The self-regarding arguments (number one, five and eight in the list) tend to be equally unpopular among Brussels and Stockholm consultants. It was also demonstrated in Table 4.2 that the picture changes when the context is switched from private lobbying meetings to public speeches. In the public arena, contrary to the expectation of the theory of publicity's civilising effect, self-regarding arguments become somewhat more popular.

In this section I will first make a few notes about the methodological thinking behind the list of arguments. I will also demonstrate in a bit more detail how the interviewed consultants chose between the different arguments. Thereafter I will describe how they motivated their choices. The tables should be interpreted as illustrations of the main results of this chapter. The methodological point of letting the interviewees select and reject three arguments was not primarily to produce figures, but to get the process of discussing different types of arguments going in the interviews. What goes through consultants' minds when they are sorting arguments? I wanted to be able to see their 'footing,' especially with respect to the force of the better argument norm and the non-selfishness norm. To what extent do they recognise and follow these norms when they approach officials and how does that affect the mode of communication (arguing versus bargaining) and the types of justification (self-regarding versus other- and ideal-regarding)?

The list of arguments
The main purpose of having a list of arguments was, first, to make clear during the interviews what we should mean by an 'argument'. During the background interviews with association representatives, companies, public affairs consultants and civil servants I noted that several interviewees talked about facts and figures as arguments. Many of the interviewed consultants were more or less experts on transport and environment issues (a policy field which makes up a substantial part of the public affairs business) and I understood from the background interviews that I could easily be drowned by facts and figures on emissions, logistics, road-rail combinations, etc. Instead, I wanted to focus on arguments in terms of

justifications—self-regarding, other- or ideal-regarding—for a particular policy option.

I made clear to the interviewees, therefore, that I was aware that facts and figures are important when lobbying civil servants, but that the arguments listed here should be considered equally well underpinned factually. It was the 'essence' of the argument, I told them, that I wanted them to consider, not whether they could be credibly backed up by facts. From time to time I had to remind interviewees who questioned for instance the political viability of a tax, or the amount of freight which would be switched from road to rail etc., that they should not let their field expertise get in the way of their evaluation of the core substance of the arguments. Generally I believe this worked out well.

A second important point with having a list of arguments was to get the discussion going on different types of justification and to include the self-regarding arguments in a natural way in that discussion. For that purpose I wanted to have a mix which could reasonably be assumed to cover the spectrum of arguments used in a case like this. The arguments had to be credible in order to compete at least approximately equally well.

I also included one argument which could be interpreted as a threat. The idea was that this could open up the discussion on the force of the better argument norm. Argument number six contains an implicit threat, or a warning, masked up as an implementation argument. 'The system encourages cheating at vehicle inspections, which will be difficult to control,' could be interpreted as saying 'if you legislate, we will refuse to comply'. On the other hand, it could also be perceived as a normal implementation issue—'this legislation will not work at ground level'. In the interviews both interpretations were discussed, with completely different evaluations as a result.

The background research for the list of arguments included reading position papers, press releases and other policy documents from companies and trade associations within the transport sector. I also tested the credibility of the arguments during the background interviews.

Nine arguments seemed to be a reasonable number to handle during the interview. The number of self-interested arguments included was matched with the question of selection and rejection of three arguments. If the interviewees were really concerned about the non-selfishness norm, they could choose to reject all three of them. As already demonstrated, that did not happen. The self-regarding argument number five ('the European [Swedish] haulage industry needs less trouble and cost burdens, not more') was the least popular argument, both when lobbying officials in private meetings and in public speech, but it was not rejected by all interviewees. The sum of selected minus rejected for the three self-regarding arguments was −12 for the closed meeting both in Brussels and in Stockholm (Table 4.3), whereas a maximum low would have been −24 in Brussels (eight interviewees) and −21 in Stockholm (seven interviewees).

To include three self-regarding arguments is basically to say the same thing in three different ways—'don't do this to us'. Arguments number one ('it will be a serious hit to the European [Swedish] haulage industry') and five are quite straight-forward in that respect. Number eight ('it is unreasonable to sacrifice the hauliers like this, when it is obvious that the sources of air pollution are complex and thus are the responsibility of the whole society') adds a touch of fairness, while keeping the hauliers as the central reference group. The 'simplest' of the three—argument number one—turned out to be the least unpopular self-interested argument.

The other arguments in the list, with the exception of number six, depending on how it is interpreted, are other- and ideal-regarding. Normally, two major public interests are used as reference values in debates over transport and environment: economic welfare and the quality of the environment. Two macroeconomic arguments were included in the list: number four ('the industry employs a lot of people directly and indirectly – jobs will be lost') and seven ('the European [Swedish] economy is dependent upon letting companies have access to road transport at reasonable prices'). Arguments number three ('a vehicle tax is an ineffective means to reduce emissions from the transport sector') and nine ('the heavy focus on road transports prevents the search for a comprehensive approach to air pollution, which has many sources, ultimately hindering effective environmental protection') focus on the environment as the major justification for policy.

During the background research phase I noticed two arguments, one in the EU context and one in Sweden, which had no specific reference group ('good for X'), but were used more like ideal principles. For the EU this was the competition/ common market argument, which seemed to be perceived as a value in itself. In Sweden, on the other hand, the idea that Sweden must seek solutions on a European or global level seemed to have similar status as an unquestionable axiom. Argument number two in the list therefore read, for the Brussels interviews; 'it will distort competition between the different modes of transportation, which will impede the implementation of an effective common market for freight transport', and for the Stockholm interviews; 'measures against air pollution require co-operation on a European or global level, not unilateral Swedish rules'.

Choosing arguments to use back stage

Table 4.4 shows the number of times the different arguments were selected and rejected by the interviewed consultants, when asked which arguments they would choose when lobbying environment officials behind closed doors. It gives a more detailed description of the prioritisation of arguments than Table 4.1 earlier. The self-interested arguments were equally unpopular in Brussels and in Stockholm, which means that there was no indication of any transparency effect.

The evaluation of the nine arguments was generally similar in Brussels and in Stockholm. The exception was the macro-economic argument, number seven ('the European [Swedish] economy is dependent upon letting companies have access to road transport at reasonable prices'). Why it was less interesting to put this argument to the Swedish government than to the European Commission was not clear from the interviews. One might, in fact, have hypothesised the opposite, given that

Table 4.4 Selected and rejected arguments in private meetings

Arguments	No of times selected		No of times rejected		Selected minus rejected		
	Bru	Sto	Bru	Sto	Bru	Sto	Total
Environment (no 3)	6	7	0	0	6	7	13
Competition/ cooperation (no 2)	4	7	1	0	3	7	10
Implementation (no 6)	4	3	3	2	1	1	2
Macroeconomic (no 7)	4	1	0	3	4	-2	2
Environment (no 9)	2	2	1	3	1	-1	0
Macroeconomic (no 4)	1	0	3	1	-2	-1	-3
Self-regarding (no 8)	2	0	4	3	-2	-3	-5
Self-regarding (no 1)	0	0	3	5	-3	-5	-8
Self-regarding (no 5)	0	1	7	5	-7	-4	-11

Note: Table 4.4 shows the results for the question 'which three arguments from the list would you select, and which three would you reject, for the meetings with civil servants in DG Environment [Ministry of the Environment]?'. Since there were eight interviewees in Brussels and seven in Stockholm, the scale ranges from 8 (all consultants select the argument and no one rejects it) to –8 (no consultants select the argument, everyone rejects it) in Brussels and from 7 to –7 in Stockholm. In total the maximum value is 15 and minimum –15. The columns do not sum up equally (ranging between 21 and 23) because, first, eight consultants were interviewed in Brussels and seven in Stockholm and, second, because a few of the consultants insisted on selecting or rejecting four, or just two, arguments.

national governments are more dependent on tax incomes, and therefore on a growing economy, than is the Commission.

Argument number two was popular both in Sweden and in Brussels but even more popular in Sweden. As described before, number two is in fact two different arguments in Brussels and in Stockholm, representing ideal-regarding principles (undistorted competition in the EU, international cooperation in Sweden).

Argument number six showed the greatest variation among the consultants (seven times selected, five times rejected), which is explained by the fact that it can be interpreted in two ways. Perceived as an implementation argument, it is fairly popular for use in contacts with civil servants. Those consultants who noticed the implicit threat ('we'll break the law'), however, immediately rejected it. The force of the better argument norm is strongly felt by the consultants, as will be seen. The 'jobs will be lost' argument (number four) was not very popular, but it was not among the first arguments rejected either (it was rejected four times). The self-regarding arguments, number one, five and eight, received the lowest scores, although not maximally low.

One thing that turned out from the interviews, however, was that the actual content of an argument is just one factor that is considered when the consultant and the client sit down to develop an argumentation strategy. What should be regarded as a 'good argument' also depends on who the argument seeks to persuade, who the messenger is, and when the argument is put forward. Finding the right voice behind an argument, as well as the right timing, is a core part of the job. Some arguments can be used by some actors but not by others. Some arguments are effective in one stage of the policy process but not in another. As will be demonstrated in this section, understanding the consultants' thinking behind the matching and timing of arguments turns out to be important for understanding the effects of publicity.

The committed partner
For companies and trade associations, according to the interviewed consultants, successful lobbying in Brussels and in Stockholm is based on constructive dialogue. This dialogue builds on proposing and listening to arguments, not threats and promises.

> What are you trying to do? You are trying to change people's minds! The NGOs try to change the decision-makers' minds in the direction of an eco-tax, and I'm trying to change them away from that. That's the process (Brussels IP 5).

Successful lobbying is about talking, but also about listening. Amateurs typically fail because they tend towards the monologic. Actors who just state 'demands' will not be taken seriously, unless they have an exceptional status of some sort, as will be discussed below.

If our consultant tour guides to politics had provided us with an accompanying guide book 'How to make your trip to politics a success,' the first entry would be a role description for the committed partner. It applies to public appearances, as will be described in the next section, but even more so for the private meetings with policy-makers. The appearance of the Secretary-General of the ERA/SRA, when taking meetings with DG Environment/Ministry of the Environment officials, should give the impression of an engaged fellow problem-solver involved in a constructive dialogue. This person, the officials should think, comes to their office with the purpose of contributing to workable solutions to the problems at hand. While the Secretary-General is desperately trying to make these officials change track it is crucial not to appear obstructive. "I don't like it' is not the start of a dialogue' (Brussels IP 8). 'We never say 'no,' we always say 'yes, but...' and then use our arguments' (Brussels IP 5).

> When you walk into a meeting with commission officials—don't just try to get messages across. Don't talk too much. Listen to their concerns, ask them questions, try to have a two-way discussion. When they have a question, surprise them by having all the data with you (Brussels IP 8).
>
> I don't think that you should start off by saying; 'this is going to be bad,' as an introductory statement. Because you're setting the tone for the rest of... not only that meeting, but your further communication with the people that you're discussing with (Brussels IP 3).

The committed partner role implies a requirement to be constructive. This applies both to the Brussels and the Stockholm context. If you do not like what is being drafted you should come up with something better. '"No" is not an amendment' (Stockholm IP 2). 'You can't just say "no," it just won't work. A political decision in a more environmentally friendly direction cannot be reversed without extremely good arguments and good alternatives' (Stockholm IP 7).

> There is a tremendous assumption and perception among regulators that industries know what they are doing, know how they're interacting with the environment, know what their emissions are, know what's going in and out of their plants etc. Wrapped up in that is that there is also a tremendous assumption that industries should be responsible. It's an over-assumption, but it's there! And you can't fight it. If you say 'it's not just us, now go away' it's not going to go very far (Brussels IP 8).

The civil servants, both in DG Environment and in the Swedish Ministry of the Environment, are referred to with respect by the interviewees. The consultants see them as competent and committed persons who want to be met with arguments which are factually based and relevant to their task. 'I would tell the client that when you meet the staff at the Swedish Ministry of the Environment, the starting point should be that they are very knowledgeable of environmental policy, that they even have a personal commitment' (Stockholm IP 5). The client must not waste their time in meetings by saying things they already know.

The option of using threats or pressure, 'banging the table', was perceived as being out of the question in the case of the ERA/SRA and the eco-taxes on trucks. Not all consultants realised at first that argument number six could be interpreted as an implicit threat ('the system encourages cheating at vehicle inspections, which will be difficult to control'). Those who did immediately rejected it. 'Number six is scoring for the other team. Who are the cheaters? Our members, of course!' (Stockholm IP 2) 'That [argument number six] is unusable! You're basically saying that you're irresponsible. It is not giving a very good image of the industry' (Brussels IP 4).

> The argument that I would absolutely not use is that the system is encouraging cheating during inspections. That is to say that your own organization consists of cheaters! It is a very bad argument. If it is true or not does not matter. You cannot say 'if you make this decision we will start cheating.' That is the argument on the list that jumps out as one that I would definitely refrain from making (Stockholm IP 1).

The force of the better argument norm—ruling out bargaining as a legitimate mode of decision-making—and the requirement to be constructive lies behind much of the thinking behind the consultants' selection of arguments. The hard currency of the lobby-corridor is other- and ideal-regarding arguments and publicly defendable alternative solutions, not threats and promises. However, self-regarding arguments also have their function, as I will show later. The challenge for the client and the consultant lies in balancing the perceived need to appear not to be obstructive, of cultivating an image of being a committed partner, bringing arguments which give added value to the officials, with the fact that the ultimate target of the lobbying campaign is to stop the present version of the eco-tax proposal. This requires careful footing.

Timing the arguments

From a public policy perspective, the scenario of eco-taxes on trucks seems to be taking place at an early policy phase. The interviewed consultants, however, perceived the fact that civil servants are working on a draft proposal as this being already late in the day. To them this case was more an instance of crisis management than of agenda setting. This perception of the timing of the case substantially affected their choices of arguments.

Generally, according to the interviewees, the earlier in the process an issue is staged the more important become the broader policy arguments, involving efforts at 'issue definition' (Baumgartner & Jones 1993: 12). Argument number nine for example, calling for 'a comprehensive approach to air pollution', was not selected, or was rejected, by several interviewees with the motivation that it was 'outdated' in this case. It would certainly be a great accomplishment if you could persuade the civil servants to shift focus from haulage to a more comprehensive approach, but that would be difficult at this stage, they argued. 'In this case, the staff at the Swedish Ministry of the Environment do not formulate policy progressively' (Stockholm IP 3). If they are actually working on a draft proposal they have already made an implicit decision to attend to the general problem of air pollution by targeting the road transport sector. The decision to go for the hauliers has informally already been taken and pointing at other sectors now will probably not be enough to escalate the issue up to the general policy level again. Having come this far, those who rejected number nine argued, the opportunity to make the drafters of the proposal look in another direction was already missed. That kind of agenda management should be a part of the client's long term security policy, which is not primarily what they are working on now.

As the situation stood, according to one consultant, argument number nine would be met by the officials saying: 'Well, we have to start somewhere':

That's always been DG environment's policy. While in an ideal world perhaps these things would be co-ordinated, and they should have a comprehensive strategy, in reality they don't. So what happens quite often is that they take one area and they say: 'Right, we'll start with this one. And then we'll do the next, and then we'll do the next, and so forth...' So they will start somewhere. And, you might say: 'Well, why us?' But then they will say: 'Well, why anybody else? You are contributing to air-pollution. Our data suggests that you are a major contributor. And so, we are going to target you.' So, I don't really see that [argument number nine] as being solid argumentation for why you shouldn't be targeted (Brussels IP 3).

One consultant calls this step-by-step approach by the political institutions 'elephant theory':

> The Commission will say 'Yes, you have a point [referring to argument number nine]. On the other hand, we have a pollution problem which is the size of an elephant—it's extremely large and complex. In order to address the problem you do not address the elephant as such, you take pieces of the elephant. And you are one of those pieces' (Brussels IP 2).

However, four consultants did select argument number nine, so there was no consensus on this argument being outdated. Second to the 'implicit threat-argument' number six, number nine showed the greatest variation among the consultants. The difference is small between Stockholm (–1) and Brussels (1), so the variation comes from individual judgements. The most important factor pointing in favour of number nine was its environmental content. As one Stockholm-consultant explained his choice of number nine for the meeting with Ministry of the Environment officials:

> I would tell the client that now you need to discuss specific issues with them and talk about environmental issues, and try to show that these proposals are not good for the environment. That is the dialogue with which I think we would have the largest chance of success. If you are able to convince them that these decisions are not good for the environment, well... I mean... the staff at the Swedish Ministry of the Environment, are making this proposition because they think that the environment in Sweden is going to get better. If you can make them doubt that, on good grounds, you have made good progress (Stockholm IP 5).

One Brussels consultant argued that the environmental content of argument number nine could be used in an attempt to stall the process:

> You could use nine to water down the eco-tax. To say: 'Oh yes, the eco-tax is perhaps a good thing, but what you really need is a comprehensive approach to air-pollution. So let's do the eco-tax, but let's not do it now. Let us also look at air-pollution by planes. Let us look at air-pollution by diesel trains, which is of course conveniently forgotten, isn't it Mr Civil Servant from the Commission? Yes it is, I can prove it. Here are the facts and the figures. A green NGO will not give you these facts and figures, Mr Civil Servant, but I give them to you.' So, I water down the issue of pollution by trucks, by bringing up other issues, and saying to the Commission: 'Basically, I agree with your eco-tax, but first you need a comprehensive approach, so please come back in five years' (Brussels IP 5).

In terms of timing, however, the dominant view of argument number nine, and to a lesser extent also of number seven ('the European [Swedish] economy is dependent upon letting companies have access to road transports at reasonable prices'), was that these were broader policy arguments which primarily should be used in early stages of policy formulation. Argument number three on the other hand ('a vehicle tax is an ineffective means to reduce emissions from the transport sector'), and, depending on how they were worded and operationalised, number two (Brussels: 'It will distort competition between the different modes of transportation, which will impede on the implementation of an effective common market for freight transportation', Sweden: 'Measures against air pollution require co-operation on a European or global level, not unilateral Swedish rules') and six ('the system encourages cheating at vehicle inspections, which will be difficult to control')—provided that it was interpreted as a pure implementation argument and not as a threat—were exactly the type of arguments one would use at this stage. When the issue has moved from the agenda-setting phase towards policy formulation the lobbyist needs foot-in-the-door arguments: factual, concrete, technical, rational arguments—'experts can deliver the message' (Stockholm IP 4)—which could have the power to stop the policy door from closing.

> At this stage, it is important to find credible and serious objections of a decent technological and practical character. One such argument may be that this goes against other processes on the EU level, that is, build on number two. It may be possible to claim that in practice this could promote a requirement for new investments in trucks, which unfairly benefits domestic manufacturers in a way that is not consistent with what is currently happening in the EU, or something like that (Stockholm IP 3).

If the responsible officials are about to close the issue and take it to a decision, the client must have something concrete to stop the process. 'A classic example of this is the Öresund bridge. You sit there, just about to make a decision, and then somebody waves a little herring and says "you haven't thought about this". Then you have to look at that thing too' (Stockholm IP 3). The controversial political decision to connect Sweden and Denmark with a bridge over the Öresund was delayed in this way, due to fear of the environmental consequences.

Timing thus affects the value of a given argument. At one point in time a given argument may be seen as highly constructive and valid, while at a later or earlier stage it may rather be perceived as obstructive. At an early stage of policy formulation, broad arguments like nine and seven may be useful for the policy-makers in the search for the right perspective on an issue, while at a later stage, when the problem is already defined, these arguments may appear as attempts to distract the process. An argument like number three, on the other hand, is less interesting when the discussion is still focused on the general problem of air pollution.

The difference between issue-definition arguments and foot-in-the-door arguments was compared by some consultants with procedural and substantive arguments in a court. Pointing at alternative solutions is like bringing in new evidence or new witnesses to the case. Putting a foot in the door by saying 'this is not going to work' is more like a process objection. You do not address the issue of whether the suspect is guilty or not, only whether he can be legally convicted. 'How many people have not saved their skins with procedures?' (Brussels IP 2)

Adding value to the process
While timing in this case pointed towards foot-in-the-door arguments, the consultants did not like the idea of basing their lobbying only on this kind of argument. The main disadvantage with foot-in-the-door arguments is that they come close to breaking with the constructive partner attitude. The reason why argument number three ('a vehicle tax is an ineffective means to reduce emissions from the transport sector') is the most popular among the interviewees is that it is both an effective door-stopper and carries with it an implicit continuation, namely the alternative solution. The first answer to the question of whether the interviewees thought there were any arguments missing from the list was the alternative solution. 'You must always try to offer an alternative' (Brussels IP 5). 'Number three is a very attractive argument. You say that you want the same thing, but not in this way. But this entails that implicitly we see that there are more efficient ways' (Stockholm IP 7).

> Argument number three is beginning a dialogue on solutions, presuming that there is a good case behind that and it's not totally negative. 'Vehicle taxes are ineffective, here are three examples of how it can be better done.' If I have no alternative and it's totally negative then it's less compelling (Brussels IP 8).

A foot-in-the-door without any serious suggestions on what to do instead is close to obstruction. It is the last step before open conflict. Responding to my question about what he would do if he did not have a credible alternative solution, the same consultant responded: 'If you don't have a good alternative solution you create it. You bring the experts in the area together. And if it doesn't exist already, you invent it. And I don't mean invent like … you know … it has to be real!' (Brussels IP 8).

One of the characteristics of the committed and constructive partner is the ability to give value added—to contribute to the process with arguments which were not already on the table. 'You should say things that nobody else can say' (Brussels IP 8). 'Which are your unique facts? That is an important question.' (Stockholm IP 5). Some arguments, especially the self-regarding arguments and the jobs-will-be-lost argument number four ('industry employs a lot of people directly and indirectly—jobs will be lost') are handicapped by the fact that they are too predictable. 'Everybody always says this' (Brussels IP 6). Even if they may contain important pieces of information about the economic effects of a proposal, and therefore have a legitimate function, these arguments are rhetorically weak because of their stereotypical character. They will not attract anyone's attention, but rather bore people. Commenting on argument number four, one consultant said: 'The relationship between industry and jobs is a bit like a nineteenth-century argument. It's Fordism: "I have so many people that work for me, I can provide schools and hospitals"' (Brussels IP 2). 'Everybody says that [argument number four]. If you have been in politics yourself, like I have, this is an argument you vomit on' (Stockholm IP 6).

> I think they [arguments number one, four and seven] are the ones which feel mostly worn. The staff at the Ministry of the Environment may say to each other before the meeting; 'now they come here and say that the trucking industry will be affected and that jobs will be lost' and then they can just mark that off later. That kind of meeting becomes so predictable and without any results. It is the expected objection that the staff at the Ministry of the Environment is so tired of (Stockholm IP 5).
>
> It's very much a question of style. It seems so reactionary, so old-fashioned [arguments number one and four]. You really need to say something more than that. As they stand they're dull, dry and a DG Environment official will kick back on it immediately, he will not accept it. You don't want to profile yourself as an old-fashioned industry with old-fashioned arguments (Brussels IP 6).

Clichés cannot work as door-stoppers. 'There is reluctance in the system, which I have learned from my own cost, against the argument that "the industry is going have to close down from this proposal"'. Basically the answer to that is '"come off it, don't give me that, I hear that ten times a week"' (Brussels IP 8).

At this stage in the process the ERA/SRA should use arguments which attract the attention of the responsible officials. 'You have to think of something new, something they have not thought about' (Stockholm IP 3). This is especially difficult as these officials may not be particularly keen on taking in new arguments when they are about to close the process. 'We'll be hurt' or 'jobs will be lost' is not going to help in that respect, unless the effects are remarkable and unexpected. If that is the case, on the other hand, and if it can be credibly demonstrated, then these arguments may bring something new to the process that needs to be checked upon. Most often, however, according to the consultants, it is very difficult to credibly demonstrate such remarkable and unexpected effects.

Choosing the right angle
The choice of arguments also depends on who the client is going to talk to. After the discussion following the selection and rejection of arguments for the meeting with DG Environment [Ministry of the Environment] officials, the following question was put to the consultants, which was also part of the introductory text given out before the interviews:

> If we keep all the presumptions of the case the same, but assume instead that the proposal is being drafted within DG Transport and Energy [Ministry of Industry, Employment and Communication]; do you think you would change your argumentation in any way or would it be the same?

The point of this question was to check whether lobbying officials with the primary task of improving the environment, rather than securing an effective transport market or economic growth, affects the status of the self-regarding arguments. The notion of lobbyists 'capturing' policy-makers, as developed in the economic interest group theory discussed in chapter two, applies to situations where the lobbyist and the lobbied work closely together backstage. It seems reasonable to assume that self-regarding arguments are more valid in such cases than in situations with less intimate relationships. When the case was set up I wanted to control for this factor by explicitly stating, as described earlier, that 'the people responsible for drafting the proposal are persons whom your client has had contacts with before. They know each other on a professional basis, but not personally.' To the extent that intimate relationships would be more common in Sweden or in Brussels, which was something I could not say for sure beforehand, this was an attempt at avoiding that bias.

In hindsight I do not think it made much difference. It was clear that no one even considered the possibility of the ERA/SRA having such a privileged relationship as that described by capture theory, either with DG Environment/Ministry of the Environment or any other DG or ministry. For the consultants such special relationships seemed to be something they hear or read about at best. 'Maybe you'll find that if you look at the farmers' (Brussels IP 7). 'The chemicals industry used to have a strong position with DG Enterprise, before DG Environment took over chemicals legislation' (Brussels IP 3). It is clearly not part of their day-to-day work, however. Capture is either generally uncommon, both in Brussels and in Stockholm, or restricted to other policy areas than environmental policy.

When I raised this issue in connection to the case of the ERA, one of the Brussels-consultants responded in the following way:

> They [DG Transport and Energy] will not have a specific worry about the road hauliers. Most often Commission officials are political scientists, public administration specialists, economists, lawyers—definitely not road hauliers. It is a very specific hypothesis that you would find someone having special loyalties because they have been working with the sector for many years. The chances of that actually happening are very low. If you find such a person he would probably rather be bored with an industry basing their argumentation on 'we're the victims, help us.' I think he would say; 'Listen, I've been working with your sector for a long time and I think you really have to think out something more constructive than that.' And even if you would find a transport official who would be more inclined to accept that argument personally, he would be less inclined to publicly state it during an inter-service consultation (Brussels IP 6).

The ERA/SRA can not count on special understandings from DG Transport and Energy [Ministry of Industry, Employment and Communication] officials, according to the interviewed consultants. Nevertheless, the different tasks of the different DGs and ministries substantially changed the prioritisation of the arguments. Table 4.5 indicates that the major change when switching from DG Environment and the Ministry of the Environment to DG Transport and Energy (TREN) and the Ministry of Industry, Employment and Communication is that macroeconomic arguments become more important while environmental arguments are used to a lesser extent. It definitely makes a difference who has the dossier, but not because of special understandings for the industry's perspective, but because of the division of labour between the DGs/Ministries. The self-interested arguments, number one, five and eight, show little change.

Argument number seven ('the European/Swedish economy is dependent upon letting companies have access to road transport at reasonable prices') was more popular, both in Brussels and in Stockholm (+3 and +2 respectively), when the client met DG TREN [Ministry of Industry, Employment and Communication] officials compared to meetings with DG Environment [Ministry of the Environment]. The 'jobs will be lost' argument, number four, is more popular with the Swedish consultants lobbying the Ministry of Industry, Employment and Communication (+4 compared to Ministry of the Environment), than it is with Brussels consultants lobbying DG Transport and Energy (no change from DG Environment). One explanation for that may be that creating jobs is not DG

Table 4.5. Differences in the choices of arguments between different DGs/ ministries

Arguments	No. of times selected (Environment)		No. of times selected (TREN/Industry)		Difference from Environment to TREN/Industry		
	Bru	Sto	Bru	Sto	Bru	Sto	Total
Macroeconomic (no 7)	4	1	7	3	3	2	+5
Macroeconomic (no 4)	1	0	1	4	0	4	+4
Self-regarding (no 1)	0	0	0	1	0	1	+1
Competition/ Cooperation (no 2)	4	7	6	5	2	-2	0
Self-regarding (no 5)	0	1	0	1	0	0	0
Self-regarding (no 8)	2	0	1	1	-1	1	0
Environment (no 9)	2	2	3	0	1	-2	-1
Implementation (no 6)	4	3	4	1	0	-2	-2
Environment (no 3)	6	7	2	5	-4	-2	-6

Note: Table 4.5 shows the differences in the consultants' choice of arguments depending on which DG or Ministry the client was meeting with. They were asked to select the three arguments from the list which they would prefer to use. (The first four columns do not sum up equally (ranging between 21–25), first because there are eight interviewed Brussels-consultants and seven based in Stockholm, and second because a few of the consultants insisted on selecting four, or just two, arguments.)

TREN's primary task while it is an important part of the mission of the Swedish Ministry of Industry, Employment and Communication. The result might have been different if the question had concerned DG Enterprise, but that is difficult to say for sure. One consultant claimed that 'the employment argument is much less important for the Commission than many people think. Unemployment is a problem for national governments, not for the Commission' (Brussels IP 5).

The environment arguments number three ('a vehicle tax is an inefficient means of reducing emissions from the transport sector') and nine ('the heavy focus on road transport prevents the search for a comprehensive approach to air pollution, which has many sources, ultimately hindering effective environmental protection') drop in popularity (–6 and –1 respectively) when the ERA/SRA met officials whose brief did not include the environment to the same extent as did the DG Environment and the Ministry of the Environment.

The fact that the arguments used varied depending on who the client was talking to is closely related to the requirement to be constructive and to bring added value. 'When you speak to somebody in a specific DG you talk strictly to the brief of that DG. You will put in front of them the arguments that are most pertinent to their job' (Brussels IP 6). Among the Brussels consultants, the upcoming inter-service consultations between the DGs was an often cited as a factor to be considered when choosing which arguments to bring. 'Internal market officials want to know about internal market implications. "What's my angle here?" they will ask. "What can I add?" You will focus on that so that they have something to say on this proposal in the inter-service consultations' (Brussels IP 4).

One Brussels consultant explains how he would distribute the arguments between DG TREN and DG Environment in the case of the ERA and eco-taxes on trucks:

> Wallström [the Environment Commissioner] needs transport and economic arguments in order to face de Palacio [the Commissioner for Energy and Transport] at the Commission meeting. But she primarily wants the transport arguments for the proposal, cause she's going to defend the proposal, and you're not going to give those arguments to her, right? So you'll talk to Wallström's officials about the environmental aspects and provide de Palacio with the transport arguments against the proposal (Brussels IP 6).

However, there is a risk in shifting arguments too easily. This concerns the 'committed partner' attitude. Credibility as a committed partner would be challenged if clients came to be seen as paying mere lip-service to the concerns of everyone they meet. The importance of consistency is strongly emphasised by the consultants. 'Nobody should be able to come later and say that you have had different messages' (Stockholm IP 2).

To find the right balance between giving added value by speaking strictly to their brief and, at the same time, giving the impression of having a consistent message, which signals seriousness and earns respect, is part of the necessary 'footing' in the lobby-corridors. In the next section, this challenge will be pushed to the extreme extent by the introduction of the public speech situation, with a broad audience. With respect to the private lobbying meetings, there were some differences between the interviewees in their judgements on how much emphasis should be put on consistency versus flexibility. The main story that emerged was that you do not put different *arguments* to different DGs or Ministries—especially not contradictory arguments—but that the *focus* of your arguments will be different. 'The same arguments would be presented in a different way' (Brussels IP 5). 'I make sure I have the same message to all targets. I want my clients to be able to have a line that holds up for everybody, but the presentation, the focal point, changes' (Brussels IP 1).

> You have the same arguments the whole way, but you put a different focus on them. If I speak to a departmental deputy at the Ministry of Finance or the Ministry of Industry, Employment and Communication, which are more strongly focused on work places, the Swedish competitiveness and so on, the Swedish competitiveness may be the first thing I mention. And then I say that, from an environmental perspective, there are also more efficient methods. When you turn to the civil servant at the Swedish Ministry of the Environment, the argument about more efficient methods for reaching this environmentally positive development should be emphasized in the first hand. 'But also' you say 'we will fall behind in the competition with continental Europe'. It will be there also, but it is not particularly highly prioritized (Stockholm IP 7).

The fact that the decision-making is collegial in the European Commission and in the Swedish government is emphasised both by Brussels and Stockholm consultants. 'You have to think about the fact that even if DG Environment drafts the proposal it goes to inter-service consultation, and then on to cabinet-consultation, and then it's finally agreed by the whole Commission' (Brussels IP 5). 'The government is a collective organ and there is talk between the ministries even if there are different opinions on certain things' (Stockholm IP 1). That means that there is a risk, or a chance, that the client's arguments will spread between the DGs or Ministries. If any contradictions are revealed credibility will be lost.

> It's like if you try to sell me your Sony recorder. You cannot use sales-arguments which are different from the sales-arguments which you use with my colleague in the opposite office, because we will talk to each other. And if I hear you say something different to him than to me, you will lose your credibility, your trust and two potential clients (Brussels IP 5).

This applies to spoken communication at meetings but even more so to written communications. 'You don't want to be in a situation where you are on paper presenting different arguments to different DGs, they sit down and compare your different arguments and realise that you are saying different things, perhaps you're contradicting yourself' (Brussels IP 3).

The concept of transparency is also popular among public affairs consultants. Appearing to have nothing to hide is part of building the 'committed partner' image. Many letters, therefore, as will be seen in the next chapter, have multiple addressees. 'If you're sending a letter, it would be addressed to the people sitting on the dossier, the Air and Noise Unit in this case. But you would also typically copy in other DG's, and other units, that may be interested in the dossier, in order to show that you are transparent' (Brussels IP 3).

This, in turn, may affect the choice of arguments. One Stockholm consultant explained why he would bring the macroeconomic argument number seven to the Ministry of the Environment, even though 'it's not really their thing, they don't really care a lot about it. But you say it because you want to be transparent. You want to be straight and honest and have the same message everywhere. Therefore you have an arsenal of arguments, but you emphasize different aspects depending on whom you are talking to' (Stockholm IP 2).

Using 'unnecessary' arguments in order to be consistent and transparent conflicts with the objective of adding value and not wasting officials' time. Again, this judgement would have to be made on a case-by-case basis. Moderating this dilemma is the fact that there is also a certain understanding and acceptance of the need to acknowledge the different roles of the actors involved. Emphasising transport arguments towards DG TREN and environmental arguments towards DG Environment is not going to upset anyone, as long as there is no contradiction. 'They know that this is the way it is done. They'll know that you're speaking to them not as Mr Smith but as MR DG Environment' (Brussels IP 6).

Choosing the right messenger

I think there is an over-reliance in the content of arguments; I think the main task is to get voices behind arguments, allies. One tends to find that the self-interested party defending its own interest has a limited impact on the political understanding of the issue. If you don't have third parties saying that this is not just important for the X industry it's also important for a wider range of interests, broader industry interests or public interests, then there is a limit to what you can achieve. You need to sit down with other stakeholders on a one-to-one and say 'this really affects you, we're doing this, what are you doing?' (Brussels IP 8).

The persuasiveness of a given argument varies depending on who the sender is. That has important implications for the kinds of justifications that can be used. 'In the modern communication society the sender of a message is sometimes as important as the content of the message' (Stockholm IP 3). The public affairs consultant's job thus also includes sorting out who should deliver which argument. Creating broad alliances with other actors, preferably actors with a different status as stakeholders, is a core part of lobbying campaigns. This is not just a question of getting 'bigger' by increasing the number of voices behind the arguments. A variety of different voices make a greater impression than many voices coming from the same direction. 'The multitude of aspects has a value in itself. That is why there is a referral system. If many different actors with different positions arrive at the same conclusion, it has a much larger value than if it only comes from one direction. Politics is about weighing different aspects' (Stockholm IP 3).

Equally important is that forming alliances makes it possible to distribute the arguments between the coalition partners. 'You have to think about who you are presenting the argument as whether or not this argument will be better coming from you as an individual company, or you as an association, or maybe from other people' (Brussels IP 3). Ideally the consultants would like to form a coalition where they can fine-tune who says what. 'When you've decided on your ten key arguments you should sit down and analyse who is the most credible voice of these arguments? On air quality and emissions maybe you find a leading scientist in Switzerland. He has written these papers, he is independent' (Brussels IP 8).

Technical arguments should be delivered by people with technical competence, preferably independent experts. Self-regarding arguments, on the other hand, should be delivered by actors who may arouse sympathy. A Secretary-General of an industry association is usually not in that category.

> It depends on the industry. Are these issues concerning small companies? Are we talking about businesses in sparsely populated areas? Is this a line of business mainly pursued by immigrant women? It is an enormous difference to say 'this is something that harms the trucking industry'—then you imagine dirty trucks—compared to if you say 'this will harm businesses in sparsely populated areas' (Stockholm IP 3).

The same Stockholm-based consultant gives the following example of how the social construction of the messenger, to use Schneider and Ingram's term (Schneider & Ingram 1993), matters for a lobbying campaign:

> During the budget negotiations one year the Green Party and the Left Party had strongly increased the tax on diesel fuel, for environmental reasons. The Green Party had been after the trucks, but what they had not quite understood was that it would have a very large impact on the public bus transportation. We helped the bus industry with this issue and got the Green Party to work with us. Instead of trucks as the 'wounded party' we got them to envision the people who ride the bus—retired people, immigrants, young people, low income people. The result was not that the tax on diesel fuel was lowered, but the next year there was compensation when the tax on public transportation was lowered (Stockholm IP 3).

One Stockholm-consultant claims that the Swedish fishing industry tends to get away with relying primarily on self-regarding arguments because of their romantic image. 'We envision that quaint old fisherman who sits by his red hut, mending his nets and telling stories' (Stockholm IP 4). The ERA/SRA, on the other hand, will have a hard time engaging political support for their private sake. 'Who loves trucks? Do vacationing Swedes love trucks? "Yippee, we are behind four trucks!" In this case we have to work on trying to change the image of the business before asking for sympathy and support' (Stockholm IP 3).

An important reason for not lobbying only the environment directorate or ministry, even if they are responsible for the drafting of the proposal, is that other directorates or ministries may be used as voices for some particular arguments towards the lead DG/ministry. The quality of economic arguments can be guaranteed by DG Transport and Energy or the Ministry of Industry, Employment and Communication. 'Distorting competition is more a DG Internal Market-argument than a DG Environment-argument. DG Environment will have to deal with it seriously when they hear it from DG Internal Market' (Brussels IP 8). One consultant rejected argument number two ('it will distort competition between the different modes of transportation, which will impede on the implementation of an effective common market for freight transportation') as an argument to use for lobbying the DG Environment.

> If we want to establish a number of parallel tracks in the process, and one of the tracks would show how this impacts business, the question is, who has the most credibility in convincing the Ministry of the Environment? Does the Swedish Road Haulage Association have the most credibility or the Ministry of Business, Employment and Communications? Most likely it is the Ministry of Business, Employment and Communications (Stockholm IP 3).

Even the 'jobs will be lost' argument can be used with the right sender. In that case the most legitimate messenger is the trade union.

> If you're going to engage emotional arguments, like the job-argument number four—and you'll have to engage emotional arguments because people in the system, even in the Commission, are emotional people and they have to recognise why this is important, that it is going to affect peoples' jobs—in order to carry those messages into the system, the producing industry is not the most credible. If there is going to be massive job losses then sit down and talk with your trade union (Brussels IP 8).

The Brussels-consultant who called the 'jobs will be lost' argument a '19th century argument' later qualified that by saying 'Sometimes we do use it, but then we work with the trade union. The job-argument is a union argument' (Brussels IP 2).

The key to 'who should say what' is the different types of legitimacy that actors have. Social organisations or grass-roots workers should not engage in technical argumentation or broad-based social analyses, in which they would have little credibility. If they have a positive social image to rely upon they should say 'this is bad for us,' and leave it at that. Trade unions and other social actors who have cause with public sympathy behind their concern may also be allowed to be more emotional in their attitude and rhetoric than industry representatives. It is easier to accept a trade unionist becoming upset while defending peoples' jobs than a businessman who is worrying about his profit. A trade-association liaison officer has to be correct and factual. For an industry representative to use the argument 'this is bad for immigrant women in sparsely populated areas' would probably be counterproductive, because s/he would have low credibility; but having an immigrant woman from a sparsely populated area saying 'this is bad for me' might be effective.

Generally the consultants prefer to use CEOs and company-employees rather than industry-association employees as voices behind arguments. The credibility of individual business leaders explaining the effects and practical consequences of a regulation on their particular companies is stronger than that of association bureaucrats. 'The Commission appreciates information that comes straight from the companies rather than from the industry associations. It is more tangible and concrete when the trucker himself describes his problem. One appreciates that there is more knowledge about details and a more genuine commitment in the companies' (Brussels IP 1).

> One experience that I got from working for X [a business association], is that politicians got up from their chairs a little bit when we arrived with representatives from the companies. A delegation could consist of the chairman and the managing director of the industry association, a staff member and one or two spokespersons from Z and Y [large companies]. First, the chairman says what he is expected to say, the managing director elaborates on that and the poor staff member has to contribute with some kind of facts. But when Z and Y say, 'let us describe how this would affect us,' well then the politicians lean forward a bit. It was also much easier to get a minister to visit a production plant than to drag them to X's office on K-street. There is a fascination with being close to reality, which we should try to use correctly. Representatives of reality have more authority when they speak. 'I have both feet on the ground, I am in the driver's seat, I know what I am talking about.' (Stockholm IP 5).

Even within a given company some people may be more effective as messengers than others. Sometimes this can be just a matter of charisma and rhetorical capability. One consultant complained that their clients usually insisted that their CEO or Secretary-General should be their leader in meetings with ministers and other top-level decision-makers. 'They say: "Now it is important, now the minister is coming," and we know that there is another employee, at the wrong level of the hierarchy however, who knows about the issue and who is really interesting to listen to, but who they will not let in, because of course the really boring CEO has to speak' (Stockholm IP 6).

Trade associations—the Eurogroups—generally have a rather unfavourable reputation in Brussels. One reason for that is that the associations tend to be held back by the most reactionary companies, when it comes to working constructively together with the institutions regulating the sector. The positions of the Eurogroups are commonly perceived to represent the 'lowest common denominator' within the sector. Reactionary companies who oppose change, and who prefer to try to prevent new regulations rather than to influence their content, sometimes try to hide behind the trade association. Working through the trade association becomes a way for these companies to act obstructively and at the same time avoid bearing the full cost of breaking with the 'committed partner' role, which costs then fall on the whole of the sector. 'The conservative companies will not present positions on their own. They will do it through their trade association. They are the ones pressing the position of the trade association towards the minimal common denominator' (Brussels IP 4).

You have to draw a line somewhere
Timing affects also the value of being constructive and remaining loyal to the force of the better argument norm. In some cases, a client may come to a point where he or she realises that the 'committed partner' attitude, the ideal- and other-regarding argumentation and the constructive formulation of alternative solutions just will not help. The door is closing and the client's arguments have not persuaded the officials to reformulate the proposal. At this stage, when the client knows that they are about to lose, there may be a calculation of the costs of violating the force of the better argument norm and ending the 'committed partner' act. Whether they actually go so far as to declare open opposition depends on what the client has to lose in the issue at hand, taking into account long-term relations with the relevant institutions. 'Somewhere you have to draw a line and say "this is becoming too painful". Then we must make a statement and take the conflict. But even in that case you have to think ahead' (Stockholm IP 2). One way in which companies can moderate the costs of norm-violation, as described above, is to get the trade association do the dirty work.

Going for open conflict primarily implies involving lawyers, according to the interviewed consultants. 'Lawyers mean conflict' (Stockholm IP 2). When the stakes are very high and the door is closing the committed partner may show a different face. If it goes that far it will be 'no more Mr Nice Guy.'

> You can discuss the validity of an environmental tax forever, but if the Commission has set its mind on proposing a tax, and if you decide to fight it, you will say: 'This is unacceptable for legal reasons, it violates a WTO agreement.' You try to force them down into negotiation by making the legal burden on them to justify their specific measure unbearable (Brussels IP 2).

This is the point at which the 'fellow problem-solver' turns into a 'pressure group'. How much pressure can be applied obviously depends on the case and the actors. It is not possible from this interview study to specify how often that happens in reality. By the consultants, however, such a situation was perceived as exceptional. In their view, starting a fight was the last-resort option, justified only if the situation was desperate, and closely connected to failure. They would try as hard as possible to avoid this option. 'Conflict-laden aggressive speeches, full opposition situations, usually result in isolation. If you are isolated you can scream and kick but you don't get anywhere' (Brussels IP 2). Future long-term relations with regulating institutions weigh heavily in the other side of the scale.

Some consultants referred to the 'see-you-in-court' strategy as something typical of American companies who have not yet learned how to play by European rules. 'American companies rarely have any arguments, or just bad arguments. They don't know Europe' (Brussels IP 6).

> There is a large difference between American companies and Europeans. The American instinct is to call in lawyers, the fighting spirit, which is not appropriate in Europe. It is more about consensus here, one should not make trouble. You enter a dialogue rather than a fight, you should contribute. In Washington you could pursue a public affairs case where the best man wins, in Europe things don't work that way. Most American companies that are established in Europe have learned that by now, but in a crisis situation it is a reflex (Stockholm IP 2).

Apart from the fact that it violates the force of the better argument norm, one consultant claimed, the threat 'we're going to take this to the WTO' is usually ineffective:

> Unless you truly have a case, the Commission, will say: 'OK, you can say that, but we know that you are not going to challenge this.' It is typically American companies who do that, and the Commission calls their bluff every time— whether it's on hushkits, whether it's on substance bans on electronic equipment—there are examples of that over and over again, and it undermines the credibility of these companies. The Commission knows that if anything is ever going to happen it's going to be three or four years down the line, in which time positions will have evolved. Maybe individual companies will have done an analysis internally and said 'maybe this directive is interesting for us after all, maybe these substance bans are interesting for us, because we may get a competitive advantage if we can introduce alternatives to this particular substance. So maybe we don't want to push this trade argument too hard' (Brussels IP 3).

For the case of the ERA/SRA and the eco-tax starting a fight was out of the question, according to the consultants, despite the fact that timing was against them. The road hauliers should prioritise their long-term relations with the institutions, even if the tax was about to go through. 'Even when you are dealing with an emergency crisis you have to vaccinate for the future. They want to come back and still have good will and credit' (Stockholm IP 2). 'For the road hauliers it's best facing that they're in this for the long haul, not just the road haul' (Brussels IP 8).

Self-interested justifications – legitimate and unpersuasive

As described in Table 4.4, the self-interested arguments were the least popular arguments on the list for private meetings with civil servants. One explanation, as already mentioned, is the perceived need to give decision-makers added value in order to gain their ear. Decision-makers want to be told something they don't already know and 'this will affect us badly' is not usually a new idea. 'What you're saying there [self-interested argument number one] is obvious' (Brussels IP 4). Such grumbling is predictable from stakeholders who stand to lose by the proposal. In order to function as a foot in the door argument, 'it will be bad for this industry' has to show that the damage would be both unexpectedly bad and connected to a wider public interest.

The fact that, historically, industry has often 'cried wolf' has made policy-makers especially suspicious to these arguments, according to consultants. Due to this scepticism, the 'hit' must be extremely well grounded in the facts. 'It is almost like when the children say "but everybody else has one!". It is not credible if you cannot provide very clear proof' (Stockholm IP 2).

> You could perhaps do something with [self-interested argument] number five if you got very specific, but then you need to demonstrate, ideally with a third party assessment, how the cost structure of the industry is affected, trends of taxation perhaps. If you can land at some good numbers like 'ten years ago 17 per cent of the costs of transporting goods in the EU was taxation, now it's 34 per cent,' then you can use it. But if it's just a general statement, and it's something which is applicable to every industry in the European Union, then it's not going to have very much of an impact on the policy-makers (Brussels IP 8).

Producing credible data on 'the hit', however, is often difficult.

> As soon as a contradiction or an inaccuracy is exposed in that argumentation [economic impact on a given business] it's undermined. And the Commission is very good at doing this. It would get arguments from people saying 'so much,' and then they say 'oh, we received something from an individual company or a national association, or from the EU umbrella association, saying it would only cost this much, can you explain the difference?' And immediately your credibility is put in question. And quite often it's very difficult for you to make a truly accurate calculation of what that economic impact is going to be (Brussels IP 3).

But even if it can be credibly demonstrated that there will be a serious hit to a particular industry, that is not automatically a strong argument. In fact, standing on their own, self-regarding arguments coming from the industry are usually are of little use in terms of persuasion. The role of policy-makers in the European Commission and in the Swedish governmental ministries, consultants emphasised, is not to look after industry's profitability. The profit margin of a single industry is not particularly interesting, *per se*, to uncaptured policy-makers. The 'hit' to the industry has to have wider implications if it is to cause concern to them. 'The way these arguments [self-interested arguments one and five] stand here [in the list], they're completely unconstructive. The response will be "so what?" (Brussels IP 4).

As explained earlier, the extent to which policy-makers will care about the client being 'hit' depends largely on the status of the actor. Two different sources of status can be derived from the interviews. One is the positive social construction of an actor as being worthy of support for some reason. Immigrant-lead SMEs in sparsely populated areas, for instance, will be heard more sympathatically than the ERA/SRA. A second source of status is having a clear connection between private and a wider public interest, such as when a company is developing environmentally-friendly technical solutions. 'What is good for General Motors is good for America' is another famous version of such a private interest—public interest link, where the focus was on macro-economic impact.

A common perception among consultants was that there had been an evolution in government-industry relations over time, which made self-regarding arguments more difficult to use. Some consultants in Stockholm referred to the Swedish government's long and costly effort to save the shipbuilding industry during the 1970s as a symbol of a failure that policy-makers are afraid to repeat. 'There has been a change in perspective when it comes to competition issues and a change in attitude towards support for business. In the climate we have today concerning policies towards business, the special interest arguments have become less useful than they were before' (Stockholm IP 4). While the common market and the common competition policy of the EU usually is assumed to be pro-business, and even containing a neo-liberal bias, (Scharpf 1999: chapter two)) the responsibility of single companies and industry sectors to look after themselves in a competitive market has grown, according to this view. Restructurings involving plants closing down are seen as natural consequences of this basically healthy competition. If a given company or sector has difficulties competing, the dominant view of European competition authorities and governmental ministries (especially finance ministries) is that they should look at their internal cost-structures rather than complaining to the government or European institutions.

There is no sign of 'capture' or tightly-knit policy communities in which 'we' is a natural reference group in the minds of the consultants when they talk about industry's relationship with political institutions. Thus, for the ERA/SRA, which lacks a sympathetic public image, sympathy can only be gained by pointing to their contribution to the public interest.

This argument [self-interested argument number 1] is usable, but then you have to put yourself in a context. Why do we have a trucking industry? What function does it have? Otherwise nobody will think it matters if you are forced out of business. If we would have made a PR campaign for typographers, it would have been fairly useless, in the light of history, because the entire profession has disappeared. The typographers disappeared because nobody needed their services. I would guess that while they were disappearing they probably attempted to claim that they should remain, but they disappeared and were replaced by computers. You have to describe why the trucks are needed. It is not for the sake of the trucks that the politicians will make a decision that is positive for the hauliers, it is not for the industry, it is not for the risk of unemployment among truckers, but for the ensuing consequences if the industry cannot survive in Sweden (Stockholm IP 5).

The ERA/SRA has an especially difficult task since they are facing a strong public interest counter-argument. 'The long-term protection of the environment is more important than economic disadvantages for a certain sector' (Brussels IP 6).

In environmental policy there is a tremendous boot on the other foot. There is a strong political momentum behind environmental policy, which means that you don't have to have all the science there, you have the precautionary principle, the benefit of the doubt, etc. And acting in that policy environment with the attitude of 'we're going to defeat that because it's costly' is maybe very reassuring, it's what you want to say, but it is not going to go far (Brussels IP 8).

Self-interested arguments coming from the industry affected are not persuasive in and of themselves. The ERA/SRA will not stop the eco-tax proposal with arguments one, five and eight, unless the negative effect is dramatic and clearly connected to broader economic interests. That does not mean, however, that these arguments are illegitimate or that they should not be used. What makes them predictable in the first place is the fact that they are being used by most actors most of the time—not only by unsuccessful amateurs but also by the most professional public affairs consultants.

In fact, these arguments have to be used, according to the consultants, in order for a company or a business association to be perceived as a serious and trustworthy actor. Bringing only other- and ideal-regarding justifications is simply not credible. As an industry representative you cannot pretend that you have engaged in the issue for other reasons than your own interest. 'You can't cover up your economic interest; it's why you're there' (Brussels IP 6). 'The commercial interest is the foundation and you should never try to hide it' (Stockholm IP 7).

Instead, the fact that the industry believes that the proposal 'will be a serious blow to the haulage industry' should be made clear from the beginning. That is the reason why representatives of the ERA/SRA are sitting in the civil servant's office. Moreover, that is the reason why the ERA/SRA is a legitimate partner in the dialogue, a group who should be listened to.

I'll be very clear about that [the potential damage to the industry] and have facts and figures, but I wouldn't dwell on it very much. It's the context, that's why I'm here, that's why we turned up today, that's the backdrop, but you don't need to go on about it for a long time. 'This is who we are, this is how many road hauliers there are', that type of thing, costs and tax burdens, put it all on a couple of pages and point out that you have far more detailed information when and if they require it (Brussels IP 8).

Private interest is nothing to be ashamed of. There is no non-selfishness norm active here, censoring self-interested justifications. 'There's an acknowledgement in Brussels that interests matter. And everyone's interest, within reason, is legitimate. So if you never talked about your own interest, possibly you wouldn't be talking about your own qualifications for speaking to this audience in the first place. They would say 'well, why are you here?''' (Brussels IP 6).

However, after having made clear your stake in the issue, having explained why you are concerned and—therefore—why you should be listened to, you present the real arguments: those which will persuade others.

> Everybody understands that self-interest is an important force behind what you are saying and of course things can become a little silly if you pretend that it is not. But self-interest is not sufficient. The politicians, or the civil servants in this case, who are to write the proposition, are looking for arguments. Then you cannot just say that it is a lot of trouble and that the trucking industry will be harmed, you have to give them an argument for the public interest (Stockholm IP 6).

If clients disguise their self-interest so that officials do not understand why they are engaged in the issue, the officials will become suspicious about what the company's real motives are. The argument should be 'transparent' with respect to the connection between the public interest and clients' private interests.

> The effect on the company, or on the business sector you're in is one type of argument. What the proposal does to the European single market is another. These are two types of arguments and if I have to make a choice, I'll choose the last one, the societal argument, but if I can, I will always try to use both. Because the last one tends to be a bit woolly and I don't want to appear woolly. Link the two—show that it's good for me and for the rest of Europe—that's a winning argument (Brussels IP 5).

Conclusion: egoistic is fine, egocentric is not
In one respect, the private lobbying meeting at first seems to confirm the hypothesis of the theory of publicity's civilising effect concerns a backstage negotiation area: there is no non-selfishness norm forcing the actors to hide their self-interested motives. To the contrary, if they did try to hide their self-interest they would undermine the legitimacy of their role as 'partners in the process'. However, in the next section it will be demonstrated that the lack of a non-selfishness norm is not a question of backstage or frontstage. Self-interest is a

legitimate motivational base for lobbyists both in Stockholm and in Brussels, in private and in public.

Furthermore, the logic of the forum is, in fact, present in the lobby-corridor, with respect to the force of the better argument norm. The appropriate role for industry lobbyists in their contacts with officials is that of the 'committed partner', who uses arguments that add value to the process. While being egoistic is nothing to be ashamed of, being egocentric is not acceptable. Committed partners, while legitimately self-interested, must seek solutions that are acceptable to others as well as themselves. Moreover, those solutions should be argued for, not sold or imposed under threat. The lobby-corridor is not a market place for buying and selling policy proposals or pressuring and demanding. The dialogue 'with which I think we would have the largest chance of success' as one consultant quoted put it, is to 'try to show that these proposals are not good for the environment' (Stockholm IP 5). The legitimate mode of communication is arguing rather than bargaining.

Self-interested parties are welcomed to the policy process by the officials, if they identify themselves as such but contribute other- and ideal-regarding arguments. The reason why self-regarding arguments have the lowest rank in the list is that they are not persuasive, not that they are illegitimate. What distinguishes amateurs from professionals, with respect to the types of justification, is how they use self-regarding arguments. Amateurs, unaware of their own limited importance for others, make a major point of them. Professionals, on the other hand, use them to present themselves; 'this is who I am, this is why I'm concerned, i.e. this is why I have a right to speak.' The emphasis of professionals' arguments, however, is on constructive other- and ideal-regarding arguments which may persuade the decision-makers.

Depending on the timing the persuasive arguments may be broad policy arguments or 'foot in the door' arguments. The content is largely determined by who the target is, naturally, but also by who will be the voice behind the argument. Even such a seemingly irrelevant change of messenger as when sending a company representative, rather than a trade association employee, may affect the officials' reception of the 'this affects us' argument.

The fact that the identity of the presenter determines the persuasiveness of self-regarding arguments has important implications for the generalisability of the theory of publicity's civilising effect. Depending on the presenter's public image or social construction 'this is going to be bad for us' may be the most 'civil' thing to say. The grass-root activists with positive public images studied by Eliasoph, as discussed in chapter two, seem to do the right thing from a public affairs perspective when they play down their public interest motives and focus on their personal needs, interests and fears, when media are around. In particular, groups with a more positive image among the general public than with elite actors that they meet behind closed doors will have stronger reason to emphasise their stake in the matter in public than in private. Industry lobbyists, however, are rarely in that category.

The fact that the logic of the forum is present in the lobby corridor should be seen as a positive result from a deliberative democratic perspective. There is a clear presumption for arguing rather than bargaining and a requirement of taking the perspective of others into account in developing arguments. However, one must recall that lobbyists are still strategic rather than deliberative actors. The 'committed partner' role is played for a purpose. It is created because it is assumed to be the best strategy for influencing public policy in the private interest of the client. What is important for the client is not to *be* a constructive partner, but to *appear* to be so. To what extent the act affects the actor in the long run, transforming his or her genuine preferences by a dissonance reduction mechanism or the 'voice of reason,' as discussed in chapter two, is beyond the scope of this study.

In the short run, however, exposure to reason will not prevent clients from abandoning the 'committed partner' role and violating the force of the better argument norm if they believe it is in their interest to do so. When the immediate threat to the client outweighs the long-term political costs of violating the force of the better argument norm, the committed partner may turn into a pressure group. The fact that this is perceived as a possible option, although only in exceptional circumstances, demonstrates that the force of the better argument norm is not internalised but followed for strategic reasons.

Using threats and pressure is not just another lobbying tactic, however. When this happens it constitutes a violation of what is considered appropriate behaviour in the lobby corridor. The costs of such norm-violations, in terms of political credibility are high, according to consultants.

LOBBYING FRONTSTAGE

After the discussion of the private meetings with civil servants the consultants were presented with a new situation, representing the move from backstage to the frontstage of the political sphere. This is the second part of the introductory text for the hypothetical case, as it was written for the Brussels interviews, with adaptations for the Swedish context shown in square brackets:

> Now, I would like you to focus on a second arena. The Secretary-General of the ERA [SRA] will give one of the opening speeches (approximately 30 minutes) at the big annual Transport Conference. The new developments within transport policy, including the environment and economic incentives, will be among the topics of the conference. Basically, everyone interested in the field will be in the audience: politicians and civil servants, competitors from other modes of transportation, environmental organisations, several of the ERA's [SRA's] members, journalists, etc. The Secretary-General will take the opportunity to criticize the proposed model for eco-taxes on trucks being considered within DG Environment [Ministry of the Environment]. The set of arguments is the same as before.
>
> If you were to select three arguments from the list to use in the conference speech, which three would you choose? Why? Is any type of argument

missing from the list? If you would reject three of these arguments—the arguments you would be least eager to use in the conference speech—which three would they be?

Table 4.6 compares the selection of arguments, from the same list of arguments as before, for the private meeting with civil servants and the public speech. The first four columns are the same as Tables 4.1 and 4.2 in the introduction to this chapter. The last three columns illustrate the effect on the choices of arguments of shifting from a closed meeting to a public speech. The change is small for most arguments, the exceptions being number six ('the system encourages cheating at vehicle inspections, which will be difficult to control') and number one ('it will be a serious hit to the European [Swedish] haulage industry'). The sum of the changes for the three self-regarding arguments is +6 both in Brussels and in Stockholm, as showed earlier in Table 4.3.

Table 4.6. Choosing arguments for private meetings and public speech

Argument	Selected minus rejected in the private meetings		Selected minus rejected in the public speech		Difference; from private meetings to public speech		
	Bru	Sto	Bru	Sto	Bru	Sto	Total
Self-regarding (number 1)	-3	-5	2	-2	+5	+3	+8
Macroeconomic (number 7)	4	-2	4	1	0	+3	+3
Self-regarding (number 5)	-7	-4	-5	-4	+2	0	+2
Self-regarding (number 8)	-2	-3	-3	0	-1	+3	+2
Environment (number 9)	1	-1	2	-2	+1	-1	0
Environment (number 3)	6	7	7	6	+1	-1	0
Macroeconomic (number 4)	-2	-1	-3	0	-1	+1	0
Competition/Cooperation (number 2)	3	7	2	6	-1	-1	-2
Implementation (number 6)	1	1	-4	-4	-5	-5	-10

Note: Table 4.6 shows the results of the selecting and rejecting of three arguments, from the list of nine arguments presented to the consultants. The first four columns were presented earlier as tables 4.1 and 4.2. The last three columns illustrate the changes in the consultants' choice of arguments between private meetings and public speech.

Contrary to the theory of publicity's civilising effect the self-regarding arguments are more popular among the consultants in the public speech than in the private meetings. The dramatic fall in popularity of argument number six is explained partly by the fact that some consultants, who initially did not notice the implicit threat in that argument, became aware of that interpretation during the course of the discussion. But even as an implementation argument number six would be weak in this setting, according to the consultants, since it is seen to be too technical for a public speech.

As before, the figures in Table 4.6 should be seen as illustrative of the major findings of this part of the study, which are to be found in the motivations of the choices given by the consultants in the discussion following the selection and rejection of arguments. Self-regarding justifications are perceived to be more relevant to use frontstage than backstage. Why is that so?

The representative's triple dilemma
A public speech of the kind described here is a true public affairs challenge. To the consultants this public audience is not a public, but several publics. The consultant writing the speech for the Secretary-General must take into account and find a balance between three different requirements, which all pull in different directions. First, there is a strong consistency constraint forcing the actors not to deviate too much from the committed partner role played backstage. Second, a speaker at a conference should for rhetorical reasons address the whole audience, however heterogeneous it may be. Third, as a representative of an organisation the Secretary-General of the ERA/SRA is under pressure to acknowledge the organisation's members. This final point explains the increase of self-interest in the rhetoric.

The consistency constraint
The requirement to be consistent between public speeches and private meetings was strongly emphasised by the consultants. This consistency constraint was an important factor behind the small change in arguments from backstage to frontstage, in spite of the dramatically different audiences in the two situations. It would weaken the credibility of the ERA/SRA if the officials going to the conference were met with a different message from the one they had previously heard in their office. 'The civil servants are there [at the conference] as well. They see if I am saying something other than what I said to them in the office last week' (Brussels IP 1).

The arguments that were worked out in the first meetings between the client and the consultant were intended for both private meetings and public speeches. One consultant said he would use 'exactly the same arguments' in the public speech as in the closed meetings, because:

> You will be singled out in two minutes if you are not living up to your messages. When you have defined the three things you want to say you do not move from that. You can adapt your points slightly, move them around in the debate, which shows intelligence, you can tailor your messages to different

audiences—the way in which you will deliver them, the rhetoric around it—but not fundamentally the content of a message. You can stress one more than the others but you're not suddenly saying that it's a job issue, you're still saying it's a competition issue. The ground for your argument stays the same. Otherwise they'll see through you (Brussels IP 2).

While the rhetorical formulations may vary, the core content of the argument should stay the same. 'It is a different audience so there will be changes in how you present your arguments, but my experience is that the basic fundamental of the argument will stay the same' (Brussels IP 3).

> You need to be consistent, because people are informed. If I argue with the Commission, DG Environment and DG TREN with my three favourite arguments and then the Secretary-General goes to a conference in another part of Europe and says different things—they will know. We have a problem with that right now, that's what we were discussing when you came. It is a client we've been working with for a year now on a particular issue. Now, some idiot on the board of that company has said, publicly, that the issue is not a problem. Now, obviously that person has been ill-informed internally, but the results are dramatic. Every Member of Parliament and Commission official, to whom we've been saying 'no, we don't want this,' now says 'but your client said in a conference that it's not a problem, so what is this?'. It is very, very important that you have a consistent, coherent, political message (Brussels IP 5).

The same consultant gives the following example of how one can 'tailor the message' to different audiences, but still keep the basic argument—no eco-tax because of the macroeconomic effects (argument number seven)—the same:

> If you go to a conference in northern Europe you say 'The Nordic countries are basically empty outside one or two large cities, therefore they need road haulage. The people in the isolated villages of Kiruna and Lapinranta, they depend on the truck', you give a nice sentimental story. Doesn't work in Italy of course, but in Italy you find something else. You say 'It's very beneficial to the industry of the small- and medium-sized enterprises in Italy and their intensive communication. They're located all over the little cities of Tuscany—how can they communicate but by road freight?' So you develop a coherent set of arguments, which always have the same message where you play on the major economic interests (Brussels IP 5).

Seeking common ground

While the consistency constraint works against changes in the selection of arguments, public speeches require a different type of rhetoric from private meetings, according to consultants. Those members of the frontstage audience who also have access to the backstage should recognise the message, but they will also accept that, in public speeches, speakers are addressing a broader audience. In a conference speech, the consultants explained, the appropriate thing to do was to address the audience as a whole. The Secretary-General should try to define the broadest possible 'we'. 'It is important to find something that everybody can be interested in' (Stockholm IP 6), one consultant was motivated in her choice of argument number seven ['the Swedish economy is dependent upon letting companies have access to road transport at reasonable prices'].

The effect of this perceived need to seek common ground is not, however, a change in the types of justification, towards more other- and ideal-regarding arguments. Rather, the attempt to address the whole audience, while at the same time holding on to the basic other- and ideal-regarding messages used in the private lobbying meetings, tends to result in what negotiation theorists call a 'lower degree of specificity' (Walton & McKersie 1965: 94). The argumentation becomes vaguer and shallower, less focused on concrete decision-making.

The Secretary-General goes to private meetings with sleeves rolled up, ready to solve problems, suitcase loaded with facts and solutions. In the public speech, on the other hand, the purpose is not primarily to change people's minds about the proposal; 'you're not going to get the proposal revised there' (Brussels IP 4). Rather, it is an occasion to work on the industries' social representation. The speech will be used to a large extent to create a positive atmosphere around the industry and the Secretary-General, which will be an asset later on in the process. The rhetoric and the style, the ability of the speaker to make the audience feel at ease—'to make sure that the speech is interesting and exciting, that the audience preferably applauds in at least two places' (Stockholm IP 6)—is equally or even more important than the precise content of the arguments. A public speech is an occasion for the Secretary-General to draw the bigger picture, define future challenges and show, 'in an elegant way' (Brussels IP 4), that the ERA/SRA has a vision of a transport policy for the 21st century. It is less an occasion for concrete discussions of the present version of the eco-tax proposal. The different purposes of the occasions naturally affect the content of the messages.

> A public event, covered by journalists and a broad audience, is not the place to negotiate on your position, or to talk about your proposal as if it was a working session with the Commission. You will not go in depth at all on facts, you have to be general. You make your principled points, but you make it lighter in the speech. A meeting with the Commission is more focused. There is a purpose for the meeting. In a conference it is more diffuse (Brussels IP 4).

Such a speech necessarily must be less substantial in terms of facts and complexities of the argumentation.

> If you want to deliver a message that not just experts understand, but also a broader audience, the media, MEPs or whatever, then the scope you have in terms of going into technicalities is reduced. You might choose the same

arguments [as in the private meetings with officials], but you would need to refine your arguments so they become a lot more political and less technical (Brussels IP 3).

The speech can be used to promote the presentation of the ERA/SRA as a committed partner, by referring to the Secretary-General's dedication to a constructive dialogue with all legitimate stakeholders.

You will say 'we saw the Commission officials on this issue last week and we're happy to report that they're happy to engage in a dialogue. They want to hear from different interested parties, we accept our responsibility in that.' In that you have the engagement of industry in solutions and engagement in policy dialogue (Brussels IP 8).

The fact that the speech is 'lighter' in its content also makes the choice of arguments less sensitive overall. In a meeting with civil servants, exactly the right things have to be said in order to get to the details of the proposal—talking 'strictly to the brief' of that DG or ministry. In a speech the substance of the message is less important. 'I am much more flexible when it comes to this type of occasion. A lot of this rhetoric [referring to the list of arguments] may be used' (Stockholm IP 7). The rejection of arguments for the public speech seemed to be a less delicate task to the consultants, as long as those arguments which form the ERA's/SRA's basic message, in private and public, are included. 'Well, the truth is that it is very difficult to discard any arguments [on the list]. Apart from the cheating during inspections, which is to admit that my members who sit here in front of me, will do everything they can to circumvent the law, this speech may contain everything it says here' (Stockholm IP 5).

Even though in this case there would be policy competitors in the audience, such as the rail-lobby and representatives from the air transport business as well as environmental NGOs, the consultants argued that the speech should try to include even them in the public 'we.' Ideally, 'we' should all be concerned about eco-taxes on trucks.

I would try to show that what is proposed [in the eco-tax draft proposal] entails a kind of general system problem. My dream here would be to find a common denominator where the entire Swedish transportation industry can say: 'We disagree on most things, but on this one we're united. Here, is something that is obviously unreasonable considering what is our common task.' To get acceptance from the airways and the railways, so that from this transportation-political Bosnia, an agreement may be reached, that Sweden cannot keep seeking separate solutions, but that it has to consider the European perspective [argument number two]. Then I would have done something really strong (Stockholm IP 3).

Building on the 'committed partner' image implies that the Secretary-General must avoid seeming to pick on others. Even though it may be tempting to try to shift the burden by saying 'why don't you tax air transport instead, they're even worse than us?' or by ridiculing the capabilities of rail transport as a nineteenth-century transport mode, to do this explicitly would not fit the 'serious committed partner' image. The speech should be surrounded by an aura of seriousness and pleasantness. No one in the conference hall should have to feel uneasy at having to witness an open dispute between representatives of different modes of transport. They should be cooperating as committed partners in finding common solutions. One consultant rejected argument number nine ('the heavy focus on road transports prevents the search for a comprehensive approach to air pollution, which has many sources, ultimately hindering effective environmental protection') because 'people from the rail industry have a completely different agenda' (Brussels IP 3). Another consultant selected argument number nine for the speech, because of its environmental content, but underlined that the wording of this argument is a delicate matter:

> Nine is a good argument, because you show that you understand and share the environmental objective of the proposal. To fulfil the objective, the choice of means must be looked at and road transport is just one bit. But you must avoid talking openly about other sectors. You can't say 'go for that industry too,' when the guy from that industry is sitting there, it wouldn't be appropriate for a Secretary-General to do that. Even if everyone knows that they have conflicting interests—look at the oil and the car industry for another example—you don't expect them pointing at each other in an opening speech at a conference. They're supposed to be working together! ... If you want to shift the burden onto them you have to be more elegant than to say 'take them instead'. In that case you'd start with the objective and say 'look, you're not going to fulfil your goals just focusing on road hauliers, the polluter pays principle says...' and so you let them draw their own conclusions on what needs to be done. You don't openly point out the other polluters, but you let them read that between the lines (Brussels IP 4).

Committed partners are not troublemakers. The Secretary-General is not there to start a fight. The speech should communicate that the ERA/SRA is willing and able to take responsibility for a transport policy of the next millennium, in co-operation with other responsible partners.

The nested internal game
The real challenge of the speech, however, lies in balancing the consistency requirement and the requirement to be perceived as seeking common ground with the expectations of the ERA's/SRA's members. Depending on the internal situation within the association, the consultants argued, the leadership might have to include arguments that will 'keep the members happy', in order to defend their own positions.

> The leaders of these types of organizations have a fairly difficult task. On the one hand, they have to keep their own comrades happy and 50 percent of their own group, and maybe more, demand blood: 'Tell that damned Environment Minister what a damned idiot he is'. That is a difficult balancing act, because he has to maintain a conciliatory tone toward the outside. The members' demand for action, blood and war, is in contrast with the results you may be able to achieve through quiet diplomacy. If the Secretary-General of the organization is up for re-election six weeks later, his tone toward the government may be a bit sharper (Stockholm IP 1).

This is the main reason why self-regarding arguments are more likely to be used in a public speech than in private meetings with officials. Those arguments are for internal rather than external use. 'In this speech he will say "it will be a serious hit to the hauliers industry". It is an argument that will not work on decision makers, but you put it in there to make the members happy. It is a way to unite your own people' (Brussels IP 1).

The problem with giving weight to self-regarding justifications in a speech, from an external public affairs point of view, is not that they violate a non-self-ishness norm. Just as in the private lobbying meeting, there is no fear among the consultants of 'revealing' their clients' private interests to the broader audience. The reason why the Secretary-General is concerned about the eco-tax proposal— that it affects the hauliers' economic margins—is uncontroversial. Rather the problem lies in holding on to a consistent performance from the backstage, where self-interested arguments should be used as a means for presentation rather than persuasion.

To find the right balance between the internal and the external audience in a situation like this is a delicate matter. 'I think you have to be extremely sensitive if you stand up in a conference, at the same time as you are working with the Commission directly on its proposal, not to say things which may compromise your negotiations with the Commission' (Brussels IP 3). From the information they had on the case of the ERA/SRA it was difficult for the consultants to say for sure whether they would actually advise their client to avoid addressing the members or not. Their judgements varied depending on how they prioritised the internal coherence within the ERA/SRA, compared to the external audience. Some of them chose to select self-interested arguments, while others did not.

> Taking the members into account I would use number one ['it will be a serious hit to the haulage industry']. Even if you're a more advanced thinker than that, you'll have to put it in, or they'll wonder what kind of representative you are. You also got the member solidarity in number eight ['it is unreasonable to sacrifice the hauliers like this, when it is obvious that the sources of air pollution are complex and thus is a responsibility for the whole society']. 'Don't sacrifice the hauliers' you say and they'll go 'Yeaa!' – they'll be right behind you. OK, the people from the other modes of transportation will think that this

guy is trying to pick on us, that would be a weakness of that argument, but they're not going to be surprised and it's not going to be too much damage (Brussels IP 6).

If it is an internal conference he addresses the members. If it's not an internal conference he should not address the members. You don't preach to the converted, you preach to the infidels. You preach to those who do not yet believe that road haulage is the best mode of transportation. If you want to show to your members that you're working for them you do that at the annual conference members-only. But if you want to sell a political message to the whole of Europe—the Commission, the Parliament and the governments—you don't talk at the same time to your members, you talk to them [the Commission etc.] (Brussels IP 5).

The consultants' first advice to the ERA/SRA would be that internal communication be managed separately so that the public speech can focus on the external audience. 'They should energize their members at the Christmas party, not here. As a leader, you have to get an acknowledged acceptance from the members, that they have confidence in the way you handle it. If you don't have that there may be enormous problems' (Stockholm IP 3). They should try as much as possible to handle their internal problems internally, preferably before any external lobbying campaign starts.

I would take great care in anchoring the line that will be pursued on this issue. 'You have chosen me as a chairman and I believe that I have the authority to decide how we should address this issue. I am happy to listen to your arguments and there are probably things that may be added to the discussions, but when it comes to the main arguments, this is the line that works and for these reasons' (Stockholm IP 1).

The stronger the authority and legitimacy of the organisation leader, the less need there is to use public appearances for internal purposes. If the Secretary-General is in a position to focus on the external audience, fewer self-regarding arguments need be used. Companies therefore have more freedom of manoeuvre and can be more straightforward in their arguments than associations. 'In the speech a company can be exactly direct to the point. It wouldn't need the arguments which are there to keep the members happy' (Brussels IP 6).

You have a lot more flexibility if you're a company. Quite often you'll find that association argumentation can be a bit bland, because they are trying to strike a balance between many different people. Whereas as a company, you can be more dynamic, more to the point, more political (Brussels IP 3).

The exception to the rule that public appearances, from a public affairs perspective, should focus on the external rather than the internal audience, is the situation where the dialogue with the political institutions is not leading anywhere and the lobbying process is coming to an end. At that point the question of open conflict will arise. As described earlier, whether one actually goes so far depends on how much there is to lose from the issue at hand. That must be balanced against the potential damage that throwing away the 'committed partner' position will do to long-term relations with political institutions and public opinion. If one decides to take that step, members may have a new role to play. The speech can then be used to rally them against the proposal.

> Generally I think that the external public is more important in these types of occasions [public speeches], you rally the members at the annual meeting. But that also depends on the situation. If it is really an issue which threatens the industry and it is important to show that you have the support of your members, you are gravitating toward rallying and conflict. Unions often do that; it shows that they have a strong support (Stockholm IP 2).

William Riker has studied the art of agenda-manipulation, which he calls 'heresthetics'. Actors exercise power by manipulating the political context in which they operate—by 'structuring the world so you can win' (Riker 1996: 9). If the consultants had been able to influence the arrangements of the conference, they would have set up two conferences rather than one; one for members-only, and one for their external audience. One consultant even claimed that 'we manage on the whole by avoiding such conferences':

> I don't think they're very helpful. The outsiders shouldn't be at the members-conference and the members shouldn't be at the outsiders-conference. Because it's two different events and it's very difficult for a Secretary-General to deliver the right message to two different audiences. You will confuse both. It requires careful planning not to end up in such a situation (Brussels IP 5).

Conclusion: the challenge of balancing different publics
One effect of publicity is a pressure on the speaker to address the whole audience. In private meetings with officials, according to consultants, clients should speak 'strictly to the brief' of the official, in order to add value and not waste the official's time. The broadening of arguments in the public speech, therefore, may seem to constitute an effect crudely in the direction hypothesised by the theory of publicity's civilising effect. But, since the arguments from the backstage also rest upon other- and ideal-regarding justifications, this is not the type of change depicted by the theory. Talking strictly to the brief of officials means addressing the correct angle, not bargaining. Addressing the whole audience does not imply a move away from self-regarding justifications towards other- and ideal-interested ones.

The reason why the speaker ought to address the whole audience in the speech is not because there is a strong non-selfishness norm in public forcing a cover-up of private interests. Nor is it primarily a question of persuading different parts of the public to change their minds about the eco-tax proposal. Rather, it is a question of making the speech worthy of a responsible 'committed partner'. It is simply in accordance with ordinary courtesy, when holding a speech, to address everyone present in the conference hall. The speech as a whole loses some of its rhetorical force if the speaker polarises rather than uniting the audience.

The publicity effect therefore includes a 'lowering of the degree of specificity', to use Walton and McKersie's words (Walton & McKersie 1965: 94). Seeking common ground in an audience with heterogeneous interests necessarily implies referring to broader and vaguer principles, rather than concrete factual arguments, which can contribute to a solution of situations such as the draft proposal on eco-taxes on trucks. While public speeches still use the form of arguing, they are, to a lesser extent, genuine efforts to convince other parties of the merits of alternative proposals. In that sense, the quality of the arguing is in fact reduced. In Chambers' words, the degree of 'plebiscitory reason' increases (Chambers 2004).

The strong emphasis on consistency between private and public speech demonstrates the absence of a backstage-frontstage logic of the kind hypothesised by the theory of publicity's civilising effect. There should be no sharp distinction between the lobbyists' behaviour in the private meetings and the public speech, according to the public affairs consultants' advice. The officials do not accept being treated as backstage actors. Drawing the curtain of secrecy does not imply an embarrassing revelation of market behaviour, since the force of the better argument norm is already followed and the non-selfishness norm is weak in private and in public.

The presence of constituents, however, interferes with the external public affairs strategy. How that balance is struck—between the strategy of communicating a consistent message based on other- and ideal-interested justifications, on the one hand, and the representative's need to respond to group pressure from his or her own constituents, on the other hand—largely depends on the degree of internal discipline within the organisation. The more centralised and hierarchical the structure of the organisation—or the more capable the leadership is of explaining their course of action to their members, to put it more positively—the less need for the leadership to defend their internal position in public events. As is well known in corporatist theory, well functioning organisations, in that respect, will contribute to a less politisised public debate. The dynamics of representation, following from the fact that the ERA/SRA is a member organisation, lies behind the increase of self-interested argumentation in the frontstage compared to the back-stage.

CONCLUSIONS: DRESSED FOR POLITICS

In several respects the findings of this chapter contradict the hypotheses of the theory of publicity's civilising effect. The theory assumes that the publicity of the frontstage forces actors to show a better side of themselves than their non-public backstage character would imply. Bargaining threats and promises would be replaced by arguing as the dominant mode of communication, while the types of justification would shift from self-regarding to other- and ideal-regarding ones. However, according to these results, putting industry representatives under public scrutiny does not bring about such a civilising effect.

Using the terminology of chapter three, the results indicate a strong civilising forum effect and a contrary politicising publicity effect, both in Brussels and in Stockholm, while there has been no sign of any transparency effect in this chapter.

A backstage area in Goffman's sense is a place where social actors can relax and be themselves, shielded from the norms of the frontstage. According to the theory of publicity's civilising effect, the private regions of politics constitute such backstages for actors who are weakly socialised into the norms of the forum. These arenas, the theory assumes, are dominated by 'hedonistic' market behaviour. But private lobbying meetings are not such a place. The force of the better argument norm is not forced upon the lobbyists only when they enter the public arena. It is there already, behind the scenes. The consultants' job is, to a large

Figure 4.1. Summary of the results of the interview study

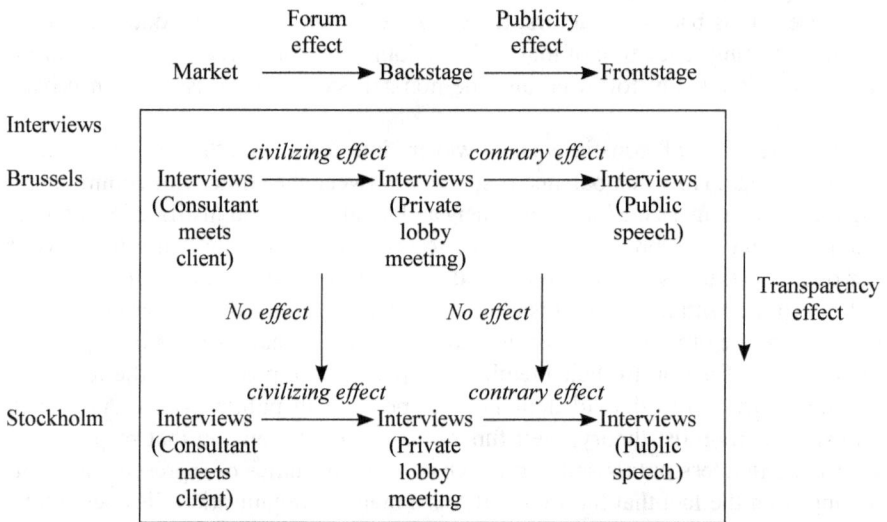

	Forum effect	Publicity effect	
	Market ———▶ Backstage	———▶ Frontstage	

Interviews			
Brussels	*civilizing effect*	*contrary effect*	
	Interviews ———▶ (Consultant meets client)	Interviews ———▶ (Private lobby meeting)	Interviews (Public speech)
	No effect ↓	*No effect* ↓	Transparency effect ↓
Stockholm	*civilizing effect*	*contrary effect*	
	Interviews ———▶ (Consultant meets client)	Interviews ———▶ (Private lobby meeting	Interviews (Public speech)

Note: Figure 4.1 illustrates the main findings of the chapter, with respect to the hypotheses derived from the theory of publicity's civilising effect. The arrows in the figure do not illustrate causal relationships but the different comparisons made in the analysis. The direction of the arrows indicates the hypothesised civilising effect. The forum effect was found in the consultants' description of the preparations necessary before the client is ready to move to the political sphere. The transparency effect was measured in the comparison between the interviews with Brussels consultants with those in Stockholm. A strong transparency effect would have implied a stronger forum effect in Sweden than in Brussels and a stronger publicity effect in Brussels than in Sweden. The publicity effect was investigated by the switching of scenarios between the closed lobby meeting with civil servants and the public speech.

extent, focused on preventing business leaders' egocentric world-views from ruining the impression that they are 'committed partners', with an open-minded attitude to the perspectives of others. The consistency requirement—which applies both to the shift between private and public arenas and to communications between different DGs and ministries—demonstrates that officials resist being treated as backstage actors. While there is a certain acceptance of the fact that the different occasions require different rhetorical styles it is not acceptable to those who have access to both stages that lobbyists radically shift arguments between the private and the public settings.

A civilising change of behavioural logic has nevertheless been demonstrated in the chapter. It occurs not as an effect of publicity but as a consequence of the move from the market to the forum. Successful lobbying—behind closed doors—requires business-people to get 'dressed for politics', i.e. to adhere to the force of the better argument norm and develop their arguments with consideration of the perspectives and preferences of others. The market actor who is a newcomer in politics tends to be too egocentric, too narrow-mindedly focused on her own costs and benefits, to manage successfully. It is the amateur client who comes closest to the pressure model of the interest group literature, as discussed in chapter two, in which 'groups know what they want and make their demands on officials accordingly, offering incentives or threatening disincentives in the event of non-cooperation' (Heinz *et. al.* 1993: 13). The image of lobbyists as 'pressure groups' is a stereotype that, in the eyes of public affairs consultants, is largely connected to failure.

Having a mind open to the perspectives of others, being prepared to evaluate the weaknesses of one's own arguments and moderate one's positions in that light, are virtues of which any deliberative theorist would be proud. While lobbyists may not fulfil other deliberative principles, such as being open to a genuine transformation of preferences in response to the arguments of others—which of course is something completely different from strategically moderating one's positions in order to optimise self-interest—the fact that the logic of the forum forces them at least half-way into the deliberative ideal is nevertheless an achievement. That, however, is accomplished by the logic of the forum, without the assistance of transparency or publicity.

The transparency effect was studied in this chapter via the comparison between the interviews in Brussels and in Stockholm. No such effect—which would have implied a stronger forum effect (less self-interested bargaining in the private lobbying meetings) and a weaker publicity effect in Stockholm than in Brussels—was found. Working towards the uniquely transparent Swedish governmental ministries does not seem to require a more sensitive 'footing' with respect to the norms of the forum than lobbying the opaque European Commission. The force of the better argument norm, which drives the mode of communication towards arguing, applies equally strongly in Brussels as in Stockholm. The non-selfishness norm, which affects the types of justification, is equally weak.

Whether these are general features of lobbying, or indicators of specific

European lobbying conditions, is not possible to determine from this study. Some consultants claimed that American companies tend to be too confrontational for European standards, more prone for instance to threatening with legal action.[3] The emphasis put on constructiveness and added value, on the other hand, may also be interpreted as being in line with American pluralist theories of interest groups as carriers of 'costly information,' as described in chapter two. Constructiveness by itself, however, should not be taken as an indicator of arguing. As discussed in chapter three, a cooperative attitude is equally compatible with (integrative) bargaining as with arguing. It is the combination of the requirement to be constructive and the force of the better argument norm which sets the standard for communication in the lobby corridors of Brussels and Stockholm.

The Stockholm and Brussels consultants also reacted similarly to the change in setting between closed meetings with civil servants and the public speech. While their sense of footing with respect to the external audience told them that what the Secretary-General said in public should be consistent with the basic arguments used on the private backstage, and that the appropriate thing to do in a public speech is to address the whole audience, their experience of working with associations also made them aware of the internal dimension of the situation. Taking the home constituency into account the publicity effect tends to become politicizing rather than civilising, in the deliberative sense. Publicity does not induce representatives to hide their base motives but rather to emphasise them even more strongly. Just like Eliasoph's volunteers and civic group activists—although for different reasons—the lobbyists, both in Sweden and in Brussels, sounded better backstage than frontstage in terms of self-interest.

Contrary to the theory of publicity's civilising effect, the force of the better argument norm was not stronger for lobbyists in public than in private. One effect of publicity was the lowering of the degree of specificity—the messages becoming vaguer and less concrete—as could be expected from negotiation theory. It seems that the actual content of the arguments matters less in public than in private. The consultants were much more careful in their selection of arguments for the meeting with civil servants than for the public speech. Only exactly the right arguments, 'talking strictly to the brief' of the officials, were allowed in the private meetings. Due to the consistency requirement, public speech should, ideally, contain the same arguments as the private meeting, but the pressure carefully to select only winning arguments was felt less in the public speech. As long as no contradictions were found, and the speech contributed to creating a positive atmosphere around the Secretary-General, the persuasive force of the arguments did not seem to matter as much in the speech as in the private meetings. Arguments, one might perhaps put it, turned into rhetoric.

One of the causal mechanisms in Elster's outline of the theory of publicity's civilising effect—the imperfection constraint—posited that the non-selfishness norm would force political actors not only to shift from self-interested bargaining to public-spirited arguing, but also to modify their positions (see page 22). In order for actors' self-interested motivations not to be revealed, they should not take a position too close to their actual objective interest, according to the imperfection constraint, as that would arouse the suspicion that the public-spirited rhetoric was a cover for self-interested motives. For industry lobbyists, however, Elster's version of the imperfection constraint turned out to be irrelevant, because of the weak or non-existing non-selfishness norm.

Furthermore, this chapter has demonstrated that industry lobbyists face another type of imperfection constraint, which works in completely the opposite direction to Elster's. Rather than diluting their positions and arguments in order to hide 'what's in it for them', in order to be legitimate partners in dialogue, lobbyists must actually show how they are affected by the proposed measures. Industry claiming only public-spirited motives looks simply too good to be true. If lobbyists overplay the 'committed partner' role by pretending that they do not have interests at stake, they will lose credibility. Self-regarding arguments, therefore, have to be included rather than disguised. The emphasis of the argumentation in the lobby corridor will, nevertheless, be put on other- and ideal-regarding justifications. These are needed to persuade policy-makers, since threats and promises are ruled out by the force of the better argument norm. But that is a question of persuasion rather than of norm-induced behaviour. Publicity has nothing to do with it.

In fact, there was even an element of a civilising force of secrecy found in the interviews. The consistency constraint impelled the Secretary-General of the ERA/SRA towards relying on the civilised arguments as much frontstage as backstage. This mechanism worked as a counter-force against the group pressure of members, which was pushing the Secretary-General towards even an more self-interested approach.

It may seem paradoxical that interest groups first have to declare their stake in order to be invited as legitimate partners but then, once engaged in dialogue, must use public-interest arguments. Such a criterion for invitation would suggest that the forthcoming interaction is also going to contain bargaining elements: 'if you want something, say what it is'. I believe the explanation is that policy-makers have a 'politics of difference' perspective rather than an 'epistemic' view of the public interest.[4] The public interest is to be found out via a discussion between the voices of different perspectives. According to the consultants, policy-makers are not searching for the 'correct' answer. The most professional industry lobbyist puts more effort into building broad alliances than to developing the ultimate 'killer' argument. If many different voices say approximately the same thing, the policy decision is likely to go in that direction.

The fact that other- and ideal-regarding justifications are focused upon, regardless of the degree of publicity, as a result of the forum effect, nevertheless activates at least one of the mechanisms of the theory of publicity's civilising effect, namely, the plausibility constraint. It implies that lobbyists may have to modify their positions in order to conform to other-regarding and ideal-regarding justifications. If, in the hypothetical scenario used here, it could not be credibly demonstrated that the eco-tax proposal would be a major setback for growth in

Europe, the ERA might have to drop their insistence on trashing the proposal. Instead they might be forced to argue that the increased risk of at least some negative effects on the European economy was sufficient to justify granting hauliers more time to prepare for the implementation of the proposal (or something like that).

A problem for the plausibility constraint, however, which also applies to Elster's imperfection constraint, is the fact that people often have difficulty distinguishing between their self-interest and the public interest. This was illustrated in this chapter by the difficulties of the 'egocentric amateur'. Wishful thinking tends to bring amateurs' perceptions of the public interest into line with their self-interest. Actors who are unaware of the weak link between their private interests and the public interest—i.e. actors having a General Motors-like perception of their own importance ('what is good for us is good for everyone')—will not change their behaviour in accordance with the plausibility or the imperfection constraint.[5]

This chapter has also demonstrated that the fact that industry lobbyists are known to be self-interested affects the persuasiveness of their arguments. It is a basic rule of common sense that, if the temperance movement argues that lower taxes on beer will save jobs, that is probably going to be true. If the same argument is given by the brewery industry, on the other hand, it is not equally credible. As Elster has argued, the perceived motives of the speaker affect the persuasiveness of a given argument, even though the argument itself is based on factual plausibility.

> To the extent that one is offering impartial arguments in order to persuade others, there is, strictly speaking, no need to prove sincerity [to impartial values]. One can, in fact, assert something like the following without violating the norms of argument: 'I do not believe in justice and fairness. I want this policy implemented simply because it is in my interest. I notice, however, that there are also purely impartial arguments for the same policy, which I offer you in case you hadn't thought of them.' Others are unlikely to give serious considerations to arguments offered in this spirit. My attempt to persuade you is much more likely to succeed if I can make you believe that I believe in the arguments I offer for your consideration (Elster 1999, p: 375f).

While Elster sees this as an absurd way of arguing for someone aiming to be persuasive, the public affairs consultants' advice is in fact rather similar to the act that Elster describes. While they would not advise the Secretary-General to be quite so explicit about it, the ERA's basic message would be 'we're in this for the profit, as you know, but we also have some other- and ideal-regarding arguments which we believe you will be interested in'. That interest groups have to act this way, in order not to retain credibility is, nevertheless, a weakness for them, as it negatively affects the persuasiveness of their arguments. In fact, the conclusion is that, as one consultant put it; 'if you only have the self-interested party defending himself, you tend to find that there is a limit to what you can achieve' (Brussels IP 8). The two major strategies for compensating this 'naturally' low persuasive power of industry are long term investments in the 'committed partner' image and building alliances with other actors who have a different type of legitimacy and credibility. A company or an organisation that has managed to build credibility with political institutions, therefore, will be very careful not to ruin that by violating the force of the better argument norm.

NOTES

1   Since there are seven interviewees in Stockholm and eight in Brussels the absolute figures are slightly misleading. Minus 12 for seven interviewees is relatively 'more' than minus 12 for eight. The difference is so small, however, that it is insignificant. Maximum low would be –24 (three arguments, eight interviewees) for Brussels and –21 (seven interviewees) for Stockholm.

2   Cf. Greenwood 2003, p: 112ff.

3   Cf. Woll, who argues that Washington lobbyists are more competitive, direct and focused on immediate interests, compared to Brussels lobbyists who are more constructive and consensus-oriented. Woll 2006, p: 463.

4   Cf. Young 1996 and Estlund 1997 respectively.

5   In this sense the amateur resembles another well-known type of actor in the interest group literature, namely the 'outsider', in the 'insider-outsider model'. Cf. Maloney, Jordan & McLaughlin 1994. While insiders, in this model, are described as having been 'domesticated' by political institutions, the outsider is 'politically unsophisticated': 'Their demands are often presented in strident and uncompromising terms.' Grant 2000, p: 20. The model assumes that outsiders either do not want, for ideological reasons, to be 'tamed' by the state, or that they are not allowed into the corridors of power. For the amateur lobbyist, however, it seems more to be a question of a lack of understanding of the terms of the forum.

chapter five | letters from backstage

The purpose of interviewing the best public affairs consultants about how industry representatives should behave in public and private political settings was to study whether transparency and publicity produce an incentive structure that induces lobbyists to act more in line with the norms of the forum. The results of the previous chapter indicated that this is not the case. While there was no sign of any transparency effect in the comparison between Brussels and Stockholm, the switching of scenarios between private and public appearances increased the degree of self-interest.

In this chapter, the interviews are complemented by a study of 'real action', in the form of written communications from lobbyists to the political institutions and the public. On the one hand, this provides a test of the results of the interviews. If the consultants (who are, one must keep in mind, professional communicators) managed to sell the author a false, politically correct, story of lobbyists using arguments rather than threats and promises, or if the interview method for some other reason did not adequately capture the transparency and publicity effects, the study of private and public letters should tell a different story. On the other hand, how real companies and organisations actually behave is a different matter from how they should behave according to the expertise. The reason why consultants are used by companies and associations is that knowledge of what constitutes successful behaviour is not freely and easily available.

A random sample of lobbying letters would include senders who varied with respect to their positions on the amateurs–professionals scale described by the consultants in the previous chapter. Consequently, such a sample would give a somewhat different picture from the consultants' best advice, probably containing a more emotional, egocentric and reactive behaviour. To collect a random sample of lobbying letters to the European Commission, however, would require a population of letters from which to draw the sample. That would be difficult even for a project with an unlimited budget. As described in chapter three, since the central archives are either non-existent or unreliable, it would require asking all Commission officials to go through their personal files.

The selection of letters for this study, therefore, has not been guided by an attempt to achieve a representative sample of interest group letters. Rather, the

sampling has been aimed at studying transparency and publicity effects by securing comparability between confidential letters, publicly accessible letters and
published position papers and press releases. When the document analysis is
compared to that of the consultants' story, some deviation would not necessarily
imply that the consultants' story was falsely idealised, since real action may not be
perfect. However, if the letters show a very different picture to that given by the
consultants, that means either that the consultants' answers were unreliable or that
their knowledge of how lobbying should be done is so narrowly spread that it is of
limited relevance for our understanding of how politics really works.

The process of collecting the letters was explained in chapter three. The result,
described in more detail in Appendices A and B, was 58 confidential letters to the
Commission from ten industry associations and companies, 41 position papers
and press releases published on the internet from the same, and similar, senders,
and 55 publicly available letters from seven comparable Swedish senders to the
Ministry of the Environment.

The sample includes senders from the chemicals, plastics, paint, batteries, electronic equipment, car, and oil industries. The European Union's chemicals policy
was up for a major revision at the time of the fieldwork (in February 2001 the
Commission presented its white paper on a strategy for a future chemicals policy).
During this period, the primary purpose of the chemicals industry's lobbying
activities was to avoid costs in relation to risk assessments and labelling of substances. The battery industry's concerns involved a proposed EU ban on Nickel-
Cadmium (hereafter, NiCad) batteries and costly collection and recycling systems
for batteries. The plastics (specifically, polyvinyl chloride (hereafter, PVC))
producers had similar worries to the NiCad battery producers, as the authorities
were considering a ban on PVC. Electronic equipment companies, in this sample
represented by Electrolux, were lobbying to influence the regulations on producer
responsibility for waste. Both the car and oil industries were primarily active on
issues concerning vehicle emissions. The two latter actors were, to some extent,
opponents. The car industry was lobbying for an environmental policy focused
on cleaner fuels rather than cars, while the oil industry wanted the regulations to
focus on cars rather than fuels. The car industry was also at the time involved in
discussions on producer responsibility for waste.

To what extent the organisations and companies in this sample are representative of the whole industry-lobbying community is difficult to say. The sample
includes both bigger and smaller actors but bigger actors are overrepresented.
Large lobbying resources probably position an actor further out on the professional's side of the scale, even though the interviewed consultants claimed that
this correlation is far from perfect. The results of the document analysis, therefore, will probably be closer to the ideal of successful behaviour described by the
consultants—a committed partner arguing with an emphasis on other- and ideal-
regarding justifications—than a sample including a larger number of small actors.

This chapter shows, first, the results with respect to the mode of communication. Do the senders of the letters argue or bargain? Thereafter the types of

justification used in the letters—self-regarding, other-regarding or ideal-regarding—will be analysed.

ARGUING OR BARGAINING?

Do lobbying letters attempt to convince the receiver of the merits of different policy options by using rational arguments (arguing), or to persuade the receiver to shift a policy stance in return for something—a positive compensation of some sort (promising/integrative bargaining) or relief from a negative consequence over which the sender has power (threatening/distributive bargaining)? Alternatively, do lobbyists just make demands without bothering to give any explicit reasons?

If politics was 'just like a market', and the closed lobby arena a place for buying and selling public policy, confidential letters would include offers such as 'if you do X, we will give you Y', perhaps followed up with 'and we can motivate it publicly in such-and-such a fashion'. If it was a naked power struggle, we would see threats and demands. I have found almost no traces at all of this type of behaviour in the confidential letters, nor in the published and publicly available documents.

Even with a generous interpretation, there are just ten paragraphs or sentences in the 154 documents (588 pages of text) that constitute potential instances of threats and promises, half of which come from the battery industry in Brussels. Since this behaviour is so limited it will be reported in its entirety. One reason for doing so is to illustrate what bargaining could look like in practice and give readers a chance to judge for themselves what should count as a threat or a promise. Most importantly, however, is the fact that there are just a handful of cases to discuss. These are the exceptions to the general rule, which is that industry lobbyists in their written communications—public and private—argue for their positions rather than bargain. The result thus confirms the story received from the public affairs consultants, with respect to the mode of communication.

In my view, among the ten potential instances of bargaining there are, in reality, only three in which the letter as a whole is dominated by a bargaining type of behaviour. These three are all confidential letters from the battery industry to European Commission officials. The battery lobbyists used both a positive offer and a negative threat in these letters, in order to persuade the Commission to abandon any thoughts of a ban on NiCad batteries and to refrain from leaving the industry with the full costs of the collection schemes for all consumer batteries. The offer consists of a voluntary commitment, whereby the industry would take responsibility for the collection and recycling of NiCad batteries. A whole new organisation—CollectNiCad—had been created by the industry for that purpose. The threat concerned non-cooperation in the collection and recycling schemes if a ban on NiCad batteries was introduced and the industry was burdened with the full costs for the collection of all consumer batteries.

The first of these letters was sent off by the CollectNiCad Secretary-General, Alfons Westgeest, to DG Environment Deputy Director General Jean-Francois

Verstrynge, and copied to ten other officials in DG Environment and DG Enterprise, on May 5th, 2000. The letter, which is two pages long, first refers to previous communications about the battery industry's proposal for a voluntary commitment, and describes the new CollectNiCad organisation. 'We are pleased to inform you ... that the CollectNiCad initiative is gaining in momentum .... Indeed, we are now in a position to assure the European Commission that the action and communication plans as set out in our letter of 1st March are well under way.' The letter ends as follows:

> The Ni-Cad related industry is committed to the CollectNiCad initiative. We must once more underline that a proposed ban on Ni-Cad batteries with a list of exemptions is an unacceptable course of action to be taken. The Ni-Cad battery is traded worldwide and is highly appreciated by the consumer without causing damage to the environment.
>
> We are offering the EU Authorities a strategy encompassing the principles of sustainable development, in which Ni-Cad batteries will be collected and recycled across the EU by industry financed systems supported by appropriate Member State legislation.
>
> All concerned, including the representatives from the European Commission and designated delegates from NGOs, will be invited to participate in the Joint Monitoring Group, allowing them to gain knowledge on collection techniques and necessary networks—a useful source of information in view of the trend towards increasing collection and recycling of consumer products.
>
> All outstanding issues have been addressed leading to a win-win situation for the EU environment and consumer.
>
> It is our duty to inform you that the final incorporation of this EEIG [the CollectNiCad organisation] will take place on acceptance of the Commitment by the European Commission and the withdrawal of the Ni-Cad ban from all present draft legislation.
>
> Should the European Commission set this initiative aside and the ban be introduced, all rationale behind collection and recycling of Ni-Cad batteries as well as the incentive for providing the related financial resources required would have disappeared, leading to a detrimental impact on both the economy and the environment. It would also send a negative signal to all other industrial sectors of the European Union.
>
> We are now anxious to finalise the proposal with you and work together towards the legal incorporation of this Voluntary Commitment.[1]

Although this letter includes references to other- and ideal-regarding principles, such as the environment and consumer satisfaction, the main message is that the voluntary commitment is something that is offered in return for the withdrawal of the ban, regardless of the merits of such an agreement. Further, the entire rationale for the industry for contributing to the collection of batteries would 'disappear' if a ban was introduced. In my view, this is bargaining, including both a threat (non-cooperation) and a promise (commitment to recycling).

However, this is just one of several letters from the battery industry during this period, around the summer of 2000.[2] One other letter includes one sentence with the same bargaining offer as in the letter of May 5th, 2000: 'This strategy [the CollectNiCad initiative] can only be implemented if the concerned industries ride out the negative economic effects of the ban'.[3] That letter, however, is an eleven-page-long argument for why a voluntary commitment would be superior to a legislative approach (including a ban) for 'environmental, trade, safety, technical and economic reasons':

> The aim [of the industry's proposed commitment] is to develop best available techniques to be implemented across the EU and to ensure maximum efficiency in collection and sorting. … A ban on Ni-Cad batteries would increase the risk of adding primary and secondary Cadmium to the environment. The Commitment provides confidence for maximum collection and recycling thus reducing the risk of environmental damage.[4]

The other letters from the battery industry from this period are dominated by arguing. The voluntary commitment is promoted in these letters not as an offer in return for avoiding the ban but because it is the most rational solution for environmental and economic reasons. In July 2000, a letter with similar content was sent to commissioner Erkki Liikanen (DG Enterprise) and commissioner Mario Monti (DG Competition), arguing the merits of the voluntary commitment:

> We have attached, for your information, an overview fiche (one page) describing briefly our voluntary approach. We also wish to assure you that industry is convinced that this initiative presents substantial advantages over the proposed regulatory ban in the best interests of European industry, environment and consumer.
>
> During the last few months, the battery industry has carefully examined the environmental issues related to the use of cadmium in NiCad batteries. Not only have production and marketing issues been considered, but also waste management. It is the industry's opinion that the NiCad battery does not create either a general or a specific risk to the environment if its introduction on the market is controlled according to the basic principles of precaution, product and market stewardship.
>
> The Voluntary Commitment proposal has an impact which goes well beyond the advantages of the proposed ban in the draft battery directive, and indeed falls in line with the priorities of the draft legislation.[5]

Thus, on the whole, arguing dominates the communication from the battery industry during this period, with the exception of the two instances of bargaining described above.

As it turned out, the Waste Unit of DG Environment was not persuaded by the voluntary commitment proposal. In March 2001, it decided instead to include a ban on NiCad batteries in its draft proposal, with certain limited exemptions. The draft of March 2001 set a 75 per cent collection target for all consumer batteries and left it open for each member state to decide how the collection systems would be financed. The industry believed the 75 per cent target to be much too high and was worried that they would have to finance the national collection schemes themselves. The March 2001 draft was followed, in this sample, by nine letters from SAFT (a French battery producing company), CollectNiCad and the European Portable Batteries Association (EPBA) between April and June 2001, two of which included bargaining language.[6] The first is a letter from the SAFT General Manager, Gregoire Olivier, to Commissioner Wallström (DG Environment), and copied to Commissioner Liikanen (DG Enterprise). This letter was sent on April 23, soon after the draft was circulated. Olivier refers back to an earlier meeting with Wallström on March 27 and complains that 'this draft reflects very little of the discussions we had a few weeks ago'. In the first part of the letter, which concerns industrial applications of NiCad batteries, Olivier strongly advocates the collecting and recycling scheme proposed by the industry. In this part of the letter Olivier is arguing, using one environmental justification ('for the benefit of environmental protection in Europe, this opportunity should not be allowed to go unexploited') and one self-regarding ('the administration of an exemption mechanism to be determined at a later date ... creates an uncertainty which is absolutely unacceptable from a business perspective'). In the second part of the letter, however, concerning portable batteries, Olivier uses bargaining language. A ban would imply that industry would no longer be willing to contribute to collecting historical waste:

> On portable batteries also, the industry strongly disagrees with the principle of a ban. Battery manufacturers and users constituted CollectNiCad to speed up the implementation and effectiveness of collection schemes all over Europe. I believe that, in the interest of the environment, this initiative from the industry should be given some support: more than 10 years of portable NiCad batteries are currently hoarded in households, and a ban, which would immediately kill all collecting schemes, would precipitate those batteries in the municipal waste stream.
>
> Unless you want to send 20,000 tons of cadmium to the municipal waste stream, you must support the CollectNiCad initiative to collect those consumer batteries. Longer term, as you know, lithium-ion and nickel-metal-hydride batteries are slowly taking up market share. There is thus room for an agreement with the industry for a phase out of nickel-cadmium batteries at a reasonable pace, as long as key segments where, for technical reasons, nickel-cadmium is the only available technology, are clearly exempted from this phase out.[7]

While the 'interest of the environment' is still included as a justificatory principle, the main message of these last two paragraphs is that, if the Commission turns down the industry's offer, the industry will not contribute to a solution to the problem of historical waste.

The second letter dominated by bargaining from the battery industry during 2001 is a letter from EPBA on June 20. It had been sent to all Commissioners. It is reprinted here in its entirety since it illustrates self-interested bargaining in practice. This was what I was searching for and, apart from this exception, could not find.

Dear Commissioner,

As a responsible and forward-looking industry, the European Portable Battery Industry is seriously concerned with the socio economic impact of the DG Environment proposal for a directive on batteries and accumulators.

On the 18th April the EPBA sent comments on the DG Environment proposal to all Directorate Generals and Commissioners consulted during inter-service consultation.

This four-page paper clearly referred to the disproportionate cost of the proposal; this is not a new element and is of crucial importance to the battery industry.

EPBA commissioned a study on cost impact to examine the potential effect on the battery industry should the industry be faced with the financing of collection and recycling of all batteries in all Member States. The study clearly points out that the battery industry would be seriously affected by the measures as proposed.

The cost impact of the collection provisions would account for approximately 30% of the annual industry revenue.

In order to ensure that the environmental aims of the Directive can be satisfied, the measures therein must bear some relevance to industry realities. The success of implementation of the Directive is dependent on the participation of industry actors.

You will understand that, despite our proven policy of support for environmental solutions, *the Battery Industry will not be in a position to assume its part of the responsibility in the collection and recycling schemes, unless the establishment of financing tools is included in the proposal.*

We note that adoption on the proposal is approaching and urge you to consider this information in the forthcoming discussions. We would welcome a meeting with you to discuss this vital issue.

Please do not hesitate to contact us at the EPBA secretariat should you require any additional concise information on cost impacts or suggested wording for the relevant provisions [Emphasis in original].[8]

If the closed-door lobby arenas had been dominated by market behaviour, this is what it would have looked like. The emphasis in the argumentative part of the letter is self-interested, apart from vague references to 'socio economic impact' and 'the environmental aims of the Directive'. The breaking of the force of the better argument norm lies in the threat of non-cooperation unless it is made clear in the directive that the industry must not be fully responsible for the financing of the collection and recycling schemes.

Even though this is an exceptional letter in the sample it is important to note that this type of behaviour exists. Furthermore, the battery industry's lobbying strategy is not led by amateurs. The Secretary-General of both CollectNiCad and EPBA—Alfons Westgeest—was at the time a partner of Ernst & Young Association Management, one of the largest public affairs consultancies in Brussels. The rest of the written communication from the battery industry in this sample is based on arguing and follows closely the committed partner role as described by the consultants in the previous chapter. But the three letters quoted here are examples of conscious norm-breaking, aimed at putting pressure on the Commission. The reason why the professional battery lobbyists chose conflict is probably, just as described by the consultants, that they were close to losing the battle over a draft proposal in which the stakes were exceptionally high. The proposal included both a high collection rate, which the industry claimed would cost a third of annual industry revenue if they would have to finance it, and a ban on NiCad batteries. DG Environment was aiming at the heart of their business, especially that of the main NiCad battery producer, SAFT.

The three letters quoted above are the only documents in the sample which are dominated by bargaining. Seven other cases contain elements of at least potential bargaining. First, CollectNiCad, in a letter to Commissioner Monti (DG Competition) and Commission President Romano Prodi, states that the DG Environment draft proposal of March 2001...

>...violates the rules of international trade because a ban of nickel-cadmium batteries is not the least restrictive measure available to reach the objectives of DG Environment. The absence of scientific justification creates technical barriers to trade which would be contested in the name of WTO rules. In addition the discriminatory proposal to ban nickel-cadmium is not performed after an objective evaluation of the environmental risk presented by alternative technologies that will replace the nickel-cadmium battery on the market.[9]

Is this a threat of legal action from the battery industry or just another argument about the infeasibility of a ban? It is not clear whether it is the European battery industry or someone else (Americans?) who, the sender of the letter supposes, would challenge the proposal legally. The content in the rest of the letter is argumentative, factual and primarily based on environmental risks. The trade rule argument is the last in a list of six points.

In the second case, the chemicals industry association, CEFIC, also refers to potential trade law violations in a press release, commenting together with the American Chemistry Council (ACC) on the Commissions White Paper in November 2002: 'The groups [CEFIC and ACC] said they hoped to sensitize EU policymakers to the serious economic implications and potential trade law violations inherent in the White Paper'.[10] There is no formulation here such as 'would be contested', as in the CollectNiCad letter. The rest of the press release argues against the White Paper for economic reasons and because it would create 'a complex, burdensome and largely unworkable system that would fail to improve human health and the environment'.

The third case involves the European Portable Batteries Association repeating the need for a clear financing mechanism of the collection schemes for consumer batteries in a press release, using the following terms: 'A visible fee is a necessary condition for the producers to be economically able to shoulder their responsibility under this directive.'[11] It is not clear how this should be interpreted. If the directive does not include a visible fee, will the battery industry refuse to comply? Or does the press release suggest that the industry will be economically destroyed and for that reason will not be able to 'shoulder their responsibility'? The rest of the press release is highly critical of the latest draft of the battery directive but, with the possible exception of the sentence quoted above, it is based on arguments—environmental, macro-economic and self-interested.

Case four is that of the paint industry organisation in Brussels, CEPE, beginning a letter to DG Environment Director General James Currie in the following manner:

Dear Mr. Currie,
After having consulted our members concerned we are confirming our commitment to pursuing a voluntary agreement to protect consumers against possible health risks, when they are spraying paints containing DEGBE [a dangerous substance], although these paints are normally not intended to be sprayed. As mentioned already in a meeting with DG Environment on April 6th 1998 as well as in several letters sent to DG Environment, we are willing to proceed further with the voluntary agreement only if a threshold for the DEGBE content in the paint is being included.
There are several scientific and general arguments to support this position.[12]

This opening of the letter is followed by other-regarding arguments, with the basic message that DEGBE is not a health risk to consumers and that the industry's toxicological data should be considered by the responsible Scientific Committee. CEPE declares that 'we would then accept the conclusions of that Committee'. Just like the battery industry, CEPE is offering a voluntary commitment to the Commission (in return for a threshold for the DEGBE content in the paint). In this case, however, there is no threat of non-cooperation if the Commission chooses to legislate instead. As a whole the letter is characterised by arguing rather than bargaining.

The fifth case likewise involves a voluntary commitment. In a letter to James Currie, the Director-General of DG Environment, the automobile industry organisation, ACEA, complains about the establishment of an expert group on a 'fiscal framework to reduce CO_2 emissions from passenger cars'. ACEA claims that such a group is unnecessary since the already existing voluntary commitment (which ACEA and the Commission had agreed to two years earlier) implies that no additional fiscal measures should be taken by the authorities. ACEA considers the setting up of the working group as constituting 'a breach of the spirit of our understanding'.[13] As a protest, ACEA declares that they will provisionally only delegate an observer to the group. Although formally the letter concerns a procedural issue the implicit message is that DG Environment must remember that they have a deal with industry that there will be no eco-taxes, and that they should stick to that.

The sixth case, again including ACEA, comes from a press release criticising the Commission's proposal on End-of-Life Vehicles, concerning the recycling of automobiles. ACEA signals that the car producers may have to take over the business of dismantling cars if the proposal goes through.

> The Commission proposal would disrupt the free market mechanism in which dismantlers compete with each other, costs are minimised and prices are the result of demand and supply. Instead, dismantlers would be encouraged to raise prices far above those resulting from a market mechanism. The need for car manufacturers to control the costs of such a system could put at risk the independence of downstream actors.[14]

Again, it is not clear whether this should be interpreted as a threat of a hostile takeover of the dismantling business or if it is just another competition argument. It is, in any case, a minor point in the three-page document which otherwise emphasises environmental and economic arguments.

The seventh and final case is somewhat peripheral but should be reported for the record. The Swedish paint industry organisation, SVEFF, protests, in an irritated letter to the Ministry of the Environment against the government's decision to allow, for cultural-historical reasons, the Årsta Bridge in Stockholm to be painted by lead-based paint, when the industry at the same time is following governmental regulations to phase out such paint. SVEFF claims, in what may be interpreted as a threat, that 'there is a risk that this decision and possible similar future decisions, means that the important work to discontinue the use of lead-based paint voluntarily, will stop for a period of time'.[15] The issue is hardly of any substantial importance to the industry, which makes this formulation a bit surprising. The letter seems to have been sent off on impulse.

The purpose of reporting all these cases, it must be emphasised again, is to demonstrate the minor role that bargaining plays in the sample of letters. These are the only examples of bargaining obtained from all the collected documents. Furthermore, the three letters from the battery industry that were discussed first are the only clear examples in which threats and promises play a central role. One could also question whether voluntary commitments should at all be counted as bargaining offers. If so, they are examples of public deals, since voluntary commitment is a recognised and frequently used environmental policy instrument in the EU.[16] If the CollectNiCad voluntary commitment had been accepted, it would have been published and acknowledged as a part of the official EU policy, rather than disguised and covered up with a 'public-regarding gloss'.

Not one letter, public or private, shows lobbyists making demands without giving reasons. Just bringing 'wants,' without trying to justify them in some way, does not seem to happen. Neither does the rhetoric in the letters and public papers contain 'demanding' terminology. The phraseology, wording, and tone of the letters are polite and correct, well suited for a committed partner. The content analysis of the documents included a coding of explicit markers of a 'we are a committed partner engaged in finding solutions' attitude, such as: 'we [Electrolux] place a great value on an open and constructive dialogue with representatives of the government';[17] 'we [the battery industry] are totally in favour of any initiative which would further improve the way our products are used and treated at the end of their life';[18] and 'we [the Swedish chemicals industry] have a common interest in supporting and promoting the work for a sustainable chemicals- and environmental policy'.[19] A majority of the letters included an explicit marking of that sort: 67 per cent of the confidential letters in Brussels, 66 per cent of the public position papers and press releases and 53 per cent of the letters in Stockholm.

There are a handful of examples in Brussels, both public and private, where the sender 'urges' the commission to, for example, 'accept and support the Voluntary Commitment of the NiCad industry',[20] or 'address the scientific basis of the environmental risk assessment in the appropriate manner'.[21] Apart from this terminology of 'urgency' there are just three cases which—again interpreting generously—involve 'demands'. First, the Swedish Chemicals and Plastics Federation in a letter to the Ministry of Environment explains that some of their member companies have difficulties getting rid of their industrial waste, since new regulations have resulted in too few incineration facilities certified by the authorities. The sender finishes the letter as follows: 'I expect that the Ministry of the Environment will soon find a solution to this problem. This is an urgent issue, which demands action now.'[22]

The second case is a letter from the Swedish Automotive Industry Association (Bilindustriföreningen), which begins: 'There are too many abandoned junk cars in the countryside—increase the salvage payment to SEK 1200. As soon as possible. We can manage that with the money in the Vehicle Salvage Fund.'[23]

The third and perhaps most clear example of a demand is also from the Swedish Automotive Industry Association. The background is a legal argument saying that a new government proposal on producer responsibility on cars will stand in conflict with EC law. The Automotive Industry Association claims that the government must notify the European Commission of this proposal.

The proposition on producer responsibility thus extends far beyond both the EU's current legislation and the future producer responsibility within the Union. The Automotive Industry Association therefore repeats the demand that the government fulfils its duties and reports the proposition to the EU Commission.[24]

This is the closest to tough, demanding rhetoric as it gets in the sample. The dominant tone of the letters thus is far closer to the committed partner role than the pressure model.

TYPES OF JUSTIFICATION

Arguing is clearly the dominant mode of communication used by lobbyists, both in Brussels and in Stockholm, in public and in private correspondence. Not one letter, press release or public position paper contains a position on behalf of the sender without an argument backing it up. Attempts at bargaining appear on very few occasions. These results thus confirm the public affairs consultants' story with respect to the importance of the force of the better argument norm. Contrary to the assumption of the theory of publicity's civilising effect, the norm applies not only on the public frontstage but also in private backstage settings.

In this section it will be demonstrated that the consultants' denial of the existence of a public non-selfishness norm, equally contrary to the theory, is also supported by the letters. The consultants claimed that self-regarding arguments should be used by industry lobbyists for presentation but that the emphasis of the argumentation must focus on other- and ideal-regarding arguments. They also indicated that self-regarding arguments would be used more, rather than less, in public settings, compared to private meetings. The content analysis of the documents described in this section confirms that picture. Self-regarding arguments are being used in the confidential letters but not so frequently as environmental arguments. Furthermore, there are more documents containing self-regarding arguments among the public documents than the confidential letters.

The content analysis is based on simple counts of the number of letters, including self-regarding, other-regarding or ideal-regarding justifications, intended to back up the positions promoted by the senders. The basic unit of analysis is the letter. As described in chapter three, those letters which did not contain a particular policy position but instead included requests for meetings, invitations to conferences, etc., were not included in the analysis.

Three categories of other- and ideal-regarding justifications were used—environmental (including public health and references to 'sustainable development'), macroeconomic (including benefits for consumers) justifications, and references to undistorted competition (including free trade). On a few occasions the arguments in the letters fall outside these categories. One such example is the legal argument on the incompatibility of EC law with a new Swedish regulation, used by the Automotive Industry Association in the quote above. Also, a few letters are purely factual, without any explicit reference to the environment or the economy. Following here are some examples of how the categorisation was made.

Self-regarding justifications include cases like the following, from the Brussels chemicals industry association CEFIC: 'The chemicals industry wants workable and practical legislation to maintain its competitiveness in an already highly regulated environment. Some vital aspects of the White Paper do not meet these criteria.'[25]Another example, from the Swedish Paint and Printing Ink Makers Association (SVEFF): 'To establish national regulations for Sweden in order to reach this goal faster [the environmental policy goal of 'an environment free from toxins'] will only cause problems, especially for companies which are active on the Swedish market.'[26] The paint industry's Brussels association CEPE, as a third example, argues that the EU chemicals policy 'will present significant technical and commercial challenges to the coating and printing ink industry'.[27]

Macroeconomic justifications include arguments like the following:

In summary, a short term general prohibition of hexavalent chrome would jeopardize an important production that involves 1500–2000 people, primarily in Motala and its surroundings. It would also mean that competitors outside of the EU would quickly take over the market and the Swedish income from the exports would be lost.[28]

Another example of a macro-economic justification is the CEFIC President quoted in a press release as saying:

Tomorrow is an important day for industrial policy in Europe. The European Commission's debate on chemicals policy is a test case for how serious it is in its aim of turning Europe into the world's most competitive economy. The Commission must make an important decision: It can either give Enterprise Commissioner Liikanen the opportunity to initiate a departure towards higher growth and more employment with his promising approach of 'a new industrial policy in an enlarged Europe', or it can unleash a 1,200 page bureaucratic regulation that will massively impair growth and innovation throughout European industry.[29]

The consultants explained that it is quite common to link self-regarding arguments with macroeconomic justifications. An example is the following from the Association of Swedish Chemical Industries, describing the burden of high electricity taxes for the company Gränges Metall. This paragraph was coded as including both a self-regarding and a macroeconomic justification:

More than 92 per cent of Gränges Metall's use of electricity is used as a raw material for the manufacturing of aluminium. The possibilities to make the use of raw material more efficient are almost non-existent. It is therefore not surprising that Gränges Metall in Sundsvall has stopped its investments due to the taxes on electricity production. 550 people work there. Every summer 200 young people get jobs at Gränges in Sundsvall. An additional 1300 people are indirectly dependent on Gränges Metall's not going out of business. No investments during a longer period of time make it increasingly difficult for the company to survive.[30]

The following example of a competition argument comes from Electrolux: 'We sincerely hope that DG Enterprise will fight with European industry for a directive that safeguards competition and does not give industry a retroactive responsibility for historic appliances.'[31]

Environmental justifications include references to public health and sustainable development. The Swedish plastics industry defends PVC with references to the environment in the following way:

[The industry] believes in PVC as a material of the future because it is a unique kind of plastic, with a number of good technological and environmental characteristics. It may briefly be mentioned that PVC among other things saves on the non-renewable natural resources in its production. In addition, PVC may be described as energy efficient because less energy is generally used in the production of the products compared to other plastic materials. If it is used right, PVC may today give environmental advantages compared to alternative materials.[32]

An example of an exceptionally self-sacrificing use of an environmental argument is the following from the battery producer SAFT. This paragraph was coded as containing both a self-regarding and an environmental justification:

Independently of its dramatic impact on SAFT, which wouldn't survive as a European company, such a ban [on NiCad batteries] is not the best available solution from an environmental perspective. ... Nickel Cadmium battery activity accounts for less than 5 per cent of all cadmium emissions.[33]

Some cases are more difficult to categorise than these. Content analyses always imply a certain degree of subjective judgement on behalf of the coder. Initially, an attempt was made to code also the most important type of justification in the letters, rather than just the existence of a category. Typically, a letter included two types of justifications, and it would have given added value to study their relative weights. However, this procedure was not followed through since the judgements about the 'centrality' of the different arguments became too arbitrary. In too many cases it was impossible for an outsider to decide which argument should be considered the most central.

The results of the analysis are shown in Tables 5.1 and 5.2. The hypothesis that the non-selfishness norm would produce a transparency effect, encouraging Swedish lobbyists to use less self-interested justifications, is not supported by the data in Table 5.1. On the contrary, the results show that the most significant difference between Brussels and Stockholm is that the number of letters containing self-regarding justifications is higher in the publicly available letters in Stockholm letters than in the confidential letters in Brussels.

The comparison between confidential letters and press releases and public position papers from the Brussels organisations investigates the publicity effect.

Table 5.1. The transparency effect: confidential letters in Brussels compared to publicly available letters in Stockholm.

Types of justification	Stockholm (publicly available) (55)	Brussels (confidential) (58)	Difference (Transparency effect)
Self-regarding	53 per cent (29)	33 per cent (19)	+20
Environment	62 per cent (34)	76 per cent (44)	-14
Macroeconomic	31 per cent (17)	33 per cent (19)	-2
Competition	13 per cent (7)	22 per cent (13)	-9

Note: Table 5.1 shows the results of the content analyses of the 58 confidential letters in Brussels and the 55 publicly available letters in Stockholm. The figures indicate the number of letters containing at least one type of justification of the respective categories.

Table 5.2. The publicity effect: confidential letters compared to press releases and public position papers from Brussels organisations.

Types of justification	Brussels (public) (41)	Brussels (confidential) (58)	Difference (Publicity effect)
Self-regarding	71 per cent (29)	33 per cent (19)	+38
Environment	80 per cent (33)	76 per cent (44)	+4
Macroeconomic	66 per cent (27)	33 per cent (19)	+33
Competition	34 per cent (14)	22 per cent (13)	+12

Note: Table 5.2 shows the results of the content analysis of the 58 confidential letters and the 41 press releases and public position papers. The figures indicate the number of letters containing at least one type of justification of the respective categories.

Just as in the interview study in the previous chapter the conclusion here is that more publicity implies more self-regarding arguments rather than less. While Table 5.2 shows that all types of justifications are used more in public than in private, the increase is largest for the self-regarding arguments.

With respect to self-interest the transparency effect and the publicity effect go in the same direction: contrary to the theory of publicity's civilising effect. When it comes to the other- and ideal-regarding arguments, however, there is an increase in the use of those arguments in the public documents in Brussels (while they are used somewhat less in Stockholm) compared to the confidential Brussels letters. In relative terms, therefore, the difference of 20 percentage points in the comparison between Brussels and Stockholm is comparable to the increase of 38 percentage points in the press material.

At least a part of the explanation for the differences of the transparency and publicity effects, with respect to the other- and ideal-regarding arguments, probably lies in the fact that the letters in Stockholm and the press releases were sent to different types of recipients. Although both are publicly available, there is a rationale for using a broader spectrum of arguments in the press releases. Letters to Swedish civil servants will become publicly available but the primary target for such letters is the civil servants themselves and the government, not the broader public. In press releases or in position papers published on the internet, on the other hand, the purpose is to reach a broad audience, primarily via the media. It is consistent with the consultants' story that there is going to be a more careful selection of arguments in letters to civil servants than in press releases. When addressing a public audience, according to the consultants, it is less important to use the perfect argument, than in a private conversation with an official. Acting directly in public seems to allow more of an 'anything goes' attitude. All the arguments available are used. While the average confidential letter in Brussels contains 1.6 types of justification, that figure is 1.9 in the publicly available letters in Stockholm, and 2.5 in the public position papers and press releases.

The Swedish lobbyist must calculate the risk that an especially interested public, including the media and whistleblowers among opponents, will ask for the letter. The difference in the degree of self-interest between the Stockholm and Brussels letters is probably—again following the consultants' story—explained by the risk that the association members are among that especially interested public.

Benefit to the environment is the most frequently used type of justification in all three types of document (the confidential Brussels letters, the public press releases and position papers in Brussels and the publicly available letters in Stockholm). A seemingly paradoxical result concerning the confidential letters in Brussels, illustrated in Table 5.3, is that environmental arguments are used not less but more often in letters that are addressed to multiple directorates and not only to DG Environment. Thirty letters in the sample are addressed only to DG Environment, 16 are addressed to DG Environment and some other directorates, while 12 letters are addressed to other directorates without being copied to DG Environment.

Table 5.3. Types of justification used for different DGs. (Frequency of documents including at least one argument of respective category.)

Type of argument	Other DGs + more than one DG (28)	DG Environment only (30)	Difference
Self-regarding	36 per cent (10)	30 per cent (9)	+6
Environment	86 per cent (28)	67 per cent (20)	+19
Macroeconomic	43 per cent (12)	23 per cent (7)	+20
Competition	32 per cent (9)	13 per cent (4)	+19

Note: Table 5.3 compares the 30 confidential letters having only DG Environment as addressee with those 28 letters having other DGs, or more than one DG (including DG Environment), as addressees. The figures indicate the number of letters containing at least one type of justification of the respective categories.

It is consistent with the Brussels' consultants' picture of how the arguments would change between DG Environment and DG Transport and Energy (DG TREN) that the macroeconomic and competition arguments are used more frequently in correspondence with other directorates (+20 and +19 respectively), which would have those considerations closer to their brief. It is also in line with the results of the previous chapter that the self-regarding arguments are approximately equally common (+6). The consultants did not want to use more self-regarding arguments when dealing with DG TREN than with DG Environment. But it is less intuitively easy to understand why the environmental arguments would be less common in the letters addressed just to DG Environment.[34]

Part of the explanation lies in the fact that a larger share of the letters addressed to other DGs than DG Environment are addressed to the Commissioner, rather than to civil servants of the directorate (39 per cent and 23 per cent respectively) and that more types of arguments are generally used towards Commissioners than towards lower level civil servants.[35] But even if the letters sent to the Commissioners are removed from the analysis, there are still more types of arguments, including environmental arguments, used in the letters addressed to other DGs. One explanation could be that the increase in the types of justification in the letters sent to other DGs has to do with the fact that it is the DG Environment officials who are responsible for these dossiers and therefore know the issues best. When the lobbyist turns to another directorate there is a greater need to 'start at the very beginning', which probably implies using more types of arguments, including environmental arguments.

CONCLUSIONS

The interviews with the public affairs consultants in the previous chapter demonstrated a strong forum effect. The egocentric market characteristics of the amateur client should be concealed by the garb of committed partner in the private lobby meetings. That included adherence to the force of the better argument norm and a repertoire of arguments emphasising other- and ideal-regarding justifications. The publicity effect, on the other hand, represented in the interviews as the step out of the closed door meetings into a public speech, went in the opposite direction. The selection of arguments became less careful overall and the self-regarding arguments were emphasised more in public than in private. There was no indication of any transparency effect in the comparison between the interviews in Brussels and in Stockholm.

On the whole, the document analysis described in this chapter supports the results from the interviews. The documents in themselves can provide only limited explanations as to why a certain action is chosen, but the patterns found seem to fit with the explanations given by the consultants.

The interview study in the previous chapter was not able to demonstrate any transparency effect in the comparison between the Stockholm and the Brussels

Figure 5.1. Summary of the results of the document analysis

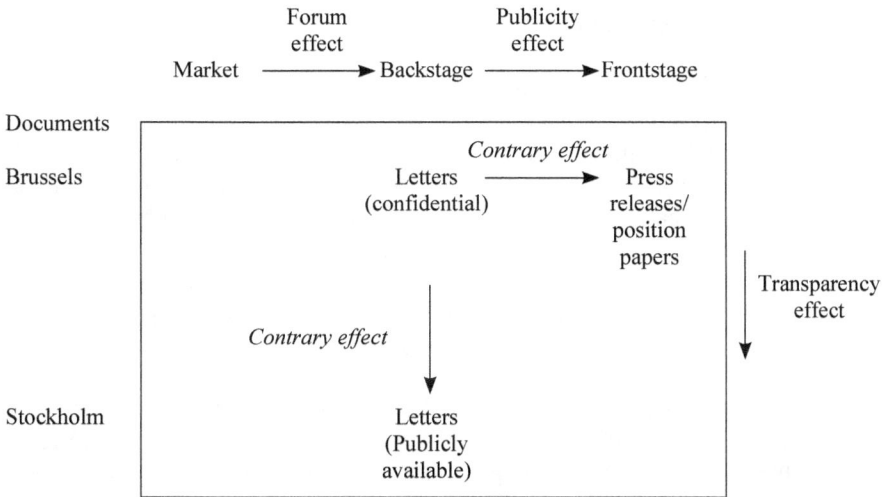

Note: Figure 5.1 illustrates the main findings of the chapter, with respect to the hypotheses derived from the theory of publicity's civilising effect. As before, the arrows in the figure do not illustrate causal relationships, but the different comparisons made in the analysis. The direction of the arrows indicates the hypothesised civilising effect. The transparency and publicity effects were measured in the comparison between the confidential Brussels letters and the publicly available Stockholm letters, on the one hand, and the press releases and public position papers, on the other hand. A strong civilising effect would have implied less bargaining and self-interest in the publicly available letters and press releases. Instead—with respect to the types of justification—the effect was contrary. The forum effect was not studied in the document analysis, since there were no comparable documents from the market sphere.

interviews. The document analysis, however, does indicate a difference between Stockholm and Brussels, which goes in the same direction as the contrary publicity effect: towards more self-interest, rather than less. While the validity of the results would have been stronger if a similar difference had been found in the interviews with the consultants, at least the two investigations are not pointing in contrary directions in this respect. It is also possible that the document analysis is more apt to find such nuanced differences between the two contexts than the interview study.

The document analysis also provides no evidence of any dressing up for the lobby corridor (forum effect), since there is no comparative data from the market sphere. Nevertheless, it can be shown that the senders are 'dressed for politics' in their confidential letters. Fifty-five of the 58 letters sent off to the Commission under the provision of secrecy are dominated by arguing. The most common argument is an environmental argument followed by macroeconomic and self-regarding arguments. Three letters from the battery industry, using the language of bargaining, were exceptions to the rule. Following the consultants' story, this can be explained by the exceptionally tough threat facing the NiCad battery producers and users.

The paradoxical—from the view of the theory of publicity's civilising effect—contrary publicity effect indicated by the consultants in the previous chapter is found also in the document analysis. This refers primarily to the types of justification, where it was seen that the self-regarding arguments are more common in public communications than in confidential letters. Again, the lobbyists sound better backstage than frontstage with respect to self-interest. The conclusion from the previous chapter that the choice of arguments is less sensitive overall in public than in private also seems to be compatible with the document analysis. The public documents contain more types of arguments than the private letters, indicating a less careful selection.

The fact that the document analysis showed that lobbyists tend to use more types of arguments in public than in private could be interpreted as attempts to broaden the argumentation in response to the broadening of the audience. A similar tendency was found in the interviews, where the consultants felt a pressure to address the whole audience in public speeches. But since the arguments in private were also based on other- and ideal-regarding justifications (although they were more selectively chosen in order to speak directly to the brief of the particular DG or ministry), this is not the type of effect depicted by the theory of publicity's civilising effect. Using more types of argument does not imply more arguing or more public-spiritedness. The fact that publicity tended to make lobbyists less careful in their selection of arguments rather seems to support the concern of Chambers and others, as discussed in chapter two, that publicity has the unwanted effect of making the substance of the arguments somewhat less important.

As a rule, according to the consultants, second to making alliances with other actors, playing the committed partner role is the best way for industry lobbyists to promote their interests. As illustrated here by the battery industry's conscious norm-violating bargaining behaviour, there are exceptions to this rule. Sometimes the dialogue breaks down and the parties end up in conflict. The fact that, in general, they choose not to do so, however, is the more significant finding. Most regulated industry sectors could take on a fight if they wanted to, for example by threatening with legal action, non-compliance or obstructing the implementation of regulations, but choose not to.

In spite of their concern for consistency between private and public speech, and the perceived need to address the whole audience as a matter of courtesy, the consultants tended to advocate more self-regarding justifications in public than in private. The reason for that was found in the internal game between the organisation leadership and its members. There is no reason to assume that this explanation is not valid also for the increase of self-interest in the written public communications. Another type of explanation could be that the increase in self-interest is a response to a 'media-logic' in which the more dramatic and indicative of conflict a press release is, the more likely the media will pick it up. While this is certainly a tactic used by environmental NGOs it is more doubtful whether it holds for industry associations, who are struggling to keep up their 'committed partner' image with the political institutions.

NOTES

1 CollectNiCad. App. B, doc 10.
2 SAFT. App. B, doc 154. CollectNiCad. App. B, doc 6, 11, 12.
3 CollectNiCad. App. B, doc 11.
4 CollectNiCad. App. B, doc 11.
5 CollectNiCad. App. B, doc 6.
6 SAFT. App. B, doc 16, 153, 19, 20. CollectNiCad. App. B, doc 7, 8, 14. EPBA. App. B, doc 72, 73.
7 SAFT. App. B, doc 16.
8 EPBA. App. B, doc 73.
9 CollectNiCad. App. B, doc 8
10 CEFIC. App. B, doc 130.
11 EPBA. App. B, doc 106.
12 CEPE. App. B, doc 78.
13 ACEA. App. B, doc 83.
14 ACEA. App. B, doc 139.
15 SVEFF. App. B, doc 92.
16 Weale 2002, p. 203.
17 Electrolux. App. B, doc 117.
18 CollectNiCad. App. B, doc 8.
19 KemiK. App. B, doc 63.
20 EPBA. App. B, doc 99.
21 CEFIC. App. B, doc 45.
22 KemiK. App. B, doc 52.
23 BIL. App. B, doc 141.
24 BIL. App. B, doc 146.
25 CEFIC. App. B, doc 126.
26 SVEFF. App. B, doc 90.
27 CEPE. App. B, doc 132.
28 Electrolux. App. B, doc 117.
29 CEFIC. App. B, doc 129.
30 KemiK. App. B, doc 55.
31 Electrolux. App. B, doc 64.
32 Plastb. App. B, doc 5.
33 SAFT. App. B, doc 17.
34 The explanation does not involve the fact that 16 of the 28 letters in the 'other DGs' category include more than one DG as addressees. There is no difference between those 16

letters which had more than one addressee and the 12 letters which were sent to just one DG (other than the DG Environment), with respect to the number of types of justification used.

35 2.2 and 1.4 types of justifications to Commissioners and civil servants respectively. There are in total 18 letters addressed to Commissioners and 40 to civil servants. Comparing letters to ministers and civil servants in Stockholm (15 and 40 respectively) shows that the difference in the number of types of justification used is smaller in Stockholm, but the tendency to use more arguments towards the political level is the same (2.0 and 1.8 types of arguments per letter respectively in Stockholm).

chapter six | the fault of deliberative theorists which demonstrates their point

The idea that institutionalising transparency will have a civilising effect on political behaviour, which has been the topic of this book, is based on the attractive idea that politics can be made to work better. According to this view, exposing political actors to publicity forces them to behave well. By opening the doors to smoke-filled backrooms, it may be possible to sweep out activities that cannot stand up to legitimate public norms.

This idea has been promoted by deliberative democratic theorists and has been common in the debate over the 'democratic deficit' of the European Union. It assumes that, while no man is an angel, most people will behave reasonably well if placed within the right institutional context. In the long run, being forced to behave well might even transform character. Eventually publicity might not be necessary to encourage these actors to behave properly. Institutionalising a high degree of transparency is also a particularly attractive means of motivating good political behaviour from a democratic point of view. The method is to let the public decide. Having faith in the power of publicity is to some extent equal to having faith in the public itself.

To deliberative theorists, behaving well in this context implies acting in accordance with the proper norms of the political sphere. The two principal norms in question are the force of the better argument norm and the non-selfishness norm. These norms are grounded in the assumption made by deliberative democratic theory that different behavioural rationalities are legitimate in the market (the sphere of commerce and consumption) from those appropriate to the forum (the political sphere). The role of publicity is to activate the norms of the forum and force them upon actors who would otherwise tend to use market behaviour in the political sphere. Lifting the veil of secrecy from the backstage areas of politics, where market behaviour is assumed to be illegitimately thriving, will help to spread the principles of the forum in their proper domain. The effect is to change the mode of communication and the types of justification used. The force of the better argument norm would induce a shift in the mode of communication from bargaining to arguing. The non-selfishness norm would force actors to use other- and ideal-regarding justifications, rather than self-regarding ones.

No matter how much sympathy one might feel towards the ideas and intentions behind the theory of publicity's civilising effect, however, the main conclusion of the previous chapters was that the hypotheses of the theory were not empirically borne out. Following industry lobbyists moving between different settings within the political sphere, characterised by varying degrees of transparency and publicity, no civilising shift in behaviour was found. The transparency effect was measured by comparison of lobbyists acting in the uniquely transparent Stockholm context and the allegedly opaque Brussels setting. The publicity effect was captured in the shift between informal backroom lobbying of officials and communications directed towards a broad public.

Rather than inducing these lobbyists to use more arguing and other- and ideal-regarding justifications, both the transparency effect and the publicity effect worked partially in the opposite direction. With respect to the types of justification, industry lobbyists sounded better backstage than frontstage, just like the civic group activists studied by Eliasoph (Eliasoph 1998) as discussed in chapter two. The degree of self-interest in their arguments was higher in public than in private and the mode of communication did not switch from bargaining to arguing. (However, the contrary transparency effect was found only in the analysis of documents. In the interview study, there was no sign of any transparency effect at all.)

There are two main reasons why deliberative theorists and advocates of transparency reforms in the EU overestimate the civilising power of publicity. The first reason concerns their assumptions about the frontstage. The theory of publicity's civilising effect overrates the public-spiritedness of the public and ignores the dynamics of representation. It idealises the frontstage by making an oversimplified assumption about the public as being, in Manin's words, a 'universal audience ... characterized by the views and values commonly shared by all the citizens'. This is a public which will only accept public-regarding justifications. Public debates therefore become 'a sort of competition for generality' (Manin 1987: 358. Cf. Bohman 1999: 178).

If representation is taken into account, as demonstrated in this study, such a competition for generality may not be the main effect of publicity. Representatives have home constituencies watching them. As described by the public affairs consultants, this domestic audience often hopes and expects to hear something different from a hypothetical abstract general public. They often want to hear that their representative is on their side, fighting for their interests. When taking into account that representatives are involved in 'nested games',[1] both external and internal games, the idea of hearing someone in a public debate saying 'Policy Y should be chosen because it is good for us' immediately comes to seem less odd.

Table 6.1. Results of the study with respect to the transparency and publicity effects.

	Mode of communication	Types of justification
Transparency effect	No effect	Contrary effect
Publicity effect	No effect	Contrary effect

It may not persuade anyone who is not a member of this particular representative's constituency but that would not be the purpose. The purpose would be to rally support in that part of the audience which determines whether this representative will be re-elected or not. The fact that publicity opens up the internal game in organisations based on representation is the most important factor behind the contrary transparency and publicity effects found in this study. Group pressure on representatives turned the civilising force into a politicising one.

The politicising force may not, however, be the end of the story. A further defence of publicity in the face of these results could be to argue that the increase in self-interest demonstrated here is merely a short-term effect. Rather than a condition of democracy, it could be seen as a symptom of a closed, elitist political system, in which the role of citizens is not to deliberate themselves but only to approve or disapprove others' deliberations. Citizens who are engaged in societal issues and who are used to taking an active part in political discussions and decision-making at different levels, on the other hand, may develop less self-regarding attitudes and a stronger acceptance of taking others' interests and perspectives into account. The long-term effect of transparency and publicity, it could be argued, may be to engage citizens more actively in the political sphere and socialise them into the norms of the forum.[2]

While this seems to be a reasonable argument one may still wonder whether transparency reforms such as sunshine acts and open debates will make a real difference to the level of 'forum-rationality' in a political system. In any case, the comparison in this study between two extreme points on the transparency scale did not find any such difference in political culture, despite the fact that the Swedish publicity principle has been institutionalised for over 200 years. The representative's dilemma was felt equally in Stockholm and in Brussels.[3]

For negotiation theorists, the politicising effect of publicity is no surprise.[4] The focus of negotiation theory, when it comes to effects of publicity, has been the effectiveness of the decision-making processes and the problem-solving capacity of political institutions rather than the direction and content of argumentation. Nevertheless, negotiation theorists do include the fact that negotiators have constituents in their calculations. 'Whether it is his employer, his client, his employees, his colleagues, his family, or his wife, every negotiator has a constituency to whose interests he is sensitive.' (Fisher, Ury & Patton 1999: 49). As discussed in chapter two, the main concern of negotiation theory with respect to publicity is the increasing 'degree of finality' of the positions. That means that there is a risk of positions becoming more rigid once they have been uttered publicly, which diminishes the flexibility and efficiency of the decision-making process. In terms of the content of arguments, negotiation theorists would predict a 'lower degree of specificity' in statements made in public. This prediction was borne out by the empirical study of business lobbyists. Not only did the rhetoric tend to become more vague, the actual substance of the arguments mattered less in public than in private to the interviewed public affairs consultants. More types of justification were used in public communications and there was less pressure to pick winning arguments for the public setting. While on the surface the form of communication in public was still arguing rather than bargaining, in reality, arguing—including genuine efforts at persuasion—was weakened rather than strengthened by publicity. The public stage was considered not so much as a place for changing people's minds about different policy options than as an arena for image-building, creating a positive 'atmosphere' around the speaker. Such a positive 'social construction' could be useful later for the lobbyist in the real decision-making arena: the backstage.

The second factor behind the overrating of the civilising force of publicity is that its defenders tend to build a straw man of what actually goes on behind closed doors. This applies both to deliberative theorists and to promoters of increased transparency in the EU. The promise of transparency and publicity for deliberative democratic theory is that it can make politics better, in terms of the mode of communication and the types of justification used. But while belief in publicity's civilising effect implies having faith in the public, and thus could be applauded from a democratic perspective, at the same time it also implies having little faith in elected representatives and civil servants. The theory assumes that murky things are happening backstage. Only exposure to the more civilised public will make elite actors behave.

Goffman's notion of a political backstage, which is the same picture drawn by the theory of publicity's civilising effect, is a place where social actors can relax and be themselves without having to care about public frontstage norms. Being oneself, it is then assumed, implies expressing market behaviour; bargaining and self-regarding justifications. Against such a view of a backstage-frontstage logic in politics Eliasoph's research has showed that American civic activists' private selves in fact tend to be more civil (in terms of self-interest) than demonstrated by their public acts. Similarily, Joerges and Neyer's research on the EU Comitology has illustrated that arguing is possible among national experts far away from the public eye.[5]

Industry lobbyists, however, were chosen for this study because they constitute a special type of actor, which puts the assumptions about the backstage made by the theory of publicity's civilising effect before a much easier test than Eliasoph's and Joerges and Neyers research. Business leaders are the market. They are genuinely self-interested actors who would not engage in politics for any other reason than improving their own opportunities for increasing profits. The private lobbying meeting seems to be an archetypal backstage. It is described in parts of the interest group literature as a hidden arena for striking political deals unable to stand public scrutiny. Of all actors, business lobbyists could be expected to feel at home in such a place if being backstage implies following the rationality of the market.

Still, not even these actors express their market selves backstage. The public affairs consultants definitely did not consider private meetings with civil servants to be home ground for business actors. Rather than constituting a norm-free backstage, private meetings turned out to require cautious footing. This footing included carefully considering the force of the better argument norm, committing the lobbyist to arguing rather than bargaining. It also involved playing the role of a constructive and committed partner, rather than an opponent applying pressure. Furthermore, according to the interviewed consultants, in order to find the persuasive arguments lobbyists must be open to the perspectives and preferences of others. To be influential, business people have to get 'dressed for politics'.

This is the fault of deliberative democratic theorists which demonstrates their point: there is a civilising effect here, similar to that expected, but it is not a transparency or publicity effect, it is a forum effect. It is democratic politics itself which forces a civil dressing upon market actors who enter the forum. The step over from the market to the forum requires a commitment to arguing and a broadening of the minds of those actors who ordinarily perceive their own cost problems as the only relevant dependent variable. This is required of business lobbyists, *regardless* of the degree of transparency and publicity.

Since politics is not just a question of eliminating inefficiency but also of 'creating justice', in Elster's words, 'the principles of the forum must differ from those of the market' (Elster 1986: 111). The trouble of the business leader who is new to politics and the pressure on him or her to dress 'correctly' before entering the political sphere demonstrate that the distinction between the market and the forum is not just an interesting theoretical standpoint in normative political philosophy. It is also an empirical reality for social scientists to study and for political actors to figure in to their calculations. In fact, this distinction is so real that it has been developed into a profitable business idea: the difficulties for business people of coping with the different logics of the market and the forum dominate much of the public affairs consultants' work. Unless these clients are willing and able to take a broader perspective, and swap the shotgun or the bargaining offer for reasonable arguments, they will fail as lobbyists.

While questioning the theory of publicity's civilising effect, therefore, this study has, at the same time, given support to a basic assumption of deliberative democratic theory, namely that politics is not 'just like a market'. In that respect, this is a contribution to the debate between deliberative and economic understandings of politics. As noted in the review of the interest group literature, the economic public choice conception of the relationship between lobbyists and policy-makers corresponds well to the backstage-frontstage logic of the theory of publicity's civilising effect. That image of lobbyists and policy-makers exchanging goods rather than arguments, and covering up the deals with a 'public-regarding gloss' (Macey 1986: 251) was not supported by this study. Assuming that all the interviewed public affairs consultants did not sell this researcher the same false story of how they are involved in 'trying to change peoples' minds'

Table 6.2. Results of the study with respect to the forum effect.

	Mode of communication	Types of justification
Forum effect	Civilising effect	Civilising effect

and, assuming also that the confidential letters are not part of a similar 'subterfuge', the public choice picture of the relationship between industry lobbyists and policy-makers is simply very far from reality. Just like the theory of publicity's civilising effect, the public choice model has much too cynical a view of what is happening behind closed doors. Private lobbying meetings are not a market place for buying and selling public policy and policy-makers do not accept being treated as backstage actors.

A similar critique can be directed towards a large part of the pluralist interest group literature, which relies on the pressure model, as described in chapter two.[6] The common picture of industry lobbyists as egocentric bargainers equipped with threats and promises describes the exception rather than the rule. Pressure groups and political merchants are norm-breakers in the lobby-corridors. Furthermore, according to the public affairs consultants they are more often losers than winners.

Corporatist theory—and especially those theorists who emphasise the deliberative character of corporatist arrangements—seems to come closest to the empirical findings of this study among the different strains of the interest group literature.[7] As noted already in the introduction in relation to the discussion of the public legitimacy argument in favour of transparency, corporatist theory would consider publicity a disturbing factor for the elite negotiations on which their model is based. On the other hand, corporatist theorists would not expect this kind of civilised behaviour to appear in informal lobbying meetings. Their argument is that if government-interest group relations are institutionalised within formal corporatist arrangements, where representatives of different groups and the government meet regularly face-to-face, then the actors may stop 'bashing each other over the head'. In a competitive pluralist interest group system, however, which relies on the kind of informal lobbying studied here, a much more conflict-oriented behaviour would have been predicted.

The contribution made in this book to the debate over the 'nature of politics' may not be uncontroversial for deliberative democratic theorists. Industry lobbyists are in many respects the complete opposite to the ideal of a deliberative actor. In fact, lobbyists do not deliberate at all, in the sense of engaging in dialogue with openness for being convinced by the arguments of others. Deliberation requires sincere reciprocity.[8] But while successful lobbyists have open minds to the perspectives of others they do not have open hearts. They are interested in the arguments and preferences of others because they need that information in order to promote their interests. If it happens that they are eventually hit by a cognitive dissonance mechanism, or if the 'force of reason' in some other way manages to transform their preferences during the process, that could be seen as a positive consequence of their hypocrisy. It does not, however, make them deliberating actors.

But dismissing the hypocritical behaviour of lobbyists dressing up for politics as just another form of coercive strategic action would be the same as dismissing norms as important determinants of social behaviour. Norms make a difference only if there is a tendency towards norm-violating behaviour among at least some of the relevant actors in the first place. The discussion within deliberative demo-cratic theory on designing institutions in order to promote a deliberative behaviour must assume that all actors have not already perfectly internalised the delibera-tive ideal. Here it has been shown that the force of the better argument norm is strong even in such a sheltered backyard of the political sphere as private lobby-ing meetings. If lobbyists are not deliberative or moral heroes that only increases the significance of that result. Even the most market-oriented and genuinely self-interested actors in politics, in private communications with officials who are working in a uniquely opaque political system (the EU) and in a political institution which is democratically unaccountable (the European Commission), have to argue rather than bargain in order to promote their interests. The fact that these actors are exchanging arguments rather than threats and promises, and that the winning types of justification are other- and ideal-regarding rather than self-regarding, is evidence of the significance of the logic of the forum. That does not imply that interest group politics is not about power and interests.[9] The conclusion is rather that while it is still a power struggle, it is a fairly civilised one. The hard currency of private lobbying meetings in Brussels and Stockholm is not naked power, but dressed.

These findings do not prove that bargaining is also uncommon in other parts of the political sphere, such as international negotiations, parliamentary commit-tees, coalition government negotiations, etc. The main reason why it is reason-able to assume that these results have something to say about politics beyond the lobbying arena is that industry lobbyists could be expected to be an easy test for the proposition that secrecy harbours market behaviour. The fact that they did not exhibit market behaviour should make us especially suspicious of routinely cynical assumptions about the backstage (such as those of public choice theory). Always assuming the worst is not always the most realistic.

Presuming that deliberative theorists are right in that rhetoric is not just rheto-ric—that there is a tendency for hypocrisy to entrap its own users and force them into positions which are optimal rather than maximal, and that not even lobbyists are totally immune to the voice of reason—then the requirement to argue other- and ideal-regardingly should make a real difference to the process and output of politics. If political actors are induced to 'talk the talk' at the forum, the chances increase that they will eventually also 'walk the walk'. John Stuart Mill has given support to this view—that we should prefer dressed power to naked power—in the following way: 'If any one thinks that the mere obligation of preserving decency is not a very considerable check on the abuse of power, he has never had his attention called to the conduct of those who do not feel under the necessity of observing that restraint.' (Mill 1861 [1928]: 199).

The requirement to get dressed is in itself a question of both norms and power. In private meetings the choice of mode of communication—arguing or bargain-ing—is largely determined by the force of the better argument norm. It is not appropriate for serious committed partners to try to sell a deal. They should argue for the best solution in order to be perceived as serious and credible. The strong emphasis put on other- and ideal-regarding justifications, on the other hand, is primarily a function of the need of the lobbyists to persuade the officials, who at the end of the day have the ultimate say over the decisions. While self-interest is legitimate, and making clear 'what's in it for us' is necessary in order to be perceived as a stakeholder to be consulted in the process, self-regarding justifications are seldom useful as means of persuasion for industry lobbyists.

Deliberative theorists overestimate the inappropriateness of using self-regarding justifications. Elster asserts that 'the presence of a public makes it especially hard to be motivated by mere self-interest. Even if one's fellow assembly members would not be shocked, the audience would be.' (Elster, 1998: 111). Self-interested motives therefore must be 'hidden' or 'disguised.' In reality, however, there are probably few cases in politics where revealing political actors as having self-interested motives will be shocking to anyone. Not only because we suspect that this is indeed a motivational force behind much political action,[10] but also, as one of the interviewed public affairs consultants put it, because 'everyone's interest, within reason, is legitimate' (Brussels IP 6). Deliberative theorists assume that publicity forces actors to use arguments which are 'mutually acceptable' (Gutmann & Thompson 1996: 53) or which 'no one could reasonably reject' (Chambers, 1996: 81). But the argument 'because it is good for us' is not necessarily unreasonable or unacceptable. It may not be persuasive either, but that is another story.

Mutually acceptable reasons thus should not be confused with persuasive reasons, which is often the case within the deliberative democratic literature. The reason for this confusion is probably the fact that the ideal model of deliberation, which lies behind much of the thinking in the literature, pictures the deliberators as equal partners seeking to reach an agreement. The non-selfishness norm then becomes a logical consequence of the combination of the force of the better argument norm and an effort on behalf of the actors to reach consensus. If the actors are genuinely trying to reach consensus, and if they are forbidden by the force of the better argument norm to bargain on the decision, then purely self-regarding arguments obstruct that process. They will not persuade anyone and will therefore not bring the actors closer to a decision. If one drops the consensus-requirement, however, self-regarding arguments become less controversial. If the final decision is taken by a vote or by a bargain, persuasion is no longer necessary to bring about a decision. In that case such arguments can be ignored by the other actors.

Furthermore, if one also drops the assumption of the deliberators as being 'equal partners', self-interested arguments may have a positive role to play. First, the notion of being partners seems to imply that the deliberators know each other, or at least know who they should be speaking to, but that will not always be the case. As described by the interviewed consultants, self-regarding arguments may be useful as means of presentation and for establishing who the deliberating partners should be. Second, the assumption of equality means that no deliberators' preferences weigh heavier than any others. In reality, of course, to paraphrase George Orwell, some actors will always be more equal than others. Actors with a positive 'social construction'[11] or with a clear link between private and public interests may rely completely on self-regarding arguments also for persuasion.

Dropping the assumptions of having to deal with equal partners involved in reaching agreement by consensus, which is a normative model rather than an empirical one, certainly brings us closer to the real world. Most deliberative theorists probably would agree that the primary role of deliberation in modern politics is to precede and complement, rather than supplement, voting and bargaining. The latter methods are, by necessity, used to actually make decisions. However, at the same time as these assumptions are lifted the non-selfishness norm fades away.

THE DEBATE ON TRANSPARENCY IN THE EUROPEAN UNION

Returning to the debate on transparency, democracy and legitimacy in the European Union, which was the starting point of the study, what have we learned? The civilising effect on elite behaviour did not turn out as expected. The point made in the introduction about taking transparency seriously by critically examining the arguments made in the debate has been confirmed. The civilising effect cannot be taken for granted and may instead turn out to be a politicising effect. That is not to say that we should stop working for increased transparency in the EU.

First, from a normative point of view it is not at all evident that a stronger emphasis on self-regarding justifications is bad. As discussed above self-regarding justifications may have a positive role to play, even from within a deliberative perspective. The idea of a non-selfishness norm may be criticised for being based on a much too rigid and mechanical assumption about all parties to the process being so 'equal' that their individual perspectives and experiences become irrelevant.

Furthermore, the deliberative conception of 'civilised behaviour' has been formulated in opposition to economic and pluralist theories of democracy. From a pluralist perspective the notion of a collective public interest as something more than the sum of individual interests is rather suspect in the first place. Open conflicts of interest are considered healthy and should be welcomed rather than avoided. If transparency makes hidden compromises among elites more difficult, from a pluralist point of view that would be a strong argument in favour of transparency and publicity. On the other hand, the politicising effect found in this study should have been more welcome if the elite behaviour had been characterised by introvert bargaining rather than arguing. In private meetings it was arguing that dominated, which renders the notion of using transparency to prevent unsound elite bargains somewhat less pertinent.

There are also other arguments being made in favour of transparency beside the civilising effect, as discussed in the introduction. While I have argued that these arguments (transparency as a fundamental right and as a promoter of public legitimacy and accountability) should be scrutinised better than has hitherto been the case that does not mean that they are wrong. Clearly transparency increases the chances for democratic accountability, even though it is not a sufficient condition. In order for the EU to attain functional mechanisms of accountability, however, transparency reforms must be complemented by reforms focusing on the ability of the electorate to impose real sanctions on policy-makers.

One important lesson from this study with respect to the debate on the democratic deficit of the EU is the following: increasing transparency with the purpose of civilising elite behaviour—strengthening the democratic legitimacy equation from the 'output side' in Scharpf's words—should not be used as an excuse for not starting to look seriously at the accountability mechanisms on the input side (Scharpf 1999: 7f). If the EU, on the other hand, should choose to go for government by the people, not just for the people—for instance by strengthening the political accountability of the European Commission, or political parties starting to compete on European issues in the national and the European Parliament elections, thereby allowing citizens to both mandate and sanction those in power[12]—then transparency will have a more important role to play.

NOTES

1   See Tsebelis 1990. Cf. Putnam, 1988: 441.
2   Cf. Bentham, who defended publicity against those who mistrusted the public of being capable of judging public affairs—'the partisans of mystery'—by emphasising the unreasonableness of a logic stating that; 'You are incapable of judging, because you are ignorant; and you shall remain ignorant, that you may be incapable of judging'. Bentham 1816 [1999]: 36.
3   The tendency of decision-making to go underground, as discussed earlier (see note 16 in chapter two), also raises the question of whether it is at all possible to substantially decrease the degree of secrecy of a given democratic decision-making process. If every opened formal arena is followed by a closed informal arena, where the real decision-making takes place, the level of secrecy is in practice unchanged. Critics of the Swedish publicity principle, for example, have argued that the fact that almost everything that is put on paper becomes publicly available has implied that Swedish civil servants are using much more verbal communication than they would have done otherwise. The result, according to this view, is that the archives are less useful for reconstructing afterwards, for example by historians, what was actually going on. See Ahlenius 2004.
4   See references in chapter two, and especially note 13.
5   See Eliasoph 1998 and Joerges & Neyer 1997a and 1997b, whose work was discussed in chapter two.
6   See Heinz et al. 1993 and further references in chapter two.
7   See references in chapter two.
8   See, for example, Gutmann & Thompson 1996: 52f, Williams 2000: 131. A condition for 'communicative action', as described by Habermas, is truthfulness. See Habermas 1984: 307f.
9   Cf. Shapiro 1999

10   As discussed in chapter two, if there is no uncertainty about the motives of the actors there will be no non-selfishness norm. I am not saying that there is no uncertainty of this sort or that we are all cynical about each other's motives. In practice most political action— although this will vary a lot between different actors— is probably motivated by a mix of self- and public-interested motives. But one can not assume that a lot of people will be surprised (or even less 'shocked') when confronting self-interested motives in politics.

11   See Schneider & Ingram 1993.

12   Cf. Lord 2004: 119f., Franklin, van der Eijk & Marsh 1996

| appendix

A. Assessing the comparability of the private letters and the public documents

	Stockholm	Brussels private	Brussels public
Chemicals & hazardous substances			
	Kemikontoret (Chemicals industry association)	CEFIC (Chemicals industry association)	CEFIC (Chemicals industry association)
No. of documents	17	16	16
	SVEFF (Paint industry association)	CEPE (Paint industry association)	CEPE (Paint industry association)
No. of documents	5	3	3
		BASF (Chemicals company)	
No. of documents		1	
	Plastbranschen (Plastics industry association)	CollectNiCad/EPBA (Battery industry & users associations)	CollectNiCad/EPBA (Battery industry & users associations)
No. of documents	5	12	14
	Hydro Plast (Plastics company)	SAFT (Battery company)	
No. of documents	10	8	
	Electrolux (Electronic equipment company)	Electrolux (Electronic equipment company)	
No. of documents	5	7	
		Ericsson (Electronic equipment company)	
No. of documents		1	
Transport			
	Bilindustriföreningen (Car industry association)	ACEA (Car industry association)	ACEA (Car industry association)
No. of documents	11	7	6

	Svensk Petrolium (Oil industry association)	Europia/Concawe (Oil industry associations)	Europia/Concawe (Oil industry associations)
No. of documents	2	2	2
		Shell (Oil company)	
No. of documents		1	
Total	**55**	**58**	**41**

Note: Appendix A shows the sample of documents used in the content analysis. The purpose of the table is to give the reader a chance to evaluate the comparability of the confidential Brussels letters, the publicly available Stockholm letters and the press releases and public position papers. For example, the NiCad battery producer SAFT which is represented in the sample by eight confidential letters to the European Commission, has a comparable counterpart in the Stockholm sample, which is the PVC-producer Hydro Plast. Both companies have had their products questioned by the authorities.

B. Total sample of letters and public documents used in the content analysis

Confidential Letters (Brussels)

Sector	Sender	DocNo	Date	Receiver	Pages
Chemicals and hazardous substances					
	CEFIC	31	001108	Prodi cc: All Commissioners	4
	CEFIC	32	000817	DGEnt	6
	CEFIC	33	000622	DGEnt + DG Env	9
	CEFIC	34	000418	DGEnt	8
	CEFIC	35	001114	DGCom	1
	CEFIC	36	001106	DGEnv	1
	CEFIC	37	010529	DGEnv	1
	CEFIC	38	000222	DGEnv	1
	CEFIC	39	990915	DGEnv + DGEnt	12
	CEFIC	40	020108	DGEnv cc: other DGs	2
	CEFIC	41	010109	DGEnv	2
	CEFIC	42	010823	DGEnv + DGEnt	5
	CEFIC	43	011102	DGEnv	2
	CEFIC	44	011019	DGEnv	1
	CEFIC	45	011016	DGEnv	2
	CEFIC	46	001221	DGEnv	3

	CEPE	76	000814	DGEnv	2
	CEPE	78	000225	DGEnv	2
	CEPE	79	000327	DGEnv	3
	BASF	74	010423	DGEnv	3
	SAFT	15	011205	DGEnt cc: other DGs	1
	SAFT	154	000314	DGCom + Prodi	2
	SAFT	16	010423	DGEnv	2
	SAFT	153	010410	Prodi	1
	SAFT	17	001205	DGEnv	2
	SAFT	18	010209	DGEnv	1
	SAFT	19	010619	Prodi	8
	SAFT	20	010618	DGEnv	3
	CNiCad	6	000719	DGEnt	3
	CNiCad	7	010625	DGCom	2
	CNiCad	8	010625	Prodi + DGCom	4
	CNiCad	9	011012	DGCom	2
	CNiCad	10	000505	DGEnv	2
	CNiCad	11	000629	DGEnv	11
	CNiCad	12	001110	DGEnv cc: other DGs	14
	CNiCad	13	010223	DGEnv	6
	CNiCad	151	011108	DGEnv	2
	CNiCad	152	011211	DGEnv	5
	CNiCad	14	010521	DGEnv	14
	EPBA	72	010418	DGCom	6
	EPBA	73	010621	All Commissioners	2
	Electrolux	64	991118	DGEnt	2
	Electrolux	65	990720	DGEnt	3
	Electrolux	66	000605	DGCom	2
	Electrolux	67	990928	DGEnv	3
	Electrolux	68	000316	DGEnv	3
	Electrolux	69	010703	DGEnv	2
	Electrolux	70	000729	DGEnv	3
	Ericsson	71	990730	DGEnt	10
Transport					
	Shell	81	991206	DGEnv	2
	ACEA	82	000224	DGEnv	3
	ACEA	83	000406	DGEnv	3
	ACEA	84	000728	DGEnv	4
	ACEA	85	001220	DGEnv	4
	ACEA	86	010214	DGEnv	3
	ACEA	87	010306	DGEnv	3

	ACEA	88	010829	DGEnv	2
	Europia + Concawe	79	000731	DGEnv	6
	Europia	80	010305	DGEnv	2

Public position papers and press releases (Brussels)

Sector	Sender	DocNo	Date	Type of document PP = Position paper Press = Press release	Pages
Chemicals and hazardous substances					
	CEFIC	107	030708	PP	5
	CEFIC	108	030129	PP	7
	CEFIC	109	000310	PP	12
	CEFIC	110	980529	PP	4
	CEFIC	111	971010	PP	12
	CEFIC	112	961121	PP	5
	CEFIC	113	010213	Press	1
	CEFIC	122	020523	Press	2
	CEFIC	123	011115	Press	1
	CEFIC	124	011018	Press	1
	CEFIC	125	010829	Press	1
	CEFIC	126	010615	Press	1
	CEFIC	127	010213	Press	2
	CEFIC	128	030714	Press	1
	CEFIC	129	030506	Press	2
	CEFIC	130	021108	Press	1
	CEPE	131	010314	PP	2
	CEPE	132	021118	PP	2
	CNiCad	94	010427	Press	1
	CNiCad	95	010716	Press	2
	CNiCad	96	020312	Press	1
	CNiCad	97	031023	PP	4
	CNiCad	98	031125	Press	2
	EPBA	99	000201	PP	4
	EPBA	100	001109	PP	3
	EPBA	101	010201	PP	4
	EPBA	102	010417	Press	3
	EPBA	103	010417	PP	4
	EPBA	104	011001	PP	2
	EPBA	105	030428	PP	17

	EPBA	106	031126	Press	2
Transport					
	ACEA	114	020315	PP	11
	ACEA	135	000526	Press	1
	ACEA	136	000427	Press	2
	ACEA	137	990525	Press	1
	ACEA	138	undated	PP	7
	ACEA	139	980707	Press	2
	Concawe	133	011001	PP	4
	Concawe	134	021001	PP	2

Publicly available letters (Stockholm)

Sector	Sender	DocNr	Date	Receiver	Pages
Chemicals and hazardous substances					
	KemiK	47	930901	Min. of Env.	3
	KemiK + others	48	920522	Min. of Just.	10
	KemiK + Sv. Petrol	49	920511	Min. of Env.	4
	KemiK	50	940425	Min. of Env.	1
	KemiK	51	000901	Min. of Env.	2
	KemiK	52	000630	Min. of Env.	2
	KemiK	53	990614	Min. of Env.	1
	KemiK + others	54	971017	Min. of Env.	3
	KemiK	55	970829	Min. of Env.	2
	KemiK	56	970821	Min. of Env.	7
	KemiK	57	970828	Min. of Env. cc: Min. of Fin. & Min. of Just.	2
	KemiK	58	970822	Min. of Env.	1
	KemiK	59	961018	Min. of Env.	2
	KemiK	60	960628	Min. of Env.	1
	KemiK + Sv. Petrol	61	951221	Min. of Env.	2
	KemiK	62	961021	Min. of Env.	3
	KemiK	63	971023	Min. of Env.	3
	Sv Petrol + others	115	981207	Min. of Env.	2
	Sv. Petrol	116	990519	Min. of Env.	1
	SVEFF	89	940420	Min. of Env.	1
	SVEFF + others	90	000929	Min. of Env.	11

	SVEFF	91	981130	Min. of Env.	5
	SVEFF	92	960603	Min. of Env.	2
	SVEFF+ others	93	971023	Min. of Env.	11
	Plast-branschen	1	951017	Min. of Env.	2
	Plast-branschen	2	970219	Min. of Env.	1
	Plast-branschen	3	940504	Min. of Env.	9
	Plast-branschen	4	971024	Min. of Env.	19
	Plast-branschen	5	971022	Min. of Env.	9
	Hydro Plast	21	911015	Min. of Env.	10
	Hydro Plast	22	930119	Min. of Env.	2
	Hydro Plast	23	921210	Min. of Env.	1
	Hydro Plast	24	921126	Min. of Env.	2
	Hydro Plast	25	921119	Min. of Env.	5
	Hydro Plast	26	921029	Min. of Env.	4
	Hydro Plast	27	961028	Min. of Env.	6
	Hydro Plast	28	970611	Min. of Emp.	3
	Hydro Plast	29	970611	Min. of Env.	3
	Hydro Plast	30	960816	Min. of Env.	2
	Electrolux	117	990610	Min. of Env.	2
	Electrolux	119	980911	Min. of Env.	16
	Electrolux	121	980624	Min. of Env.	6
	Electrolux	120	981123	Min. of Env.	9
	Electrolux	118	980626	Min. of Env.	4
Transport					
	BIL	140	970121	Min. of Env.	2
	BIL	141	000908	Min. of Env. + Min. of Ind.	2
	BIL	142	000614	Min. of Env.	1
	BIL	143	980204	Min. of Env. cc: other Min.	2
	BIL	144	970507	Min. of Env.	1
	BIL	145	970504	Min. of Env.	2
	BIL	146	971021	Min. of Env.	2
	BIL	147	970922	Min. of Env.	2
	BIL	148	970526	Min. of Env.	6
	BIL	149	970220	Min. of Env.	3
	BIL	150	971028	Min. of Env.	4

| bibliography

Abromeit, H. (1998) *Democracy in Europe. Legitimising Politics in a Non-State Polity*, Oxford, Berghahn Books.

Ahlenius, I. (2004) 'Rätten att granska tomma skåp', *Dagens Nyheter*, 040423.

Austen-Smith, D. and Wright, J.R. (1994) 'Counteractive lobbying', *American Journal of Political Science*, vol. 38, no. 1.

Barro, R. (1973) 'The control of politicians: an economic model', *Public Choice*, vol. 14.

Barry, B. (1965 [1990]) *Political Argument*, Berkeley, LA, University of California Press.

Baumgartner, F.R. and Jones, B. (1993) *Agendas and Instability in American Politics*, Chicago, University of Chicago Press.

Baumgartner, F.R. and Leech, B. (1998a) *Basic Interests. The Importance of Groups in Politics and in Political Science*, Princeton, Princeton University Press.

Baumgartner, F.R. and Leech, B. (1998b) 'Lobbying friends and foes in Washington', in A. Cigler and B. Loomis (eds), *Interest Group Politics*, 5th edn, Washington DC, Congressional Quarterly Press.

Beetham, D. (1991) *The Legitimation of Power*, Basingstoke, Macmillan.

Bellamy, R and Castiglione, D. (2000) 'The uses of democracy. Reflections on the European democratic deficit', in E. Eriksen, and J. Fossum (eds), *Democracy in the European Union: Integration Through Deliberation?*, London, Routledge.

Benhabib, S. (2002) *The Claims of Culture: Equality and Diversity in the Global Era*, Princeton, NJ, Princeton University Press.

Bentham, J. (1816 [1999]) *Political Tactics. The Collected Works of Jeremy Bentham*, James, M., Blamires, C. and Pease-Watkin, C. (eds), Oxford, Oxford University Press.

Berry, J. (1997) *The Interest Group Society*, 3rd ed., New York, Longman.

Birkinshaw, P. (1997) 'Freedom of information and open government: the European Community/Union Dimension', *Government Information Quarterly*, vol. 14, no 1.

Bohman, J. (1997) 'Deliberative democracy and effective social freedom: capabilities, resources, and opportunities', in J. Bohman and W. Rehg, (eds),

Deliberative Democracy: Essays on Reason and Politics, Cambridge, Mass., MIT Press.

Bohman, J. (1998) 'Survey article: the coming of age of deliberative democracy', *The Journal of Political Philosophy*, vol. 6, no. 4.

Bohman, J. (1999) 'Citizenship and norms of publicity. wide public reason in cosmopolitan societies', *Political Theory*, vol. 27, no. 2.

Bohman, J. and Rehg, W. (1997) 'Introduction', in J. Bohman, and W. Rehg (eds), *Deliberative Democracy: Essays on Reason and Politics*. Cambridge, Mass., MIT Press.

Bouwen, P. (2002) 'Corporate lobbying in the European Union: the logic of access', *Journal of European Public Policy*, vol. 9, no. 3.

Brennan, G. and Pettit, P. (1990) 'Unveiling the vote', *British Journal of Political Science*, vol. 20, no. 3.

Buchanan, J. and Tullock, G. (1962) *The Calculus of Consent: Logical Foundations of Constitutional Democracy*, Ann Arbor, Mich., University of Michigan Press.

Bunyan, T. (2000) 'Access to documents "could fuel public discussion"', in Bunyan, T., Curtin, D. and White, A., *Essays for an Open Europe*, European Federation of Journalists, www.ifj.org.

Chambers, S. (1996) *Reasonable Democracy. Jurgen Habermas and the Politics of Discourse*, Ithaca, New York, Cornell University Press.

Chambers, S. (2003) 'Deliberative democratic theory', *Annual Review of Political Science*, vol. 6, no. 1.

Chambers, S. (2004) 'Behind closed doors: publicity, secrecy, and the quality of deliberation', *The Journal of Political Philosophy*, vol 12, no 4, p. 393.

Checkel, J. (2001) 'Norms, institutions and national identity in contemporary Europe', *International Studies Quarterly*, vol. 43, no. 1.

Cohen, J. (1989) 'Deliberation and democratic legitimacy', in A. Hamlin, and Pettit, P. (eds), *The Good Polity: Normative Analysis of the State*, Oxford, Blackwell.

Coleman, J. (1990) *Foundations of Social Theory*, Cambridge, Mass., Harvard University Press.

Curtin, D. (1996) 'Betwixt and between: democracy and transparency in the governance of the European Union', in J. Winter, D. Curtin, A. Kellerman, B. de Witte (eds), *Reforming the Treaty on European Union: The Legal Debate*, The Hague, Kluwer Law International.

Curtin, D. (1997) *Postnational Democracy. The European Union in Search of a Political Philosophy*, The Hague, Kluwer Law International.

Curtin, D. (2000) 'Citizens' fundamental right of access to EU information: an evolving digital *Passepartout*?', *Common Market Law Review*, vol. 37.

Curtin, D. (2003) 'Private interest representation or civil society deliberation? A contemporary dilemma for European Union governance', *Social & Legal Studies*, vol. 12, no. 1.

Dahl, R. (1956) *A Preface to Democratic Theory*, Chicago, University of Chicago Press.

Davis, R. (1999) 'Public access to community documents: a fundamental human right?', *European Integration online Papers* (EIoP). vol. 3, no. 8.

Deckmyn, V. (2002) *Increasing Transparency in the European Union?*, Maastricht, European Institute of Public Administration.

Delli Carpini, M., Cook, F. and Jacobs, L. (2004) 'Public deliberation, discursive participation, and citizen engagement: a review of the empirical literature, *Annual Review of Political Science*, vol. 7, no. 1.

Denzau, A. and Munger, M. (1986) 'Legislators and interest groups: how unorganised interests get represented', *American Political Science Review*, vol. 80, no. 1.

Downs, A. (1957) *An Economic Theory of Democracy*, New York, Harper & Row Publishers.

Dryzek, J. (2000) *Deliberative Democracy and Beyond: Liberals, Critics, Contestations*, Oxford, Oxford University Press.

Dryzek, J and List, C. (2003) 'Social choice theory and deliberative democracy: a reconciliation', *British Journal of Political Science*, vol. 33, no. 1.

Dyrberg, P. (2002), 'Accountability and legitimacy: what is the contribution of transparency?', in A. Arnull and D. Wincott (eds), *Accountability and Legitimacy in the European Union*, Oxford: Oxford University Press.

Edwards, G. and Spence, D. (1997) *The European Commission*, 2nd edn, London, Cartermill.

Elgström, O. and Jönsson, C. (2000) 'Negotiating in the European Union', *Journal of European Public Policy*, vol. 7, no. 5.

Eliasoph, N. (1998) *Avoiding Politics. How Americans Produce Apathy in Everyday Life*, Cambridge, Cambridge University Press.

Elster, J. (1986) 'The market and the forum: three varieties of political theory', in Elster, J. and Hylland, A. (eds), *Foundations of Social Choice Theory*, Cambridge, Cambridge University Press.

Elster, J. (1995) 'Strategic uses of arguments', in Arrow, K. *et al.* (eds), *Barriers to Conflict Resolution*, New York, Norton.

Elster, J. (1998) 'Deliberation and constitution making', in Elster J. (ed.), *Deliberative Democracy*, Cambridge, Cambridge University Press.

Elster, J. (1999) *Alchemies of the Mind. Rationality and the Emotions*, Cambridge, Cambridge University Press.

Eriksen, E. and Fossum, J. (2000) (eds), *Democracy in the European Union: Integration through Deliberation?*, London, Routledge.

Estlund, D. (1997) 'Beyond fairness and deliberation: the epistemic dimension of democratic authority', in Bohman, J. and Rehg, W. (eds), *Deliberative Democracy: Essays on Reason and Politics*, Cambridge, Mass., MIT Press.

Fearon, J. (1995) 'Rationalist explanations for war', *International Organization*, vol. 49, no. 3.

Fearon, J. (1998) 'Deliberation as discussion', in J. Elster (ed.), *Deliberative Democracy*, Cambridge, Cambridge University Press.

Ferejohn, J. (1999) 'Accountability and authority: towards a theory of political accountability', in Przeworski, A., Stokes, S. and Manin, B. (eds), *Democracy, Accountability and Representation*, Cambridge, Cambridge University Press.

Finel, B., and Lord, K. (1999) 'The surprising logic of transparency', *International Studies Quarterly,* vol. 43, no. 2, pp 315–39.

Fisher, R., Ury, W. and Patton, B. (1999) *Getting to Yes. Negotiating an Agreement Without Giving In*, 2nd edn, London, Random House.

Föllesdal, A. (2000) 'Subsidiarity and democratic deliberation', in Eriksen, E. and Fossum, J. (eds), *Democracy in the European Union: Integration through Deliberation?*, London, Routledge.

Föllesdal, A. and Hix, S. 'Why there is a democratic deficit in the EU: a response to Majone and Moravcsik', *Journal of Common Market Studies*, vol. 44, no. 3, pp 533–62.

Fossum, J. (2000) 'Constitution-making in the European Union', in Eriksen, E. and Fossum, J. (eds), *Democracy in the European Union: Integration Through Deliberation?*, London, Routledge.

Franklin, M., van der Eijk, C. and Marsh, M. (1996) 'Conclusions: the electoral connection and the democratic deficit', in van der Eijk and Franklin (eds), *Choosing Europe? The European Electorate and National Politics in the Face of the Union*, Ann Arbor, MI, University of Michigan Press.

Gambetta, D. (1998) '"Claro!": an essay on discursive machismo', in J. Elster (ed.), *Deliberative Democracy*, Cambridge, Cambridge University Press.

Gargarella, R. (2000) 'Demanding public deliberation. The Council of Ministers: some lessons from the Anglo-American history', in Eriksen, E. and Fossum, J. (eds), *Democracy in the European Union: Integration through Deliberation?*, London, Routledge.

Goffman, E. (1959) *The Presentation of Self in Everyday Life*, New York, Doubleday.

Goffman, E. (1981) *Forms of Talk*, Philadelphia, University of Pennsylvania.

Goodin, R. (1986) 'Laundering preferences', in J. Elster & A. Hylland (eds), *Foundations of Social Choice Theory*, Cambridge, Cambridge University Press.

Goodin, R. (1992) *Motivating Political Morality*, Cambridge, Mass., Blackwell.

Gosseries, A. (2005) 'Publicity', *The Stanford Encyclopedia of Philosophy (Winter 2005 Edition)*, Edward N. Zalta (ed.), http://plato.stanford.edu/archives/win2005/entries/publicity/.

Grant, W. (2000) *Pressure Groups and British Politics*, Houndmills, Macmillan.

Greenwood, J. (2003) *Interest Representation in the European Union*, Basingstoke, Palgrave.

Grigorescu, A. (2003) 'International organizations and government transparency: linking the international and domestic realms', *International Studies Quarterly*, vol. 47, no. 4.

Gronbech-Jensen, C. (1998) 'The Scandinavian tradition of open government and the European Union: problems of compatibility?', *Journal of European Public Policy*, vol. 5, no. 1.

Groseclose, T. and McCarty, N. (2001) 'The politics of blame: bargaining before an audience', *American Journal of Political Science*, vol. 45, no. 1.

Gutmann, A. and Thompson, D. (1996) *Democracy and Disagreement. Why Moral Conflict Cannot be Avoided in Politics, and What Should be Done About it*, Cambridge, Mass., The Belknap Press of Harvard University Press.

Habermas, J. (1984) *The Theory of Communicative Action. Vol 1. Reason and the Rationalization of Society*, Cambridge, Polity Press.

Habermas, J. (1996) *Between Facts and Norms. Contributions to a Discourse Theory of Law and Democracy*, Cambridge, Polity Press.

Harden, I. (2001) 'Citizenship and information', *European Public Law*, vol. 7, no. 2.

Harlow, C. (2002) *Accountability in the European Union*, Oxford, Oxford University Press.

Hayes-Renshaw, F. and Wallace, H. (1997) *The Council of Ministers*, London, Macmillan.

Heinz, J., Laumann, E., Nelson, R., and Salisbury, R. (1993) *The Hollow Core: Private Interests in National Policymaking*, Cambridge, Mass., Harvard University Press.

Héritier, A. (1999) 'Elements of democratic legitimation in Europe: an alternative perspective', *Journal of European Public Policy*, vol. 6, no. 2.

Héritier, A. (2003) 'Composite democracy in Europe: the role of transparency and access to information', *Journal of European Public Policy*, vol. 10, no. 5.

Hermansson, J., Lund, A., Svensson, T. and Öberg, P. (1999) *Avkorporativisering och lobbyism*, SOU 1999: 121.

Hojnacki, M. and Baumgartner, F. (2003) 'Symbols and advocacy', Paper prepared for delivery at the annual meeting of the Midwest Political Science Association, Chicago, Illinois, April 3–6.

Hojnacki, M., Baumgartner, F., Berry, J., Kimball, D. and Leech, B. (2006) 'Goals, salience, and the nature of advocacy', Paper presented at the annual meeting of the American Political Science Association, Philadelphia, PA, August 31-September 3, 2006.

Hoy, D. (1986) (ed.), *Foucault: A Critical Reader*, Oxford, Blackwell.

Joerges, C. and Neyer, J. (1997a) 'From intergovernmental bargaining to deliberative political process: the constitutionalization of comitology', *European Law Journal*, Vol. 3.

Joerges, C. and Neyer, J. (1997b) 'Transforming strategic interaction into deliberative problem-solving: European comitology in the foodstuffs sector', *Journal of European Public Policy*, vol. 4. no. 4.

Johnson, A. (1999) *Rätt att lobba. Om politisk påverkan efter korporatismens fall*, Stockholm, Timbro.

Karlsson, C. (2001) *Democracy, Legitimacy and the European Union*, Uppsala, Acta Universitatis Upsaliensis.

Keohane, R. and Nye, J. (2003) 'Redefining accountability for global govern-ance', in Kahler, M. and Lake, D. (eds), *Governance in a Global Economy: Political Authority in Transition*, Princeton: Princeton University Press.

King, G., Keohane, R.O. and Verba, S. (1994) *Designing Social Inquiry. Scientific Inference in Qualitative Research*, Princeton, Princeton University Press.

Knight, J. and Johnson, J. (1994) 'Aggregation and deliberation: on the possibility of democratic legitimacy', *Political Theory*, vol. 22, no 2.

Kollman, K. (1998) *Outside Lobbying. Public Opinion and Interest Group Strategies*, Princeton, Princeton University Press.

Kuran, T. (1995) *Private Truths, Public Lies: The Social Consequences of Preference Falsification*, Cambridge, Mass., Harvard University Press.

Lahusen, C. (2002) 'Commercial consultancies in the European Union: the shape and structure of professional interest intermediation', *Journal of European Public Policy*, vol. 9, no. 5.

Larsson, T. (1998) 'How open can a government be? The Swedish experience', in Deckmyn, V. and Thomson, I. (eds), *Openness and Transparency in the European Union*, Maastricht: European Institute of Public Administration.

Lax, D. and Sebenius, J. (1986) *The Manager as Negotiator: Bargaining for Cooperation and Competitive Gain*, New York, Free Press.

Lerner, J.S. and Tetlock, P.E. (1999) 'Accounting for the effects of accountabil-ity', *Psychological Bulletin*, vol. 125, no. 2.

Lijphart, A. (2002) 'The evolution of consociational theory and consociational practices, 1965–2000', *Acta Politica*, vol. 37.

Lodge, J. (1994) 'Transparency and democratic legitimacy', *Journal of Common Market Studies*, vol. 32, no. 3.

Lord, C. (1998) *Democracy in the European Union*, Sheffield, Sheffield Academic Press.

Lord, C. (2004) *A Democratic Audit of the European Union*, Basingstoke, Palgrave.

Luban, D. (1996) 'The publicity principle', in Goodin, R. (ed.), *The Theory of Institutional Design*, Cambridge, Cambridge University Press.

Macedo, S. (1999) 'Introduction', in S. Macedo, (ed.), *Deliberative Politics. Essays on Democracy and Disagreement*, Oxford, Oxford University Press.

Macey, J. (1986) 'Promoting public-regarding legislation through statutory inter-pretation: an interest group model', *Columbia Law Review*, vol. 86, no. 2.

Majone, G. (1996) *Regulating Europe*, London, Routledge.

Maloney, W., Jordan, G. and McLaughlin A. (1994) 'Interest groups and public policy: the insider/outsider model revisited', *Journal of Public Policy*, vol. 14, no. 1.

Manin, B. (1987) 'On legitimacy and political deliberation', *Political Theory*, vol. 14, no. 3.

Manin, B., Przeworski, A. and Stokes, S. (1999) 'Introduction', in Przeworski, A., Stokes, S. and Manin, B. (eds), *Democracy, Accountability and Representation*, Cambridge, Cambridge University Press.

Mansbridge, J. (1992) 'A deliberative perspective on neo-corporatism', *Politics & Society*, vol. 20, no. 4.

Mather, D. (1997) 'Transparency in the European Union', in Thomson *et al.*, *Openness and Transparency: Meaningful or Meaningless? Access to Information on the European Union*, Manchester, European Information Association.

Mazey, S. and Richardson, J. (2001) 'Interest groups and EU policy-making: organisational logic and venue shopping', in Richardson, J. (ed.), *European Union: Power and Policy Making*, 2nd edn, London, Routledge.

Milbrath, L. (1960) 'Lobbying as a communication process', *Public Opinion Quarterly*, vol. 24, no. 1.

Mill, J.S. (1861 [1928]) *Considerations on Representative Government*, London, Routledge.

Miller, D. (1992) 'Deliberative democracy and social choice', in Held, D. (ed.), *Prospects for Democracy: North, South, East, West*, Oxford, Polity Press.

Miller, D.T. (1999) 'The norm of self-interest', *American Psychologist*, vol. 54, no. 12.

Mitchell, W. and Munger, M. (1991) 'Economic models of interest groups: an introductory survey', *American Journal of Political Science*, vol. 53, no. 2.

Moloney, K. (1996) *Lobbyists for Hire*, Aldershot, Dartmouth.

Moravcsik, A. (1998) *The Choice for Europe. Social Purpose & State Power from Messina to Maastricht*, Ithaca, New York, Cornell University Press.

Mulgan, R. (2000) '"Accountability": an ever-expanding concept?', *Public Administration*, vol. 78, no. 3.

Naurin, D. (2001) *Den Demokratiske Lobbyisten* [The Democratic Lobbyist], Borea, Umeå.

Naurin, D. (2003a) 'Does publicity purify politics?', *Journal of Information Ethics*, vol. 12, no. 1.

Naurin, D. (2003b) 'Den Europeiska Centralbanken–oberoende med ansvar-sutkrävande?' [The European Central Bank–Independent and Accountable?], in Bernitz, U., Gustavsson, S and Oxelheim, L. (eds), *Europaperspektiv: Valutaunionen, författningsfrågan och Östutvidgningen* [Europe in Perspective: Monetry Union, Constitution and Enlargement], Stockholm, Santérus.

Naurin, D. (2004) 'Transparency and legitimacy', in Dobson, L and Follesdal, A. (eds), *Political Theory and the European Constitution*, London, Routledge.

Naurin, D. (2006) 'Transparency, publicity, accountability–the missing links', *Swiss Political Science Review*, vol. 12, no. 3.

Neyer, J. (2003) 'Discourse and order in the EU: a deliberative approach to multi-level governance', *Journal of Common Market Studies*, vol. 41, no. 4.

Öberg, P. (1994) *Särintresse och allmänintresse: Korporatismens ansikten* [Private and Public Interest: The Faces of Corporatism], Uppsala, Acta Universitatis Upsaliensis.

Öberg, P. (2002) 'Does administrative corporatism promote trust and delibera-tion?', *Governance*, vol. 15, no. 4.

Öberg, U. (1998) 'Public access to documents after the entry into force of the

Amsterdam Treaty: much ado about nothing?', *European Integration Online Papers* (EIoP), vol. 2, no. 8.

Österdahl, I. (1998) 'Openness v. secrecy: public access to documents in Sweden and the European Union', *European Law Review*, vol. 23.

Peters, G. (1995) *The Politics of Bureaucracy*, London, Routledge.

Peterson, J. (1995) 'Playing the transparency game: consultation and policy-making in the European Commission', *Public Administration*, vol. 73, no. 3.

Pollack, M. (2003) 'Control mechanism or deliberative democracy? Two images of Comitology', *Comparative Political Studies*, vol. 36, no. 1/2.

Posner, R. (1971) 'Taxation by regulation', *Bell Journal of Economics and Management Science*, vol. 2.

Prat, A. (2005) 'The wrong kind of transparency', *American Economic Review*, vol. 95, no. 3.

Putnam, R. (1988) 'Diplomacy and domestic politics: the logic of two-level games', *International Organization*, vol. 42, no. 3.

Remer, G. (1999) 'Political oratory and conversation. Cicero versus deliberative democracy', *Political Theory*, vol. 27, no. 1.

Riker, W. (1982) *Liberalism against Populism: A Confrontation Between the Theory of Democracy and the Theory of Social Choice*, San Francisco, Freeman.

Riker, W. (1996) *The Strategy of Rhetoric. Campaigning for the American Constitution*, New Haven, Yale University Press.

Risse, T. (2000) '"Let's argue!" Communicative action in world politics', *International Organization*, vol. 54, no. 1.

Risse, T. and Sikkink, K. (1999) 'The socialisation of international human rights norms into domestic practices: introduction', in Risse, T., Ropp, S. and Sikkink, K. (eds), *The Power of Human Rights. International Norms and Domestic Change*, Cambridge, Cambridge University Press.

Rose-Ackerman, S. (1999) *Corruption and Government: Causes, Consequences, and Reform*, Cambridge, Cambridge University Press.

Sanders, L. (1997) 'Against deliberation', *Political Theory*, vol. 25, no. 3.

Scharpf, F. (1999) *Governing in Europe: Effective and Democratic?*, Oxford, Oxford University Press.

Scharpf, F. (2003) 'Problem-solving effectiveness and democratic accountability in the EU', MPIfG Working Paper 03/01.

Schelling, T. (1960) *The Strategy of Conflict*, Cambridge, Mass., Cambridge University Press.

Schimmelfennig, F. (2001) 'The community trap: liberal norms, rhetorical action, and the eastern enlargement of the European Union', *International Organization*, vol. 55, no. 1.

Schlozman, K. and Tierney, J. (1986) *Organized Interests and American Democracy*, New York, Harper and Row.

Schmitter, P. (2000) *How to Democratize the European Union... And Why Bother?*, Lanham, Rowman & Littlefield Publishers.

Schneider, A. and Ingram, H. (1993) 'Social construction of target populations: implications for politics and policy', *American Political Science Review*, vol. 87, no. 2.

Schultz, K. (1998) 'Domestic opposition and signaling in international crises', *American Political Science Review*, vol. 92, no. 4.

Schumpeter, J. (1943) *Capitalism, Socialism and Democracy*, London, Allen & Unwin.

Shapiro, I. (1999) 'Enough of deliberation. Politics is about interests and power', in S. Macedo, (ed.), *Deliberative Politics. Essays on Democracy and Disagreement*, Oxford, Oxford University Press.

Stasavage, D. (2004) 'Open-door or closed-door? Transparency in domestic and international bargaining', *International Organization*, vol. 58, no. 4, pp. 667–703.

Statskontoret (2000) *Genomförandekommittéer*, Statskontoret 2000: 20C.

Steiner, J., Bächtiger, A. Spörndli, M. and Steenbergen, M. (2004) *Deliberative Politics in Action. Analysing Parliamentary Discourse*, Cambridge University Press.

Stigler, G. and Friedland, C. (1962) 'What can regulators regulate? The case of electricity', *Journal of Law and Economics*, vol. 5.

Streeck, W. and Schmitter, P. (1985) *Private Interest Government: Beyond Market and State*, London, Sage.

Streeck, W. and Schmitter, P. (1991) 'From national corporatism to transnational pluralism', *Politics & Society*, vol. 19, no. 2.

Sunstein, C. (1996) 'Public deliberation, affirmative action, and the Supreme Court', *California Law Review*, vol. 84, no. 4.

Truman, D. (1951) *The Governmental Process: Political Interests and Public Opinion*, New York, Alfred A. Knopf.

Tsebelis, G. (1990) *Nested Games. Rational Choice in Comparative Politics*, Berkeley and LA, University of California Press.

van Buitenen, P. (2000) *Blowing the Whistle*, London, Politico.

Walker, J. (1991) *Mobilizing Interest Groups in America*, Ann Arbor, University of Michigan Press.

Walton, R. and McKersie, R. (1965) *A Behavioural Theory of Labor Negotiations. An Analysis of a Social Interaction System*, Ithaca, NY, ILR Press.

Walzer, M. (1999) 'Deliberation, and what else?', in S. Macedo, (ed.), *Deliberative Politics. Essays on Democracy and Disagreement*, Oxford, Oxford University Press.

Weale, A. (2002) 'Environmental rules and rule-making in the European Union', in Jordan, A. (ed.), *Environmental Policy in the European Union*. London: Earthscan.

Weiler, J.H.H. (1997) 'The European Union belongs to its citizens: three immodest proposals', *European Law Review*, vol. 22.

Weiler, J.H.H. (1999) *The Constitution of Europe*. Cambridge: Cambridge University Press.

Williams, M. (2000) 'The uneasy alliance of group representation and deliberative democracy', in Kymlicka, W. and Norman, W. (eds), *Citizenship in Diverse Societies*, Oxford, Oxford University Press.

Williamson, P. (1989) *Corporatism in Perspective. An Introductory Guide to Corporatist Theory*, London, Sage.

Woll, C. (2006) 'Lobbying in the European Union: from *sui generis* to a comparative perspective', *Journal of European Public Policy*, vol. 13, no. 3.

Young, I. (1996) 'Communication and the other: beyond deliberative democracy', in Benhabib, S., *Democracy and Difference: Contesting the Boundaries of the Political*, Princeton, NJ, Princeton University Press.

Ziller, J. (2001) 'European models of government: towards a patchwork with missing pieces', *Parliamentary Affairs*, vol. 54, no. 1.

Zurn, M. (2000) 'Democratic governance beyond the nation-state: the EU and other international institutions', *European Journal of International Relations*, vol. 6, no. 2.

| index

| subject index

www.ingramcontent.com/pod-product-compliance
Lightning Source LLC
Chambersburg PA
CBHW072131020426
42334CB00018B/1759